MATTERS OF CHOICE

A Test Selector's Story

JOHN BENAUD

SWAN
PUBLISHING

First published in 1997 by
Swan Publishing Pty Ltd
Suite 14C, 81 Waratah Ave. Dalkeith, W.A. 6009

National Library of Australia
Cataloguing-in-Publication data

Benaud, John, 1944- .
John Benaud . matters of choice.

ISBN 0 9586760 2 X.

1. Benaud, John, 1944- . 2. Cricket players - Australia -
Biography. 3. Cricket. I. Title.

796.358092

Printed in Australia by McPherson's Printing Group

Designer: Stan Lamond, Lamond Art & Design

Copy-editor: Dawn Koester

Cover photos: Richie Benaud, Dean Jones,
Sir Donald Bradman, Rick McCosker, Doug Walters (FAIRFAX);
Merv Hughes, Mark Taylor (ALL SPORT); Steve Waugh,
Dennis Lillee, Shane Warne (VIV JENKINS).

MATTERS OF CHOICE

A Test Selector's Story

In memory of Lou.

CONTENTS

John Benaud

Cricket has been a way of life in the Benaud family for 70 years. Fortune, rough and smooth is reflected in the cricketing lives of Lou Benaud, and his sons Richie and John.

Lou, the talented father, was denied an opportunity in his cricket career by a stingy government bureaucracy, and made a vow ... that his two sons would get a better chance than he did to play in the 'baggy green' of Australia.

Richie defied the odds to become one of Australia's greatest all-rounders and finest captains, and today is the acknowledged maestro among the game's television commentators.

John played for Sydney club teams Cumberland, Randwick and Penrith, Sheffield Shield for NSW and then for Australia under Ian Chappell's captaincy. He was an Australian selector from 1988 to 1993, and was appointed a NSW selector in 1997.

He is a journalist by profession. He covered Bob Simpson's tour to the Caribbean in 1978 and has contributed cricket columns to Sydney's *The Sun-Herald* and London's *Sunday Independent*.

FOREWORD
by Richie Benaud

Cricket is about people, meeting them then getting to know them, playing fiercely and fairly in their company and then socialising with them in conversation with a glass or two of your favourite hard or soft nectar; it is about loving the game. Characters abound, the secret is to find them. It's not just a matter of someone saying Fred, or Charlie or Jock is a great character, he actually needs to be one. When you find them the secret is never to let them go. I know most of the people in this book because many of the characters are from Sydney, but geography is incidental. In every cricket club, sporting club, office and selected walk of life, these characters live. I know them because some are first-class or Test cricketers, others have provided associations at club level or in administration. Harold Goodwin I know because he and I went to school together. He played his cricket then exactly as he played it later with Central Cumberland when I was again his captain and he was my opening batsman. He was magnificent. He never played for Australia, never even donned the New South Wales cap, and was never thought about for NSW Colts' XI or NSW Second XI games. He remained, until we both retired, one of the cricketers who gave me an enormous amount of pleasure in taking part in a game of cricket.

Nowadays, when I am in Sydney, I go through every match in the club cricket results in the Sunday newspaper. I always glance first at Northern District to see if a young lad, Matthew Schenke, has done anything that day because Lou helped him with advice a few years ago, then Parramatta which used to be Central Cumberland, then

Randwick which is where I now live and Bankstown to see what happened that day to Ken Hall because, as a youngster he originally played with Cumberland. I have never lost the belief that the Australian game completely revolves around the club matches which are the prelude for some to the Sheffield Shield. I retired from Test cricket the year 'Emu' started his career as a 12-year-old, playing in a morning competition and then being driven to the seniors' match in the afternoon where he would watch hoping desperately someone might not turn up, just as I had done as a 12-year-old in 1942.

Throughout the pages of this book there is a delightful cross-section of cricketing characters, including Doug Walters who came down from the country to play with the club where John and I were playing and Jack Chegwyn who found him. 'Cheggy' is owed an immense debt by NSW cricket because he was the one who started all the short tours to the country where a place in the team was so prized by the young cricketers in the Sydney area. Unsung heroes like Cheggy abound in cricket. One such is Laurie Sawle who certainly had no pretensions to play for Australia but did a great job at Test level when he was Chairman of Selectors, some 40 years after I had been on the receiving end of the century he made against NSW. If the pen-picture of Emu had me chuckling and reminiscing, the one about Tom Morris and East Lydeard held me fascinated. Humour and fascination and then certainly a tear or two because the story about young Michael is one of the saddest and, at the same time most inspiring, I have ever read. It follows on from the notes 'JB' has made about some of Lou's thoughts on the game of cricket, how it should be played on the field and perhaps, more important, *how it should be played*. We were both lucky to have him as a father, and Rene as a mother, each of whom loved cricket and supported us in our cricket careers and in our more normal lives as well. Their influence in those spheres and many others appear in the following pages and I hope you enjoy reading it as much as I have done.

DEANO

*When the selectors abruptly interrupted the Test career
of Dean Jones 'why?' was the most-asked question.
The most peddled answer was that it had to be something
other than cricket that upset the selectors. This is
what really happened.*

When a high profile cricketer is dropped from a team — Dean Jones,
Michael Slater — or he fails to make one when he's been the hottest of street-corner tips — Mike Whitney, Ashes 1989 — a lot of fans get edgy. They
believe an injustice has been done. The most popular scuttlebutt is the con-spiracy theory.

One of Australia's former captains, Kim Hughes, was one who seemed to
think Dean Jones received less than a square deal. Maybe his opinion was the
dividend of Kim's own career, a roller coaster ride that bottomed out at the
'Gabba in 1984 when he resigned as Test captain.

That particular gut-churning moment raised a few eyebrows about Kim's
temperament for the top job, as it should have done. But any reasonable as-sessment was buried beneath a welter of opinion that Kim was the victim of
some behind-the-scenes shenanigans. The fact was, Australia just kept on los-ing Test matches — 13 from 28 while Kim was in charge.

When 'Deano' was dropped from the Test team in 1992, Kim reportedly
said, "Jones was the victim of a mediocrity that had embraced the team …
unless you conform to a 'one bag, two bags, three bags full sir' person, they
won't pick you."

Then he dabbled in the cloak and dagger stuff: "I won't tell you who 'they'
are …" Naturally, Kim's assessment raises a few questions, not the least of
which is why do former cricketers have a penchant for peddling such
nonsense?

Did Kim really mean to imply that the Australian team at that time,
1992–93, was mediocre and filled with bended-knee bag-fillers, players like
David Boon, Mark Taylor, Steve Waugh, Shane Warne, to name just a few?

The only time I'd ever seen them on their knees, with tongues hanging
out, was before that great god of fitness, physiotherapist Errol Alcott, after

he'd put them through a session of sinew sizzle.

Kim's reference to 'they' implies that somebody other than the selectors was choosing the Australian cricket team at that time. Does Kim know something that nobody else does? I don't recall any strangers waltzing into the selection room and banging a fist on the table.

Where's his evidence that the selection process at that time was tainted? Kim's comments might have carried some weight, been worth further consideration, if he had publicly identified 'they' — named a few names.

The conspiracy theorists want the cricket public to believe that the dropping of Deano was really a plot by a bunch of shadowy string-pullers and their four puppets — two selectors from New South Wales (Simpson and Benaud) one from Western Australia (Sawle) and one from Victoria (Higgs) — to rid the national team of one of its most popular cricketers for reasons other than cricket.

Deano wasn't the victim of a conspiracy. He might have been the victim of circumstances. Or, was it all his own work?

November 9, 1992

I'm talking to Deano in the Members' Bar at the Sydney Cricket Ground. It's about nine in the morning and, on the other side of the long, plate-glass picture window play will soon be underway in the Sheffield Shield match between NSW and Victoria.

Naturally, neither of us is having a drink, but we're both totally pissed off, Deano slightly more than me, and rightly so … Melbourne's weather has been vile, in October 106 millimetres, well above normal, and his club cricket has been a washout.

To make matters worse, the program for the 1992–93 season devised by the Australian Cricket Board, in cahoots with the Boards from the two touring teams, is going to allow him just two Sheffield Shield matches in which to find touch for the First Test against the West Indies at the 'Gabba, then only 18 days away.

We agreed that the program was ridiculous, so ridiculous that prior to the Test the visiting West Indians could actually play more cricket than some of Australia's Test players, even though Richie Richardson's men would arrive in Australia nearly a month after the Australian season had hit off.

So, Richie Richardson would spend more time in the middle than David Boon. As a selector I was thinking, "This is terrific. What a great way to help our blokes toughen up for our tilt at the long lost Frank Worrell Trophy!" Sometimes you wonder what makes administrators tick.

While Deano had been getting down in the mouth watching the rain down south, up north in the sunshine at the 'Gabba a new kid on the block, Damien Martyn, hardly past his 21st birthday, was belting twin centuries (133 not out and 112) for Western Australia against Queensland, who had a strong attack, McDermott, Rackemann and Tazelaar.

Martyn's most obvious talent was hitting into the gaps, a true mark of class, and he timed the ball beautifully, too. He was a precocious type, probably with a large head-size, but certainly a big talent, too. His 112 came quickly, off 162 balls, and in a team total of 184. It gave WA the opportunity to push for victory.

Some selectors like players who can turn matches. Doug Walters was a batsman who could do that. At the SCG nothing much went Deano's way. He was a single off double figures when Mike Whitney dug one in short. Deano bent at the knees and swayed to avoid it, a sensible and acknowledged method of playing such a delivery.

But the two-tone SCG pitch nobbled 'Whit's' intended rib-tickler and suddenly Deano had to cope with not a quick bouncer, but the unexpected — a slower, ballooning ball with half the bounce. As he tried to adjust his footwork and bat and body position for a defensive shot the ball got into the tangle of shirtsleeves, gloves and armguard, then ricocheted down onto the stumps.

By coincidence, the NSW No.3 batsman Steve Waugh was the victim of a short ball, too. Merv Hughes showed his grunt by digging one in on the corpse of a pitch on the first morning; it snaked back at Steve and made him jump and jerk up his gloves into a defensive position to protect his thrown back head, the pose that makes fast bowlers smile, wickedly.

There are other observers who cringe at it; they see the reflex jump and think, "How can you play him against the West Indies?" Some have advised Steve, "Learn to hook, you mug!" My only wish was that he'd learned earlier in his career to do what he did so well later — not get his feet so planted, his body so side on.

So, a duck for Waugh, caught by Nobes at short forward leg, and such a dolly he could have swallowed it. How should a selector judge a dismissal like that — top marks to the aggressive Hughes, or a black mark against Waugh, who was desperately wanting to get back into a team that he'd been out of for 10 Tests? On the latter point a fair question might have been: it looks bad … but how many times has he actually been out that way?

Half a dozen days later, in Hobart, Steve offered a forceful reply to those critics who had suggested he should be banned from any match where batters might have to dance to the drumbeat of a tall West Indian quartet. Batting at No.4 for the Australian XI against Richie Richardson's team he fought hard to make 95 and followed up with an unbeaten, even 100. There were moments of discomfort against the pace and bounce of Ian Bishop, but his character remained unbent.

Damien Martyn made 39 and 44 in the game. Any selector judging the merit of each performance needed to be conscious of the fact that sometimes opponents can indulge in a little sandbagging in Test 'trials', as that match was.

This happens because they are keen to "play someone into" an upcoming Test, on the basis that they believe they have the suspect player's measure. Bishop was the only frontline quick the West Indies played. They rested Ambrose, Patterson and Walsh.

A couple of days before that match Deano had made 76 against the West Indies, batting at No.3 for the Prime Minister's XI. How should a selector rate that innings against Waugh's and Martyn's in Hobart?.

Does he take the flavour of the game into account — a one-dayer against a four-day match? Who batted under the most pressure, the batsmen in Hobart or those in Canberra?

A few days before the selectors were to choose the team for the First Test, Steve Waugh again played against the West Indies, this time for NSW at the SCG.

At the same time, Deano played in a 'home' Sheffield Shield match against Queensland. But it wasn't programmed for the Melbourne Cricket Ground, which Deano had called 'home' for all his long career, and therefore where he probably felt happiest, most relaxed under less pressure.

The MCG was out of action, under renovation after a long, wet winter of Rules football and the match had to be played at a less grand suburban club ground, St Kilda. During the game it rained — some of the 139 millimetres that fell in the month, almost double the average.

This was an important match for Deano, and only a cricket observer completely out of touch with reality could have suggested otherwise. The player himself would have been pumped up for the occasion.

But, a club ground and more rain ... those two ingredients, a relatively lacklustre venue and grey, weeping skies, must have cast a cloud of depression over Deano. If they didn't, if Deano was content that they were merely glitches of no consequence, then his scores, 14 and one, must have pricked him.

After all it was a fact, that for one reason or another — weather, controversial early season program or opposing bowlers — Deano had spent hardly any quality time in the middle. He might have been happy to stand on his Test record, but probably he'd have been a lot happier if his current form was more competitive.

Meanwhile, at the sunny SCG, on a belter of a pitch, Steve Waugh made 22. In the same game Mark Waugh made 200 not out. It was a timely reminder of 'Junior' Waugh's talent. In the first Sheffield Shield game at the SCG, when Deano and Steve Waugh had failed, Junior had made 88.

Yet, Junior was coming off a Test series in Sri Lanka where he'd made four ducks in a row. His Australian teammates had acknowledged the feat — only the sixth player in the game's history to 'achieve' it — with a new nickname, 'Audi'.

Audi was a great advertisement for the team's reputation as quick wits, but a player would be testing the selectors' senses of humour if he offered such a record as the basis for a spot in the next Test team they were going to choose.

Sawle, Simpson, Higgs and I chose all four batsmen, the two Waughs, Jones and Martyn in the twelve for the First Test. The Test was to start on November 27, but as usual the twelve was announced days earlier, in this case on the 23rd.

Another 'usual' habit was for us to announce an extra bowler in our twelve, a cover against any injury problems that might crop up during training, or, as a precaution against a weather change, or the type of pitch the curator might eventually roll out.

So, nominating the 12th man had generally become a straightforward exercise, and was sometimes even telegraphed to the media by the team hierarchy well before the Test began.

But in this twelve the 'extra man' was a batsman — we chose seven (the four plus Taylor, Boon and Border), and media speculation as to which middle-order batsman would mix the drinks raged right up until the first morning of the Test.

"The 12th man won't be Border", wrote a media wit, but that merely masked his frustration. There was much criticism levelled at the panel over its determination not to reveal which player would miss out.

But there was a simple reason for our shyness. We were keen to try to keep the West Indians guessing, off-balance tactically; they were playing under a new captain, Richie Richardson, and he had no Gordon Greenidge, no Viv Richards, no Jeff Dujon, no Gus Logie, no Malcolm Marshall.

Would delaying our final combination give Richie and Co. less time to formulate tactics? It possibly didn't matter because West Indian bowling game plans had been fairly stereotyped through the '80s and '90s — hand the ball to one of four fast bowlers, bowl him for six overs, spell him, bowl another one for six overs, and so on.

And, would keeping our own players in the dark confuse and frustrate them, even leave them unnerved by the constant media speculation? Or, would it create a sharper edge to their preparation?

We had decided to go back to David Boon as one of the openers (regarding him as a better option against the West Indies pace quartet than any of the fringe opening candidates, or the veteran Geoff Marsh who had been dropped the previous series against India), which meant we had to find a new No.3.

So, if we had announced the final eleven a few days before the event the new No.3 would have come under intense media pressure — "Does Curtly Ambrose like you … will you be wearing one suit of armour, or two …?" And so on.

Selection is a bit of a jigsaw. There are any number of factors that might influence the final choice — form, a player's past record, temperament under pressure, enterprise, allround flexibility, team balance, playing conditions and, the opposition and the game plan to try to win. The last few mentioned are often covered by the 'horses for courses' theory.

In 1992 the feeling among the selection panel was that the West Indies were vulnerable, more vulnerable than they'd been for a long time — new

A reasonable enough plea from Dean Jones, but … as a general rule, is it really wise for selectors to explain to players why they missed out? How detailed should such an explanation be? What if there is more to a selection judgment than a form comparison? For instance, what should a selector tell a player whose temperament, or character he considers suspect? And, in this era of accelerating litigation what might the consequences be for a brutally honest selector? The wisest course for any selector is to offer the player the chance to work it out for himself. Most cricketers are smart enough to do that.

Exiled Jones wants selectors to open up

DEAN JONES yesterday called for more communication between national selectors and players.

The stand-in Victorian captain was responding to a newspaper article by former Test captain Allan Border, which said Jones had been exiled from international cricket since 1994 because he had offended too many establishment figures.

players have to work with them on where the team is heading."

Jones said he held no grudges against Border and thanked him for shedding some light on the matter.

"It's cool. He's spoken his mind and now we can get on with life," Jones said. "I've been looking for a couple of reasons myself.

"I'd hate

captain, new batting order, but most important no Marshall. Marshall had no peer as an aggressive, smart, fast bowler who majored in intimidation.

There was a feeling on the panel that the time was right for Australia to try to change 'the psyche' a bit, to make the West Indies think "what are they up to?", to throw them a few curve balls.

In five seasons the make-up of our batting hadn't varied much from Marsh, Taylor, Boon, Border and Jones plus one other. That's not to say Australian cricket was in a rut, or we were losers; but every so often we seemed to lack that 'edge' that might have tipped the Frank Worrell Trophy our way.

I believe one of the strengths of the selection policy under Laurie Sawle was its consistency, its faith in players. Those two ingredients allow for a proper examination of a player's talents under real pressure.

But there is a danger in such a philosophy, too — you can become too relaxed, too comfortable, and the predictability of your selection can be reflected in the way in which the team performs.

In fact, the jigsaw pieces didn't look much different this time — except Marsh was out, and add in the two Waughs and Damien Martyn.

Martyn and Mark Waugh were the in-form players. Young Martyn had exhibited a lack of respect for his cricketing peers, sometimes recklessly but in the main fearlessly. On that evidence, and weight of runs, a selection panel could reasonably expect that Martyn was unlikely to be intimidated by Ambrose, Walsh, Patterson and Bishop.

Steve Waugh's temperament had undergone a severe test. After his Ashes glory in 1989 he had been dropped for his brother Mark from an Ashes Test in 1991. Not long after that in the Caribbean he'd even been chosen for a single Test as a No.7 batsman who bowled — a bowling allrounder!

Whilst in Test oblivion he had batted with some success at No.3 for NSW and had toured Zimbabwe with Mark Taylor's B team. With all that, and his current form in mind, a selector had to decide: is he a better, tougher player now for surviving all those setbacks?

Jones was out of form, although 'out of luck' might have been a reasonable observation, too; but, the saying about 'making your own luck' stands firm when it comes to selection.

Deano might have had a thought that his 76 runs from 106 balls at No.3 in the PM's game was a strong pointer to his chances, because amidst all the conjecture before the Test he was reported by one newspaper as saying, "I've got a fair idea where I'm going to bat."

But realistically, in the absence of good form in the Sheffield Shield, Deano's most recent Test form and his overall Test record were always going to be his best allies.

Statistics can reinforce any argument, no matter how sensible or how spurious, even to show that black is white! The most commonly quoted statistic in Deano's record is his Test average — 46.55; some say that any selector who drops a player with a record like that must be a space-brain.

It's important to realise that a player's career average doesn't necessarily reflect his current form, but in Deano's case he was coming off a statistically strong three-Test series against Sri Lanka in Sri Lanka — 276 runs at 55.20 — including an unbeaten even century in the Second Test. That's a strong case for retention.

As a matter of course, questions would be posed at the selection table … was it a quality performance? What was the state of the games when Deano batted? What influence did his performance have on the games and on the team's performance?

This excerpt from a media report on the Second Test was less than kind to Deano.

Dean Jones top scored in the innings, but he wouldn't have got past one if it hadn't been for one of many vital misses by the Sri Lankan fieldsmen. Jones went on to score 77 and then in the second innings was reprieved on nought and 40 on his way to an unconvincing century.

So what? There's not been a batsman take strike who hasn't needed a lucky break, or two. When selecting I'd sometimes read a media report on a day's play and wonder if I'd been at the same game.

Media reports never carried any weight whatsoever in our selection process. The question armchair selectors have to ask is this: what if, on this occasion, the media report turned out to be a fair assessment of Deano's performance and in 'synch' with the tour report?

Statistically, Deano's career had soared in the home summer that followed the Ashes glory tour of 1989, in Tests against New Zealand, Sri Lanka and Pakistan. In the Adelaide Test against Pakistan he made twin centuries and his career Test average reached 53.41; he was truly at the peak of his form.

But it was to be another 26 innings before he scored his next Test century, an unbeaten 150. That was in the 1991–92 season in the second innings of the last Test against India, the Test from which Mark Waugh and Geoff Marsh were both dropped for poor form.

It could be strongly argued that Deano deserved to be on the outside with them. In six innings in the first four Tests of that Indian series he'd made only 153 runs. Despite his 150 in the last, only his most ardent fans could have denied that his form was suffering a fairly dramatic decline.

The Indian series had preceded the tour to Sri Lanka where he had done well. What we had to assess at the selection table was whether the quality of his Sri Lankan performance had really done anything at all to reverse the decline that had started against India.

One final statistic that could be considered was Deano's record against the West Indies. He'd batted against them 19 times for one fifty (81 at St John's, Antigua in 1991) and one century (216, his highest score in Test cricket, at Adelaide in 1989).

The fifty and the century had both been scored in what are called 'dead Tests' — the series has been decided — as was his 150 against India. How much should that aspect of his record influence a selection panel if it was being asked to place high value on that record?

If we selectors were determined to pursue a more flexible philosophy against the West Indies, if we were determined to do what might be termed 'break the mould', then selecting an in-form Damien Martyn offered us the opportunity of a new, bold face and a player about whom the West Indies knew little, if anything.

Deano's record was immaterial in any comparison with Martyn. So, his record would have to stand against the current batting form of the Waughs.

Selection is not always as simple as Batsman A versus Batsman B; if their talent is rated the same, 'bells and whistles' might swing the argument. The Waughs could both bowl, Mark Waugh was a brilliant slips fielder, possibly the world's best, Steve was smart in the gully.

We needed a strong slips cordon for McDermott, Hughes and Bruce Reid. Jones could field there, too, but — he couldn't bowl if Bruce Reid broke down, always a real possibility.

That left only one other aspect to the selection to be considered: the No.3 batting spot. Jones had spent some of his early Test career there and his record showed he had done well there, averaging 48.63; in 1989 he had moved down to make way for David Boon. Neither of the Waughs had held down the Test No.3 spot.

But in the end the simple fact was that Deano, for one reason or another, had spent no major time in the middle, and was out of form. The opposite was true of his batting adversaries, the Waughs.

For Deano it was a summer *horribilis*. Early, his sense of humour remained intact. On the third day of the Test a hailstorm broke over the 'Gabba prompting 12th man Deano to don his helmet, go to his teammates' kits for more helmets and rush them out to the groundsmen who were frantically covering the pitch.

It raised a laugh among a crowd hunched miserably under plastic tarps and umbrellas, although it also raised the eyebrows of one or two of his teammates who were pondering the sodden fate of their gear!

There were more raised eyebrows at the SCG in January when in a World Series Final Deano asked Curtly Ambrose to remove his familiar white sweatband from his bowling wrist, and Curtly, after some unhappy arm-waving complied with the request and as well, removed five Australian batsmen for 32 runs.

Of course, Deano was entitled to register his concern about the sweatband — but was it smart, or only half-smart?

Deano's disappointing Sheffield Shield aggregate at summer's end (383 runs at 31.91 with a high score of 72 not out) was probably a true reflection of his state of mind all summer long. Down. Worse was to come — we selectors decided to leave Deano out of the 1993 Ashes squad.

I remember Jim Higgs said afterwards, "You're ending his Test career." Jim's words have stuck in my mind simply because it seemed to me to be an over-dramatisation of the situation, and a contradiction of Jim's usual, not-so-serious nature.

Jim's an old legspinner, and a smart one — in that unforgiving profession he recognised that the need to develop a sense of humour was just as important as the need to develop a well-disguised flipper.

I reckon Jim Higgs shared a fair bit of my father Lou's cricket philosophy. They both learned about the game in the country, Jim on weekends with the Kyabram fire brigade cricket team, north of Melbourne, sort of on the road to Simon O'Donnell country, Deniliquin.

"I play for fun," he said, not long after breaking into the Victorian Sheffield Shield team, but possibly still thinking of Saturday 'fire duty'. Lou maintained 'enjoyment' was a major factor in any successful cricketer's outlook.

Jim's bowling action was like Lou's, a rocking motion where the 'ball hand' started near the right hip, then swept up and over, allowing the ball to be flung out. "Fling the ball out, son," was Lou's coaching advice if a bowler wanted to achieve maximum spin.

Jim graduated into engineering with first-class honours in maths and physics, and listening to him doing an 'autopsy' on a legspinner was sometimes to imagine him planning a motorway around Mt Everest — 'apexes', the 'angle of the ball's axis', the 'square line of flight' all got a mention.

But when it was all boiled down he shared Lou's philosophy — "Accuracy and length come with practice. Spin's the main thing you need to accomplish when you're young," Jim said, "otherwise you'll have trouble learning it."

Then, just to reassure you that he hadn't lost his devil, he'd add, "And anyway, spinning the ball is more interesting than just tossing it up and worrying about accuracy."

On the panel Jim had always been the one of us least likely to lean towards any "in the name of the Son, the Father and the Holy Ghost, amen" speeches about any player in the shadow of the axe.

As it turned out, Jim was right about the demise of Deano — mixing drinks at the 'Gabba in that First Test against the West Indies was indeed his last Test. Why should Jim have had such a premonition?

Perhaps he realised that England were still so unstable in 1993 that anyone in the Australian batting line-up could do little else but enhance his career prospects. But that's a cynical outlook, and Jim was not given to cynicism when it came to Australian cricketers.

It's more likely Jim's premonition was to do with Deano's age, going on 32, and something else that was happening in Australian cricket at that time — the graduates from the Australian Institute of Sport Cricket Academy were beginning to announce themselves in a big way.

Ponting, Martyn and Bevan were just a few of the wave of bright young batsmen who were dumping on bowlers in the Sheffield Shield — and not all of them were from the Academy, for instance Matthew Hayden.

A judge as good as Jim would have recognised that Deano, even in good form, would indeed have a real struggle to make it back into the Test team, particularly if it kept winning.

Deano versus The Waughs, a comparison:					
	Tests	Runs	H'Score	50/100	Ave
Jones	52	3631	216 (WI)	14/11	46.55
M Waugh	69	4464	140 (Eng)	28/11	41.33
S Waugh	95	5960	200 (WI)	34/14	49.67

As well as playing 50-plus Tests for Australia Dean Jones played 164 One-day Internationals, a memorable career. Other cricketers haven't been that talented, nor has good fortune smiled upon them in the way they might have hoped. They played only one Test.

ROWDY

There are 58 cricketers who played only one Test for Australia. They are unkindly referred to as 'one-Test-wonders'. How can this happen? How can a panel of selectors whose reputation is to keep the faith, judge a player on one Test only?

Spare a thought for the Grade, or district cricket selector, one of a panel which might comprise a glut of self-centred skippers with a premiership on their minds, or their own 'mates' agenda. Such panels have to choose five different twelves from 70 players, a task made more difficult because it involves 'grading' the talent.

It's crystal ball stuff, because from net trials the selector has to make an instant judgment not only on talent, but talent potential and, toughest of all, temperament. Sheer guesswork, really. Like doing Lotto.

For instance, judgment on a 16-year-old batsman who can hit them out of sight might be influenced by the fact that he also throws his bat out of sight when things don't go right. But who's to know he won't grow out of that at 21 and, at the same time retain his talent?

Just how difficult the job can be at that lower level is reinforced by this note in the 1939–40 annual report of the Central Cumberland club in the Sydney grade competition: "T. Urry registered a unique performance by commencing the season with the Shires and ultimately reaching the First grade eleven."

Urry went from the bottom to the top … a poor pre-season net trial, perhaps?

The State selector in Australia has a tough job, too. He is the one who has to have the true eye for potential, the gift of spotting the player who will one day strengthen the winning chances of the Australian team.

It can be a difficult balancing act because simultaneously he has to address winning the Sheffield Shield and, depending on certain match conditions, that might tempt him to omit a particular style of bowler, even though he might be of Test potential.

That's the 'horses for courses' theory. But doesn't that raise an important point — shouldn't cricketers be able to handle all conditions? The early career progress of Shane Warne provided a fascinating insight into some Victorian selection philosophy on spin.

The fact is, unless the State selectors get it terribly wrong, the Australian selectors should always be observing the cream of cricketing talent. That doesn't make it an easy job for the national panel, but it's certainly not as difficult as trying to choose 12 'potentials' from 70 rookies.

At national level some players are rated 'certainties' — Allan Border in peak form, for instance — and other players fill specialist positions, like the wicketkeeper, or the opening batsmen, or the spinner. And, if you're really lucky, spinners plural!

For instance, in Australia's 119-year Test history there have only been 27 wicketkeepers chosen, and 10 of those played less than 10 Tests. Such positional influences in the national selection process considerably improve the odds about the selectors getting it right.

But when an Australian selection panel creates a one-Test-wonder you can rightly question the original judgment.

Wayne Phillips was a diminutive Victorian opening batsman. In modern cricket parlance the 'suits' in marketing would package him as 'unfashionable'. A caricaturist might have portrayed him as two eyes under a helmet, peeping out from an oversize pair of þads.

His batting style was slightly ugly, but well organised, and he was a run accumulator rather than a run machine. When he was chosen for Australia he was balding, and 29 years old. In the horse racing game that's 'aged'. He was a quiet type, hence the predictable nickname 'Rowdy'.

The selection panel had on its hands a problem near the end of the 1991–92 season — the complete lack of form of the vice-captain and courageous opener Geoff 'Swampy' Marsh.

Marsh had been an integral part of the rebuilding of Australia's strength through the '80s, and a major player in our success at both forms of the game, but after four Tests against India he had less than 200 runs at 25.

This slump had been preceded by a poor series against the West Indies.

If the numbers had been stacked up on a graph the trend line would have resembled a slippery slide. In such circumstances the options for selectors are limited — stick with the player and hope he comes out of it, or drop him.

If the series against India had been line-ball, and we'd needed to win or draw the Fifth we might have been tempted to stick with Marsh on the score of his past record and experience.

Or, we could have applied the 'horse for the course' theory, as the Test was to be played in Perth, Marsh's home town. But we were three-up in the series, and unbeatable.

And anyway, the theory that you never change a winning team is misguided — the trick is to keep trying to improve the combination. So, all the ingredients were there for a team change, even though Marsh was the vice-captain. If he'd been the captain the process would have been handled in an entirely different way.

Marsh was 33 years old, and, the West Indies were coming back to Australia for a five-Test series the following summer — what if Marsh remained out of form? To retain him could compromise the future performance of the team. We'd have missed the perfect chance to address a potential weakness.

The team was chosen via telephone hook-up, never the best way, but necessary because the Fourth Test was being played in Adelaide and the selectors were scattered, at the Sheffield Shield or some other level of cricket, such as Second XI.

Phillips came in for Marsh, to continue the right-left combination with Mark Taylor; his gritty character had been noted when he helped Victoria tough it out to win the Sheffield Shield Final against NSW the previous summer — a selection panel can see such determination as a plus should he ever get into a tangle with trouble-making Test quicks.

The other option was to 'spec' a young player, Matthew Hayden, 20 years old, from Queensland. He was fashioning the first of three successive 1,000-run seasons, but the selectors weren't to know that.

He was a left-hander — should the prospect of a left-left combination (with Mark Taylor) have been a worry? He was young and inexperienced, and his style was almost completely half front-foot — should that have been a concern with the West Indian tour just around the corner? We could afford to wait and see how he played at the start of the next Sheffield Shield season.

The dropping of Marsh sent out a message — there is some doubt about one opening batting spot. The choice of a player of Phillips' age and moderate performance suggested we hadn't necessarily found a stand-out candidate. The fallout from the Phillips' selection, unfortunately, was ill-considered and sometimes bitter. Its catalyst was the high esteem in which Marsh was held within the team.

A few years later, coach Bob Simpson described Phillips' promotion as "the biggest mistake we made as selectors". In his book, *The Reasons Why*, Bob said, "I did not go along with his (Phillips') selection because at that time it seemed like too much of a one-off. Our policy had been to give players an extended run and Phillips' selection went against that strategy."

He doesn't offer an alternative to Phillips, but he does comment on the dropping of Marsh: "The decision was made no easier by the fact that Geoff Marsh had to be dropped in order to fit Phillips in. When I went to that selection meeting, I knew Swampy probably shouldn't survive, but it was still a tough one. My hardest one of all."

What's Bob saying there — apart from "It wasn't me!"? A mixed message it is and you get the impression Bob would have liked Marsh to stay, even though he "knew he probably shouldn't survive".

The selection was done the night before the last day of the Adelaide Test; selectors prefer not to make announcements about team changes — negative ones, anyway — midway through a Test. It can sap team morale.

Bob subscribed to that philosophy, because occasionally when advocating it he would use as an example the low point in my career — being sacked, whilst not out overnight, in the middle of my second Test against Pakistan.

But on this occasion, if we are to believe Shane Warne, Bob decided the team should know about the changes.

In his book, *My Own Story*, Warne reveals: "That morning before we began our warm-up, Bob Simpson called us together and told us Swampy and Mark Waugh had been dropped. Everyone was stunned and the warm-up and fielding practice before play were pretty ordinary."

And, as we later found out, captain Allan Border, was particularly filthy. Via telephone hook-up to Perth, he tongue-lashed chairman Laurie Sawle over the Marsh dropping.

Three points can be made about that: one, it shows Australian captains don't always get the team they think they deserve; two, Border's pro-Marsh outburst, which became public, certainly could not have helped debutant Phillips' pre-Test build-up.

The third point is this: should a captain be on, or off, a selection panel? Had Border been sitting in on the panel would his public reaction to the Marsh dropping have been more moderate? Does being part of a reasoning process automatically defuse aggression?

What if Border had been on the panel, and presented to the rest of the selectors the same ultimatum he offered Laurie Sawle? What might the panel have done — sacked AB, too?

In my view, selection needs to be a dispassionate process. I subscribe to former American President Harry S. Truman's theory about selection; he once said, "When you appoint someone to the Supreme Court he ceases to be your friend." The danger of having captains on selection panels is they can be blindly patriotic to their teammates. There needs to be a 'separation of powers'.

Consultation with the captain, before and after, remains the best way to go.

In the final Test Kapil Dev cemented his reputation as one of the world's great swing bowlers by passing 400 Test wickets, none of which was Wayne Phillips, but the Victorian made only eight runs and 14.

Immediately following the series against India we selectors named an Australian team to tour Sri Lanka — Phillips' name was missing. Who knows what thoughts might have gone through his head when he heard the news? "Gee, what happened there?" might have been one. To draw again on an inference made by Bob Simpson in his book, didn't the non-selection of Phillips seem to go against the panel's 'extended run philosophy'?

No opener was chosen in Wayne Phillips' place. Not Marsh, not Hayden. If the original dropping of Marsh had sent out the message that we were on the lookout for a new opening batsman, this decision hurled in a couple of qualifications, loud and clear: we're not sure about Phillips, or anyone else for that matter.

There was another one — all is not lost, Swampy. The cricketing public was entitled to criticise us for a high-risk strategy, entitled to question why we weren't trying to blood another opener on the tour. After all, immediately after concluding the three-Test tour to Sri Lanka the Australian team would fly home to take on the West Indies.

It didn't seem sensible to be leaving the opening batting combination up in the air. The stratosphere, even.

The only regular opener chosen for the tour was Taylor. It was left to the tour selectors to decide who would fill the other spot, but David Boon, who had opened successfully until 1989, when Taylor was brought in, was certainly well tried and, more than anyone else, likely to do well.

But the tour selectors left Boon in the No.3 slot; Tom Moody, a batsman who had been chosen in five Tests as a middle-order player, was now asked to open the batting, and in foreign conditions. A tall order, even for a skyscraper like Tom. He made 71 runs in six innings.

Some observers made the point that the Moody decision was nothing less than a deliberate attempt by the tour selectors to leave the way open for a Geoff Marsh comeback. But that allegation looks a bit skinny if we ask the simple question: what if Moody had succeeded?

As it was, Swampy made 121 in the first match of the next summer, against Queensland at the 'Gabba, venue for the First Test, but its quality didn't convince the selectors. Phillips accumulated 205 in 585 minutes for Victoria against NSW and then opened with Hayden for the Australian XI against the Windies in the pre-Test trial in Hobart.

It is history now that David Boon opened in the First Test against the Windies. And, it is history that the Tom Moody opening experiment possibly prematurely ended his Test career.

Hayden made his Test debut in 1994 when Mark Taylor was unfit on the morning of a Test against South Africa.

Wayne Phillips never played another Test.

Of the 58 Australian one-Test-wonders, 19 were chosen for the last Test in a series, nine of them 'dead Tests' because the series had already been decided. Two of them made a half-century, Stuart Law and Albert Hartkopf. One, Mick Malone, returned a five-wicket haul.

Still, it's better to have made it once than not to have made it at all. One who didn't make it was my cricket-loving father, Lou. He had a brilliant record as a legspin bowler, but he couldn't beat the NSW Education Department.

LOU

*Richie Benaud played 11 Tests more than Dean Jones,
Rowdy Phillips played two Tests fewer than me — could
Lou Benaud, had he been given the chance he deserved,
have been good enough to play for his country, too?*

Louis Richard Benaud. Born Coraki, northern NSW,
February 28, 1904. Died North Parramatta, near Sydney,
January 8, 1994. Lou was a country boy, who spent his
early youth in the northern rivers district of NSW. His
grandfather, Jean Benaud, was a master mariner, from
Bordeaux, France. Maybe there was French cricket in
the Benaud blood ...

Lou became a schoolteacher. In those days it
was a travelling profession, but no matter to
which farflung country town the public service
took Lou — North Casino, Koorawatha,
Jugiong — he enjoyed the game of cricket.

In these recollections of Lou's, set out as
they were in school exercise books, and
detailed in his precise, legible, upright
hand, you may see some of the determination, and success, that was to
influence the diverse careers in cricket
of his two sons ... and others.

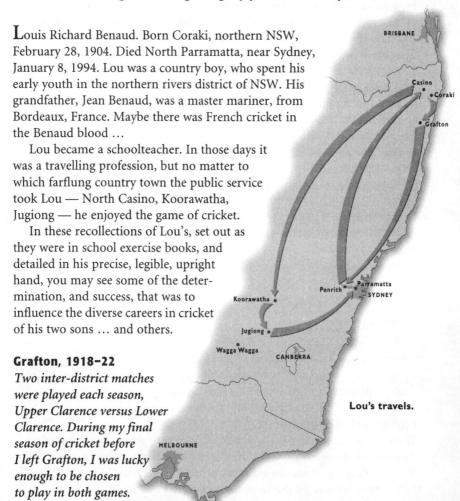

Lou's travels.

Grafton, 1918–22
*Two inter-district matches
were played each season,
Upper Clarence versus Lower
Clarence. During my final
season of cricket before
I left Grafton, I was lucky
enough to be chosen
to play in both games.*

A.O. Gray, the captain of our team, was one of the best wicketkeepers I'd seen. I didn't expect to be called on to do much bowling because Albert Ford, an experienced and capable legspinner, was also in the team.

In the Lower Clarence team was a batsman named Vic McClucas, who would now be referred to as "The Bradman of the Lower Clarence". I remember some of his scores were 404, 345 and 267. He seemed to score a century, a double century and other very high scores fairly frequently.

I was anxious to see him for I'd read about his century scoring efforts. I didn't have long to wait for A.O. Gray won the toss and sent Lower Clarence in to bat. McClucas opened and took strike.

As I watched A.O. set the field I wondered who was going to open the bowling. When he'd set the field A.O. threw the ball to me and said, "You open the bowling, Lou."

I bowled to McClucas, he moved out to drive it, missed, and A.O. stumped him off the first ball of the match.

It wasn't unusual to open the bowling with a spinner in those days. Because McClucas knew Albert Ford's style A.O. used me as a sort of shock trooper. Albert Ford's finger spin type of legspin bowling was much slower through the air than my fast wrist spin type of bowling.

uncovered concrete pitches on Fisher Park. The schoolmate who showed me how to bowl legbreaks gave me my second bit of coaching. This time it was how to stand up to fast bowlers instead of backpeddling towards square leg.

My game improved and I ...

From Lou's notes on cricket.

When Lou was 19 years old his father, Richard Grainger Napoleon Benaud, a jeweller and watchmaker by profession, chose to move the family from Grafton to Penrith, then a small town in Sydney's outer west.

Penrith 1923–25
There was an unusual arrangement re the venue of games in the B grade competition. Each match was played over two Saturday afternoons — the first Saturday's play was on the home ground of one team, while the second Saturday's play was on the home ground of the other team.

It was while such arrangements were in force that I took 20 wickets in one match. I've never bowled better in my cricket career than in the first Saturday of the game when we played St Marys B on Penrith Showground, where I took ten wickets for 30 runs and on the following Saturday at St Marys where I took ten wickets for 35 runs.

TWENTY WICKETS IN A MATCH — THE SCOREBOARD
Waratah v. St Marys

WARATAH

L Reddan	b R Morrison	2	(8)	b A Morrison	23
G Gow	b M Bennett	0		b Bennett	0
F Knight	b M Bennett	2	(4)	c&b Bennett	16
H Wright	b R Morrison	14	(6)	b R Morrison	16
L Benaud	c G Bennet b R M'son	9	(7)	c G Bennett b M Bennett	1
T Glassock	not out	49	(9)	c&b A Morrison	30
A Edwards	b M Bennett	6	(3)	c Beacroft b R Morrison	0
R Burns	c G Bennett b Moore	0	(5)	absent	8
C Thorndike	c Dollin b M Bennett	0	(1)	c Ward b Dougherty	3
L Moore	run out	5	(11)	run out	2
N Greaves	b Moore	3	(10)	not out	3
Sundries		8			9
Total		**98**			**116**

First innings bowling: M Bennett 4/31, R Morrison 3/25, G Bennett 0/21, Moore 2/13.

Second innings bowling: M Bennett 3/29, R Morrison 2/24, Dougherty 1/15, Moore 0/18, G Bennett 0/10, H Dollin 0/6, A Morrison 2/5.

ST MARYS

H Dollin	b Benaud	4	(6)	st Greaves b Benaud	10
R Morrison	b Benaud	1	(5)	c Wright b Benaud	24
E Dougherty	c Glassock b Benaud	10	(1)	c Wright b Benaud	4
M Bennett	c Gow b Benaud	4		c Reddan b Benaud	0
A Morrison	c Wright b Benaud	10	(7)	b Benaud	0
J Beacroft	b Benaud	16	(3)	b Benaud	3
G Bennett	b Benaud	0	(2)	st Greaves b Benaud	4
D Turner	b Benaud	0		b Benaud	0
W Dollin	b Benaud	0		b Benaud	18
W Ward	lbw Benaud	0		not out	11
G Moore	not out	10		b Benaud	0
Sundries		7			5
Total		**52**			**79**

First innings bowling: Benaud 10/30 (inc hat-trick), Wright 0/15.

Second innings bowling: Benaud 10/35, Edwards 0/21, Wright 0/8, Reddan 0/10.

Waratah won outright by 83 runs.

When I took my seventh wicket on the second Saturday the bowler at the other end bowled the next over so wide that the striker didn't have to play at one ball. At the end of that over I went to our captain and informed him that I wouldn't bowl anymore if the other bowlers bowled wide.

The captain stopped any further foolish bowling behaviour and I was able to take the three remaining wickets by merit and, not by favour of the other bowlers.

Some representatives from the Sydney district cricket club, Cumberland, called at our home and my father consented to their request that I be allowed to play for the club. I played all but one game in second grade — a first grade match at the hallowed SCG.

I decided to become a schoolteacher. At the end of my course I was appointed to a bush school — One Tree Farm Provisional School at North Casino (600 kilometres from Sydney). I endeavoured to have my appointment changed so that I could remain in Sydney and continue to play for Cumberland.

Permission was refused. From the time I left Grafton until I finished my teaching term at North Casino I had a great desire to become a Test cricketer. I had outstanding performances in high school cricket, junior cricket and country cricket so I felt that if I had the opportunity there was a chance I might make it.

Lou was 21 going on 25 and if you ask any good judge of cricketers they will tell you that these are the transforming years, the years when a player matures, the time in a cricketer's life when he's most likely to make it.

North Casino 1925–29

When I was teaching at North Casino what I regarded as perhaps the most wonderful experience of my cricket career was to be chosen in the North Coast cricket team to play against Alan Kippax's team on the Recreation Ground at Lismore. In Kippax's Sydney team were also Archie Jackson and Don Bradman.

We scored 212 and they scored 224, so there wasn't much in it. The match was played on an antbed pitch with a canvas mat on it and occasionally the ball kept low. Our fast bowler created a sensation when he bowled Archie Jackson and had Don Bradman, who followed him, caught behind off the next ball.

I had a good match as I scored 39 not out and took three for 65. It was quite a thrill to get the wicket of Alan Kippax with the third ball I bowled to him. Although I only bowled three deliveries to Kippax I formed the opinion that here was a batsman who could take a leg break bowler apart.

The first ball was a leg break of good length pitched on the leg stump. It was glanced to the leg boundary. The second delivery was a good length leg break pitched on the off stump. That ball was back cut very speedily to the boundary.

The third ball was a good length top spinner pitched on the middle stump. Kippax prepared to back cut the ball but it went straight on for his middle stump. But he wasn't completely beaten for he changed his stroke and followed the ball with his bat; the ball and his bat hit the middle stump at the same time.

After the match I was called into our opponents' dressing room where Kippax congratulated me on my bowling and then he added that if I was ever considering going to Sydney to play cricket he would help me join a Sydney grade club.

An invitation that Lou was forced to refuse.

While he was at North Casino, Lou was selected to take part in The Quest For Bowlers organised by the *Daily Guardian* newspaper. It was to be held at the SCG. He went to the Education Department seeking permission to attend. It was refused.

He was also twice chosen in the North Coast team to play in the Country Week cricket carnival in Sydney, an acknowledged 'talent quest'. Leave of absence was again refused. Lou wrote:

I was so frustrated by the transfer refusal and the leave of absence refusals that I took a vow: if I married and there were any boys in our family they would not become schoolteachers and, they would get opportunities that I had missed to reach the top of the cricket ladder.

The One Tree Farm school at North Casino was at the edge of 'Hillcrest', a dairy farm owned by George Saville. Lou took a shine to one of George's three daughters, Irene, but to everyone, Rene. She had watched Lou playing cricket on the property next door, where a bachelor with a love for the game prepared his own antbed pitch.

He was Jim Saville, Rene's uncle. Lou and Rene were married one January Saturday in the Lismore Presbyterian church — at 7am, so they could catch the 9am steam train to Sydney, the only train, to spend a brief honeymoon at Bondi, as popular for young lovers then as it is today.

In the year Rich was born, 1930, The Depression had gripped Australia. Lou was transferred to Koorawatha, 1,000 kilometres south from Casino and 300 kilometres south-west of Sydney.

A two-year long drought had reduced the red soil to dust for as far as the eye could see, a joyless landscape made all the more depressing by the sight of pile upon pile of dead sheep.

Lou taught at Warrandale, 11 kilometres from Koorawatha along a dirt road deeply rutted by the wheels of the bullock drays; broken axles on Lou's Chev Tourer were an occasional test of his temperament.

There was no competition cricket, but matches were arranged against cricket teams from nearby towns. Sometimes 'nearby' could be a long way. Rene remembers Lou's 'creams' were 'pinks', coloured by the red soil that impregnated the bore water supply. Lou wrote:

I think it is worth recording that during a match against Wattamondara at Koorawatha I had seventeen chances dropped off my bowling before lunch. We still won the match!

In 1932 the Education Department moved Lou on again, this time to Jugiong school, a further 70 kilometres south, on the road to Gundagai. There he remained until 1937. In any one of those five years he taught six classes, 50 children of various ages, in one room separated by a dividing curtain.

Just about any day in winter Lou and Rene could gaze out from the school residence and see a grassy hill and its pepper trees turned white, not by snow but by frost. In summer there were large brown snakes, and cricket.

The local press reported that Lou, then 28 years old, made quite an impact: "Jugiong has without a doubt the best slow bowler in the country, in the person of Lou Benaud," it said.

Some of his first season performances were: v Cooney's Creek 7 for 55; v Harden 8 for 24; v Murrumbah 6 for 19; v Bogans 6 for 24; v Cunningham's Creek 9 for 48. Meanwhile, Rich had turned four years old and was showing ball sense.

Thirteen years after he'd been sent bush, Lou was posted back to the Sydney metropolitan area, to Burnside school at North Parramatta — Cumberland Cricket Club territory. What an irony! Back in the backyard of the very club which had thought so much of his potential all those years before. Full circle, but now he was 33 years old. Lou wrote:

I decided to retire from cricket but I was persuaded to attend the Cumberland pre-season practices at Lidcombe Oval and I was lucky enough to be chosen in the First Grade team for the first match of the season at Cumberland Oval.

I had to buy a new pair of sprigged boots which had full length running spikes in the soles and heels. I used them at the pre-season practices and had them on at Cumberland Oval before we were to take the field.

The curator walked over to me and asked me to show him the spikes in my cricket boots. When he had carried out his inspection I was amazed and bewildered as to what I would do after he had finished saying that I would not be allowed to use those spikes on his pitch.

After I'd informed him that I'd no other cricket boots and I had no way of shortening the length of the running spikes he relented somewhat and said that he would shorten them.

We went to the smaller of the two grandstands underneath which he kept his equipment. He got an axe and a hammer, placed each spike on the cutting edge of the axe blade and hit each spike with the hammer.

It was a pretty rough job but I was allowed to play. After, I noticed some other members of the team had long running spikes in the soles and heels of their cricket boots ... I wondered whether the new boy from the bush had been set up!

Lou stopped playing in 1956, when he was 52 years old. In the end, at Cumberland, they called him 'Colt'. He had played 18 seasons as a leg break bowler with Cumberland in First, Second and Third grades, taking 572 wickets, 360 of them in First grade, at 20.8.

The Cumberland end-of-season reports acknowledge his great bowling talent: "L. Benaud staged some really good bowling performances … his turn on any wickets was pronounced, and he repeatedly beat the batsmen … week after week, catches were dropped off his bowling … if only a fraction of these chances had been accepted, he certainly would have broken R.C. Coogan's First grade record of 56 wickets in a season."

THE THOUGHTS OF LOU

There is something about cricket that one doesn't seem to get so strongly from other games. That something is the 'spirit of cricket', which creates a great love of the game in the heart of the person who is imbued with the spirit.

Lou Benaud Joins A Select Trio

Veteran spin bowler, Lou Benaud, on Saturday became the fourth Cumberland cricketer to take 300 wickets in first grade matches.

Les Pye (480), Rupert Coogan (337) and Mark Bosley (307) were the other three.

Benaud brought his total to 303 when he took five for 65 against Balmain and has built up his aggregate over a period of ten seasons. Duri

Cumberland Argus, 1947–48 season.

What is it about cricket that produces such love of the game and such loyalty to the game? It is the uncertainty of the game.

Those persons who refer to a promising young player as 'another Bradman' or 'another Davidson' do considerable damage to such young players; it gives a false impression of his skill and ability; they have labelled him as a cricketer absolutely devoid of a personality of his own, a shadow of some great cricketing character of history.

Cricket has been played for many years and in spite of some people is still strong. There is nothing wrong with cricket — only with those who play cricket the wrong way, those who administer cricket in the wrong way and those who select the wrong types of cricketers.

I think it's about time the 12th man's duties were confined to playing cricket instead of acting as a waiter, general dressing room useful and messenger boy.

Players seem to be regarded as too old at 30 these days. It is just the opposite with administrators who never know when to retire.

I have no time for the negative and unethical in cricket. Ethics and cricket are like true friends — never at their best when they are parted. Those who separate them leave themselves open to accusations of bad sportsmanship, while their methods are branded as, "That's not cricket."

Enthusiasm and enjoyment are necessary ingredients of a cricketer's make-up. Once he loses his enthusiasm for the game and his enjoyment of the game he should retire for he is not giving one hundred per cent team effort.

Some people maintain that batsmen should walk when they know they are out. If that is so it should be fair enough for a batsman to refuse to leave the wicket when that batsman knows he is not out, but has been given out in error by an umpire.

Some people maintain pitches should be completely covered, others that they should not be covered under any circumstances. There doesn't appear to be much sense in rolling a pitch to be hard and fast then allowing it to be wet and become a soft, plum pudding.

It is the easy way out to buy very good players from other States or from overseas countries. Why not accept the challenge and develop over a period of time potentially promising cricketers from within his own State?

Over a period of time a bowler should be judged by the number of overs he takes to secure each wicket. One would assume that a bowler who bowled 150 overs for 50 wickets was more positive than his team-mate who bowled 150 overs for 25 wickets.

Surely no umpire is expected to be so good that his judgment always correctly decides what has happened. All umpires must make some mistakes. The better the umpire the fewer the mistakes, although a good umpire like a good cricketer may have a run of outs. No umpire ever expects a cricketer to succeed all the time.

In the summer of 1947–48 Lou enjoyed his own inspirational moment — he and Rich, father and son, took the field together for Cumberland First grade. Lou matched his most successful season — 54 wickets. Rich took nine. It got better.

RICH

*Rich took 248 Test wickets for Australia, a record
that stood from 1963–64 until 1980–81, when Dennis
Lillee topped it. Rich was also acclaimed as one of the
game's most enterprising captains. It was, at times,
an uncertain career path, but Lou had most certainly
prepared him for that.*

Was Rich lucky? A fellow cricketer once said if Rich had put his head in a
bucket of pig slops he'd have come up with a mouthful of diamonds. Or was
he just tough?

There was no doctor at Koorawatha in 1930 and Rene had to travel back
to Penrith, Lou's home town, to have Rich. He was premature, and sickly,
and the doctor forbade Rene to take him back to Koorawatha.

After six weeks there was only slight improvement in his condition, but
the doctor relented. Rene, with Rich, and supported by Lou's sister, made the
long journey home by steam train, a heatwave all the way, and dusty.

When school broke up for the summer holidays, Lou and Rene brought
Rich back to Penrith and took him to the doctor for a check-up.

Rene remembers the moment, the doctor talking to Lou: "I'll tell you now
Lou, I let that little fellow go home to die. He must have wanted to live. I
could do nothing more for him." Lou wrote:

*At Jugiong public school, when Rich was about four, a very small bat was
cut from packing case timber and he began to hit a tennis ball with the bat.*

*The school residence was a huge place because one of the teachers, who
had lived there some years before we did, had a very large family so some
extra rooms had to be built on to the original residence.*

*We did not use any of those extra rooms as living quarters, but as Richie
progressed in his cricket skills, one of the empty rooms was used by him
when he played with the bat and ball.*

*In addition to having a bat and ball he also had a pencil and scorebook.
He wrote down (the names of) two Test sides and he became batsman,
bowler, fieldsman, wicketkeeper, umpire and scorer.*

Maybe he was a little patriotic, for Australia won more Tests than the other sides. It was sweet music to hear the ball being hit in that room for it signified that Rich had developed a keenness for cricket.

Towards the end of our stay at Jugiong, Rich had his first game of cricket against a team from Bookham Public School. He was only six years old and to a parent, doting or otherwise, it was a rather frightening experience to see the little chap facing up to a fast lifting compo ball (compressed cork), bowled by lads nearly twice his size, on coir mat.

I have this mind picture … I was the smallest of boys, only four years old, trailing close behind Rene as she walked down the hallway of our North Parramatta home to answer a loud knock at the front door.

Rene opened the door, and I can still hear her urgent gasp, "Oh, Rich …"

I looked up and saw Rich; his usually cricket-tanned face was black and yellow in colour. This is what had happened, related later by Lou:

In a Second XI match at Melbourne in the 1948–49 season, Rich tried to hook a bumper but he was hit on the forehead. He was taken to hospital and x-rayed. The x-ray was negative. When he returned home we were deeply shocked by the extremely bruised and swollen appearance of his face.

He went to see Dr Jack Jeffery, a great lover of cricket, and further x-rays were taken. The doctor called at our place the following Saturday morning and asked where Richie was. We told him that Rich had gone to Lidcombe Oval to watch Cumberland First grade play a match.

The doctor gave us a severe shock when he informed us that Rich had a severely shattered frontal bone in his head and then he asked us to ring the Oval and tell Richie not to practise in the nets as a blow on the injured head would result in his death. After a successful operation Rich was able to play cricket again during the next cricket season.

Later in his career, Rich wrote about this incident, and did so advisedly:

One of the most exciting sights in cricket is a fast bowler being belted by a good hooker … I still like to go for the hook myself, although it once nearly put paid to my career when I was playing for the NSW Second XI. I got right behind the line of a bumper from Victoria's Jack Daniel, missed it and was taken to hospital with a fractured skull.

You see, the bumper is one ball you must not get behind. Instead you must go further across. You need to move right inside the line of flight and that means moving quickly. If you cannot move quickly enough so that your body is across to the offside and the ball is passing

down the legside, then forget all about playing the hook. It will either get you out, or injured.

In recent times we haven't seen too many hookers, good or otherwise. The reason cannot be because bowlers are faster. Is it just the product of a modern coaching discipline — a non-percentage shot? Or, do helmets have something to do with it?

Helmets are protection against a potentially fatal head injury from the short-pitched delivery. Cricketers were once taught that their best protection against the bouncer was the hook shot. More than that, they expected to score runs from it. Counter attack.

It could be argued that the helmet is a positive safety factor but a negative game factor. Because the helmet is a comfort thing does it take the edge off the batsman's instinct to survive, the mental signal that can trigger the hook shot?

As much as the hook shot depends on good footwork and good position, so does it depend on the sharpest of reflexes. Of course, another reason for the hook being the forgotten shot is the lawmakers.

When they decided to limit the number of bouncers a batsman could receive — rather than stressing umpires should enforce the unfair play rule — the former West Indian captain, Richie Richardson, was peeved, and rightly so. He said, indignantly, "Man, they've taken away my most productive shot."

Rich was one of three cricketers the selectors chose for a Test debut against the West Indies in the 1951–52 series in Australia. It was the Fifth Test of the series, a 'dead' Test because Australia led 3–1.

In the series, Australia had used three different opening combinations. Now, they used another, Colin McDonald and George Thoms. Thoms, a solid type from Victoria, made 16 and 28 and never played another Test.

This Test was at the SCG, a postcard of a ground then and, to support Rich Lou had travelled by bus, train, tram and foot, sitting in the M.A. Noble stand, lower deck, as near to behind the bowler as was possible.

Rene remembers the day as 'hot'. It was — 105 degrees, "in the shade", as weather people are fond of adding, just to make sure everyone knows how hot they really are.

Rich made three runs. His wicket was one of 19 that fell on the first day. He took one wicket, the very last one to fall in the Test. It was not, as he might have hoped, one of the famed Three Ws, Walcott, Worrell or Weekes, who were Nos. 3, 4 and 5 in the West Indian line-up.

It was the No.11 Alf Valentine, a left-arm spinner whose eventual Test batting average over 36 matches was 4.70. The optometrist who prescribed the strength of Alf's wire-framed spectacles possibly revisited the drawing board. Rich had made a modest start.

The next summer Rich was 12th man for the First Test against South Africa, but he played in the next four. He scored 124 runs, took 10 wickets and, in the Third at the SCG, fielding in the gully, had his mouth bloodied and teeth smashed by John Waite's square cut.

After five Tests he had scored 146 runs, and not a fifty among them. Rene found it hard to listen to the radio: "If Rich was batting I used to go outside and iron."

And, he had taken 11 wickets, with a best haul of four for 118. The selectors, Bill Brown, Phil Ridings and Jack Ryder chose him for the 1953 Ashes tour. Sir Donald Bradman was missing from the panel — the only time between 1938 and 1969 — because of a family illness.

It was the longest tour since World War I. It lasted 39 matches and the players were away from home for eight months. At North Parramatta, Lou and Rene stayed up late, listening to descriptions of play via the shortwave.

Most of it was frustrating, interrupted by that gutteral, swishing sound that accompanied such faraway broadcasts, and the Ashes were lost.

We can be sure it was a defining moment in the Australian dressing room — Australia had held them for a record 19 years. Rich played three Tests, and was dropped from the third and the last. He made 15 runs in five innings. His two Test wickets had cost him 87 runs each.

Back at home, he was batting for his Sydney club team Cumberland next season and a friend of Lou's overheard a conversation: "Can't bat, never could bat, never will be able to bat." The speaker later became a NSW selector.

Rene: "Lou was worried Rich would be dropped. He used to say, 'I hope they don't drop him, he'll come good.'"

England were back in Australia in 1954–55. Rich played in all five Tests. He scored 148 runs, but again there was no fifty. He took 10 wickets, but still didn't have a five-wicket haul. What is a selector to make of form like that? Is there is a limit to a selector's patience?

But ... Rich had come back from the 1953 tour of England and, in the Sheffield Shield, scored more runs than any other NSW player (665, three centuries) and taken more wickets (30). And, around Australia only Ken

Mackay and Colin McDonald scored more runs, and only Ian Johnson took more wickets.

On the strength of that the selectors were entitled to think the tour experience might have improved him and, to choose him in the next series, particularly if their philosophy demanded they find a quality allrounder, one who could bowl legspin.

But after that 1954–55 series his Test record was as depressed as ever: 13 matches, barely 300 runs, and only 23 wickets. The selectors had to ask the tough question — did they still think Richie Benaud could make the step from Sheffield Shield to Test class?

Selectors who persevere with a player in such circumstances are often accused of being pig-headed, or of a refusal to admit that their first judgment was wrong.

And, such selection consistency in the face of player misfortune lends weight to the theory that it's tough to get into the Australian team, but it's a whole lot tougher to get out of it.

The selection process that immediately followed The Ashes series defined what sets real cricket selectors apart from armchair cricket selectors. Instead of committing Rich to Test cricket oblivion, Bradman, Ryder and Dudley Seddon maintained faith.

They chose him for the 1955 tour to the West Indies. You can ask me, as a one-time Australian selector, whether I would have picked him. Of course! Wouldn't you have?

Rich made 246 runs in five Tests and hit a century in 78 minutes at Sabina Park. And he took 18 wickets, but no five-wicket hauls. However, he did get the 'Three Ws' eight times (Weekes — whom the 'keeper had dropped off him in Rich's SCG debut Test — four times, Walcott three, and Worrell hit his wicket).

Do selectors have a hunch, or a gut feeling? How do they think? The good selector has a 'knowledge' born of years of watching and playing against cricketers of every type and every grade.

Bradman, a champion, had an 'eye' for a champion cricketer, just as the gifted horse trainer has an eye for a champion thoroughbred. Of course, neither is always on the money. Cricket is as uncertain as the racing game.

Before the Australian team left for its 1956 Ashes tour, Sir Donald gave us a hint of his thought processes. The chairman of selectors wrote in Sydney's *The Sun* newspaper:

Benaud will be called upon as the chief legspinner. So far his figures scarcely reflect the promise of his early youth in this department, and

yet he has constantly turned in useful performances.

More flight would, I think, pay dividends, but don't let us be unfair and make comparisions with say Grimmett. Benaud is there to do his job when required and his value to the team may not necessarily be judged on how many wickets he gets with his legspinners. In the batting line I feel Benaud's great potential has not so far materialised.

When a man can make 135 in 110 minutes (11 sixers and nine fours) against Bedser, Bailey, Tattersall and Wardle as Benaud did at Scarborough (in 1953, on the previous Ashes tour) it doesn't make sense that his Test aggregate for the same season, after five innings, should be 15.

Benaud scores first century of English tour

From R. S. Whitington and A.A.P.

WORCESTER, Thurs.—New South Wales all-rounder Richie Benaud today scored the first century of the 1956 Australian cricket tour of England.

Benaud and Len Maddocks added 126 runs for Australia's sixth wicket against Worcestershire.

Fifty in 27 minutes

From Lou's scrapbooks, a small turning point in a son's international career that had been languishing.

If one Test match can really turn a cricketer's career then it's possible that the Lord's Test of 1956 did the trick for Rich. In case Lou missed a ball he took two newspapers a day, scissored out the match reports and pasted them in school exercise books.

One of the cricket writers covering that tour was Arthur Mailey, the former Test player and wily legspinner. This is from his Second Test report in *The Daily Telegraph*:

> Richie Benaud's 97 at Lord's yesterday was a great challenge to modern cricket. Here at least was one player who was prepared to sacrifice a century — his first at Lord's — for the sake of his side.
>
> Benaud was the last line of the aggressive school of Australian batsmen ... thanks to a series of beautiful shots, he reached 97, at which point he tried to hit a six and lost his wicket.
>
> People around me said: 'Wasn't it a pity he didn't reach his century?' Bob Wyatt, an ex-England selector, said to me: 'What a terrible stroke — his feet weren't in position.'
>
> I staggered from the scene like a drunken man. Here was a batsman who had climbed to the nineties during a very dangerous period for Australia. He had played every shot from an agricultural swing, to hitting a Fred Trueman bouncer over square leg with a glorious hook shot, to a French cut.
>
> And at the first mistake he was being condemned.

Bill O'Reilly reported in *The Sydney Morning Herald*:

> An electrifying catch by Richie Benaud at short gully swung the Second Test Australia's way. Standing fairly short for Ken Mackay bowling to Colin Cowdrey, Benaud's assignment was to look after any edged shot which might loft in that direction.
>
> The ball, with Cowdrey's full weight behind it, was still on the way up as it reached Benaud. Both hands were raised intuitively and the ball stuck in the right one * for the most amazing snap effort one could ever hope to see.
>
> Several seasons ago Benaud, fielding in the same position in Sydney against the South Africans, suffered a severe mouth injury from a similarly hit ball.

More from O'Reilly:

> Then came Benaud, brought on far too late by captain Ian Johnson and (Peter) May began to struggle like a rat in a trap. May was beaten time and again before being bowled middle stump.
>
> This was the beginning of the end for England. Benaud dismissed Godfrey Evans stumped and Miller and Archer quickly cleaned up the tail-enders.

---

* Rich: "Cowdrey was caught two hands but because of the force of the shot I was knocked backwards and let go of the ball with the right hand."

By the time Rich was 27, he had been on tours to England, twice, and to the West Indies and, on the way back from England in 1956, toured Pakistan and India. Yet, a hard-marker might still have rated his Test career record as moderate.

But in India there was a signal, the most satisfying yet for Bradman and Co. — he took 23 wickets in three Tests.

Ten months passed, and he was chosen for his fourth overseas tour, South Africa, 1957–58. *The Sun*'s cricket writer, Ray Robinson, reported on the opening match against Northern Rhodesia:

Kitwe, October 1957 — Richie Benaud, taker of ten wickets in a day, is now known along the copper-belt here as 'Bwana Benaud'. Bwana is the Central African Tribesman's word for 'master'.

A story of sheer cricketing hard labour lies behind his development of the deadly top spinner now being used by Benaud in South Africa. Yesterday, it helped him take nine for 16 in the first inings and one for 34 in the unfinished second innings.

I have never seen a bowler prepare more thoroughly for a tour. His longest spells from bowling at practice have been his own seven-minute batting turns. The six foot allrounder's weight has come down from 14 stone to 13.8 in a week.

His confidence has risen with his control of direction, which is better than at any other time in his career.

At the end of the tour, *The Sydney Morning Herald* reported:

Port Elizabeth, March 1958 — Richie Benaud was the hero of Australia's eight wickets win against South Africa in the Fifth Test today.

During the course of the day Benaud:

- **Took his 100th Test wicket and joined the select band of allrounders who have taken 100 wickets and scored 1,000 runs.**
- **Took his 100th first-class wicket for the tour. His final tally of 105 wickets surpasses Bill O'Reilly's 95 wickets and Clarrie Grimmett's 92 wickets on the tour to South Africa 22 years ago.**
- **Took his 500th first-class wicket.**

Rich retired from Test cricket at the SCG on February 12, 1964, at the end of the Fifth Test against South Africa. Writing for *The Sun* newspaper he made this observation:

This then is in a sense a farewell. But not to worry. One of the endearing

things of cricket is that when one player goes out there is another ready to step into his place and represent the country.

I've had a good run and enjoyed every moment of it. Just ten years ago I was a young hopeful waiting anxiously for the last day of the Fifth Test against South Africa.

At the conclusion of that day when the Springboks drew the series the Australian team was announced for the 1953 Ashes tour of England. It was a tense and exciting moment waiting for the announcement to come over the air.

Consequently I know just how lots of cricketers in Australia feel today. Tonight the selectors will meet to pick the 17 to represent the country in England this year.

To those who go it will be a wonderful trip and I can only wish them as much pleasure as I have had over the years.

If I had my time over again I would do exactly as I have done — play cricket.

Rich's was a career in two phases:				
Seasons	Tests	Wickets	S/rate (Balls/wkt)	Average
1951–57	24	50	87	34.4
1957–64	39	198	74	25.1
Career	63	248	77	27.0

A long, long road from Jugiong to genius. Rich's early enthusiasm for the game was fostered by the same Central Cumberland club that offered Lou his first chance in senior cricket. The 1942–43 report said, "Richie Benaud (aged 12) scored for the seconds, collected the fees, and also filled in as a player in extreme circumstances."

CUMBOS

Central Cumberland was a foundation club when the
Sydney competition began in 1893–94. As well as Rich,
Cumberland cricketers who played Tests for Australia were
Doug Walters, Greg Matthews, W. P. Howell, F. A. Iredale,
G. R. Hazlitt and, me. Others could 'play a bit', too.

I remember him as an elderly gentleman in a hat, bespectacled, slight in build, but upright, and with a walking stick that he used mainly to prop his hands upon as he sat watching First grade cricket matches at Cumberland Oval in the '60s.

He was 80 years old then and I called him Mr Cranney, but in his much younger, more athletic days every cricketer in Sydney, and later the length and breadth of NSW, knew Harold Cranney simply by his nickname, 'Mudgee'. Mudgee opened the batting for Cumberland and in the 1911–12 season he hit — 'scored' would be an unjust observation, as you will see — 831 runs in the season. Mudgee's opening partner for many years was E. L. 'Gar' Waddy. Gar once described another of his opening partners, George Payne, an engine driver from Bathurst, as 'a left-hander who could hit like a horse kicking'.

Mudgee then, must have had the kick of a stallion. "He did not let the ball hit the bat, I can assure you," said Waddy.

History backs Gar's observation: in the 1912–13 season Mudgee carted Newton of Waverley for 6-6-4-2-2-6 in an over; in 1920–21 he took to Bert Hopkins, who a decade earlier had been playing for Australia, hitting 34 off an over, 4-6-6-4-6-2-6. Bert was silly to bowl a no-ball with Mudgee in that mood!

Mudgee's 831 runs was a Cumberland club record that was to last for 55 years and when it finally did go under, it was by only four runs, most likely via a thick edge wide of slip because the breaker was me.

I needed 24 innings to do what Mudgee did in just 16. That's the nonsense about breaking a record. We often erase from the record books the name of the true champion. Mudgee had hit five centuries in his record, I could manage only one.

Surely a record should be deemed 'broken' only if a qualifying basis for the record is bettered — that is, in Mudgee's case, his record should stand because I took so many more turns at the crease.

There was a television promotion not so long ago selling cricket bats which featured the Top Ten rungetters in Test cricket. Incredibly Sir Donald Bradman, the greatest batsman of all time, the batsman who scored about a hundred every time he took guard, was not among them. How ridiculous!

Surely Bradman's name should have been right at the very top of the list, with an asterisk detailing his phenomenal deeds, a recognition at least, of the champion's existence. Think of it this way: if Bradman doesn't rate a mention when it comes to scoring runs, who should?

It is a measure of Mudgee Cranney's greatness that after making his First grade debut in the year 1901, when he was 14 years and 11 months old, he put together a career record that still stands today.

Matches	Runs	HS	50/100	Ave
217	9414	177	60/18	36.91

Yet, Mudgee always nominated B. W. Farquhar as the greatest batsman to play for Cumberland. That may have been modesty on Mudgee's part, but having heard him reminisce about Farquhar it's just as likely to have been an awestruck recognition of his teammate's talent. "I still cannot work out how it was he never played for Australia," said Mudgee.

"One time we played Balmain and batted on a very bad wicket ... all out for 149 ... Farquhar not out 108," was Mudgee's brief summation of a genius at work. Mudgee was only 17 years old at the time, but his memory of the day's events remained clear. There was no attempt to colour the moment, or to clutter it with too much detail. Mudgee left the gaps to be filled by a young cricketer's imagination.

Imagine it. The pitch was a 'sticky' — it had been soaked by rain, but sunshine and wind had created a patchy, dried, thin crust on the surface causing the ball to either leap sharply, or skid through. Imagine the technical treat that Farquhar must have served up that day, judging perfectly his forward and back movements, when to hit and when to block.

Farquhar had opened the batting on a devilish pitch and scored a century while the rest of his team managed 40; and the records show that on the day that he batted through the innings, 20 other batsmen were dismissed for 111 runs.

To revisit the question of records, and how they should be recognised, it should be noted that in Grade cricket these days all pitches are covered.

That's a good thing for the game, and the spectator, but it should remind us just how accomplished were some of our past players whose names have gone under the eraser.

Mudgee must have been a dab hand on a crook pitch, himself.

On one occasion against Waverley we put them out for 86. Gar Waddy and myself opened up. We had 90 runs up in just over the half hour. The captain Les Pye signalled 'Have a hit'. Gar walked down to my end and said, 'He wants us to get out and get them in again on the bad wicket. If this happens too often how are we going to get into the State side?'

Now some people might think Gar Waddy was being selfish and, on the surface, a case could be made to support that point of view. But every cricketer's dream is to wear the baggy green cap of Australia, and it would be a strange personality indeed, and an unmotivated one, that was forever able to repress the thought that it would be a damn good feeling to get a spot in the NSW team.

After all, few are chosen (since 1855, there have been 649 NSW players, one of them Mudgee, who was a selector for a season, too). But what about the rest? Why didn't more of them catch the selectors' eyes, all those other talented Grade cricketers? Their success seems only to have been a 'tease' in their quest for higher honours.

For instance, Cumberland's R. C. (Rupert) Coogan was a talent. He bowled slow spin on a consistent length and with subtle changes of pace and flight. They were his tools to frustrate the batsmen, rather than prodigious spin. Not everyone is Shane Warne.

In every season Rupert played with Cumberland, from 1912–13 on (two in second grade, nine in first grade) he took the most wickets for his team — in other words, he headed the bowling aggregate eleven times in 11 seasons.

It's quite a record, but Rupert remained unchosen for NSW; the likelihood is that Rupert was unlucky enough to be in cricket at the wrong time — World War I happened and, the twirling tweakers of Arthur Mailey coincided with Rupert's deeds of deception.

There are champions, and there are champion blokes, and club cricket has more of the latter than the former. We salute our champions, sometimes with tickertape parades. In fact, in 1996 in Sydney some politician decided it would be a good idea to salute the runners-up, a football team, with a ticker-tape parade!

What sort of a mixed message does that send out? You get 'an A for effort' … or, 'second-best is OK'. Surely there has to be a pinnacle of achievement? Can the day be too far away before petty-minded politicians are giving tickertape parades to wooden-spooners because 'they did their best'?

There are no medals, or tickertape parades for some club men, the 'workers' without whom many of the champions might have had a less enjoyable time trying to negotiate a less level playing field.

Lou was a good club man — as well as playing, he was a youth team manager, a selector and a coach. Who knows what motivates 'the good club man'?

Probably, it's just the sheer love of the great game … at least, that is the reasonable conclusion that can be gathered from the following excerpts from Cumberland Reports:

"After commencing in the Seconds, Owen Smith forced his way back to the Firsts, finishing up fourth in the averages. At times he showed a decided lack of practice, due no doubt to living over a hundred miles away …" — 1938–39 REPORT.

Maybe it's because cricket has a breadth to it that can be a balm in troubled times … this cricketer remembered his mates in the middle of a war:

"It is with deep regret that I have to report that Bruce Mullinger, a long time member of the club, has been officially reported as 'presumed dead' in operations over Germany. In the last report, we mentioned receiving a cheque from Canada from Bruce to purchase a bat for the Second grade team." — 1942–43 REPORT (WORLD WAR II).

Maybe it's a determination to put something into a game that fate prevented them playing …

"Sid Teale was only 34 years old when he died. Dogged by ill health and confined to a wheelchair from his early youth, Sid's work for the young sportsmen of the district was prodigious and became something to which his whole life was dedicated. With a willing band of assistants he toiled so that each Saturday suitably graded age groups of youngsters could acquire not only the necessary skill, but also the spirit, in which the game should be played." — 1958–59 REPORT.

Maybe it's the camaraderie …

"William 'Bill' Kenney had been the official scorer for the Second

grade from 1956–57 to 1973–74, a period of 18 years during which his accuracy and attention to detail were equalled only by his enthusiasm and strong team loyalty." — 1969–70 REPORT.

Maybe it's the desire to see to it that cricket's tradition is carried on by a new generation ...

"Bill Gleadall lived to 90, and he watched First grade matches until the end. In 1925–26, the season in which Cumberland first entered a team in the Shire competitions, the then 45 year old enthusiast looked after the young team. With no home ground it was a formidable task but he made his car available each week and, acting as guide and mentor, played only when a vacancy occurred." — 1969–70 REPORT.

Smith, Mullinger, Teale, Kenney, Gleadall ... certainly they are names not as synonymous with cricket as Bradman, O'Reilly, Miller, Chappell and Border but, in their very own way, the influence they left on the game was just as indelible.

Lou said of Cumberland: "It was the very best club which could provide my two sons with their opportunities to become first-class cricketers."
He was right. Cumberland's cricket had spirit.
Rich and I were born 14 years apart, but we often shared the field with the same enterprising teammates, one of whom was Harold Goodwin.

HAROLD

*Harold Goodwin was a 'Cumbo' with a sharp eye
and reflexes. He was a smart baseballer, a fine squash
player and good golfer, respected by all. He was an
opening batsman who had scant respect for any fast
bowler's reputation.*

Harold's leisurely disrespect for fast bowlers with reputations seemed so reminiscent of that great Cumberland opening pair of the early 1900s, Mudgee Cranney and Gar Waddy.

Mudgee had handed down a story, and with it maybe the tradition.

We played Manly who had a new fast bowler named Tracey, who was meeting with good success. As Gar and I walked to the wicket, Gar, who invariably took strike, asked me to take it. I was wondering how hostile Tracey might be — Gar evidently wondered the same, and wanted a look at him from the other end!

First ball of the opening over came along and I saw he was just fast enough to be right. I laid into the rest of the over — they were six-ball overs — and hit five fours. At the end of the over Gar came tearing down and said, 'Go easy with him — I want some of him before he's taken off!'

Playing Grade cricket at Cumberland Oval in the '60s, before it became Parramatta Stadium, could be a mighty exciting day out. Sometimes though it wasn't the case; if there'd been a drop of rain overnight, not even blazing sunshine on the day of play made any difference — players would be greeted by a blackboard propped against the outer two metre high paling fence, with the words, "Oval Closed!!!" emphatically chalked on it.

In the old days, the Parramatta Park Trust, which administered Cumberland Oval, wasn't exactly rolling in money and, to improve the bottom-line, took a decision to double-lease the ground during the summer to raise more money.

The second lease was offered to a motor racing company, which wanted to conduct car races — speedway — on Saturday nights. This entailed an outbreak of what these days is termed business infrastructure.

A dirt track was graded around the inside of the oval fence, and to protect the spectators from wayward speed cars the fence was strengthened with thick wooden planks covered in sheets of tin. Goodbye picket fence.

At five o'clock every Saturday afternoon the preparation began to get the track ready for the night's racing. So the last hour of cricket was played out on the oval while a man drove a water cart round the graded track. Boundary hits made a tinny thunder clap against the fence, and the ball came back caked in reddish-brown mud.

Minor matters really, compared with the fate that befell the groundsman in the 1957–58 season. Immediately play ended it was his ritual to head for the pitch to flood it. He was hit by a speedcar doing a warm-up circuit and had a spell in hospital.

GOODWIN HITS RORKE FOR SIX

Hard-hitting Cumberland opening batsman Harold Goodwin gave his side a wonderful start to the 1960-61 season last Saturday when he hit the first ball bowled by Australian fast bowler Gordon Rorke for six.

Goodwin, who scored 50 runs in 53 minutes, followed the six with a succession of fours and hard-hitting scoring shots to all parts of the field.

• Set for win

berland Oval, was all out by tea for 109.

Cumberland Argus, March 28, 1960.

Like all folklore, cricket's has been exaggerated over time. They say Harold Goodwin once hit the first ball of a season, delivered by an ex-Test bowler, for six, into the local swimming pool. It wasn't quite like that.

Sometime in the late-life of the old Cumberland Oval the local council built an Olympic swimming pool on the southern side of the Oval, the paling outer fence of which was hard up against the high wire boundary fence of the pool.

Naturally, it became the goal of every slogging low order batsman to hit one into the swimming pool. It was at the start of the 1960–61 season and Frank Worrell's West Indians were about to make quite a splash with their enterprising batting in Test matches against Rich's Australians.

Rich wasn't available for Cumberland's first match of the season which was against Mosman, a club whose junior cricket development has died in the '90s but which back then had produced Ian Craig, the youngest ever Australian captain, and later provided the cricket springboard for Allan Border, the longest serving Australian captain.

Another Mosman player of renown was the Australian fast bowler Gordon Rorke and he was in the team for the season opener against Cumberland. Rorke was a big fellow, about six foot six inches under the old scale, which is around 195 centimetres if you're determined to fuss about the new one.

He was blond and because he bowled very, very fast and sometimes aggressively short, the imaginative press had tagged him 'The Blond Bombshell', what else? He had come through the lower grades, where one day an opening batsman had been confused by the field placements set for the young Rorke at his home ground, Mosman Oval, now Allan Border Oval. In those days the pitch was a greentop, and had a 'ridge'.

Rorke was preparing to run in from about 10 paces, but the slips and wicketkeeper were standing back about 35 paces. "What are you blokes doing back there?" chuckled the opener. "You'll see," was the serious reply.

Rorke's teammates were never shy about doing a psyche job on opponents. Once, the Mosman 'keeper Doug Ford went into the dressing room of another Sydney club, Petersham, before play began, tossed a stretcher at the feet of their opening batsmen and said, "You blokes'll need this!"

Rorke was famous for a long drag. When he delivered, his front foot seemed to stay airborne for an eternity and his drag was so extended that when he finally let the ball go it seemed as if the spiked sole of his left boot was in your face. Batting against him could be unnerving.

So, first ball of the Cumberland innings in the 1960–61 season First grade match against Mosman at Cumberland Oval … Rorke, to Harold Goodwin.

Bouncer! Harold flat-bat pulled it into the Noller Pavilion — the 'smaller of the two grandstands', where Lou had had his spikes shortened. Many of those present swear that from the other end the hit would have made the swimming pool.

'Rorkie' was a very dry customer, though. While one of his teammates was fetching the ball he turned to the umpire, Ted Wykes and, with mock-indignation and a dip of his head in Harold's direction, said, "Doesn't this bloke know who I am?"

Harold was fearless, and in a slightly ugly way. His short-arm, flat-bat style enabled him to play ferocious pull shots, over — sometimes 'through' — the fielder at midwicket, the balls flying like missiles launched. To balls pitched wider, those outside the off stump rather than in line with the body, he slashed at.

They would often go high over the slips and off to the boundary. Once, in a match against Northern Districts, he had their captain, Neil Harvey, well stuffed. In those days, an effective method of dismissing slashers like Harold was to set a fly slip — a man about 10 or 20 metres beyond the normal slips fielders — for the catch.

So, there was Harold on a moist pitch that had a greenish look, not quite timing his cut shots. Over the slips they flew, with Harvey at first slip looking more and more exasperated. Back went one fly slip ... a miscued cut fell short, then one fell wide; back went a second fly slip ... one went high, then one to the right of him; back went a third fly slip! Later, I overheard Harvey say to Rich: "How do you set a field to him?"

Northern Districts bowlers seemed to suffer at the bat of Harold more than those from any other club. Once, Cumberland played NDs in a semifinal at Merrylands Oval. This was Cumberland's No.2 ground and, to set it apart from the No.1 ground's speedway track, Merrylands had a tar and cement cycling track around it. We were nothing if not versatile when it came to choosing our grounds!

As so often happens in the finals series in Sydney it was wet, both days. NDs made 176 and when Cumberland batted Ross Taylor opened the bowling to Harold. Taylor was tall and sinewy and generated good pace, and his high arm action enabled him to bounce the ball disconcertingly.

Harold took strike and hooked the first ball of the innings high and handsomely over backward square leg, over the bike track, over a wire fence, over a paling fence and, into a swamp. There was a lengthy search, resulting in muddied creams, bloody oaths and then finally the call ... 'lost ball'.

Jim Burke, the former Test player and NDs skipper, ran to the dressing sheds and took another new ball from his bag. Harold hit it into the same swamp. There was a shorter, testier search, before Burke returned and asked Harold, who was skippering Cumberland, "Could you lend us another new ball?"

It was a short boundary, and the height of Harold's hits clearly registered in Taylor's mind as a weakness to be exploited the next time he met up with Harold. That would be especially so if the game was played at NDs home ground, Waitara, where the leg fences were longer.

And so the trap was set. In a one-day match at Waitara, on a Saturday morning after the Friday night before, a morning so bright and sunny it hurt the eyes, Ross Taylor began from the northern end. Down on the leg fence, more backward of square than fine, was John Phillips, a legspin bowler of terrific promise, someone who bowled at the same pace as Bill O'Reilly and had much the same boisterous approach to life.

John was a tough cricketer, and sociable, always prepared to have drink after the game and to have a chat at any time — even when he was on the fence at fine leg waiting for his team's fast bowler to spring a trap.

Taylor bounced Harold, Harold hooked high, Phillips got under it, hands held high … the ball hit them, went right through … hit Phillips on the forehead … and went over the fence for six. Harold got 66 in 40 minutes … with 11 fours as well.

If a first ball duck is a 'golden' in modern cricket parlance, what then should we call Harold's first ball sixers? And, Harold could never have satisfied the textbook technicians, but what is technique, when all's said and done? Some of the best eschew textbook perfection — Doug Walters, for instance.

DOUG

When Doug Walters came to play with Cumberland he boarded with Harold Goodwin's parents. In his first season he made 409 runs and by the end of the next he had passed the 'magic thousand' in 18 innings, a new record. It had been held by a Cumberland Test player, F. A. Iredale (22 innings). An omen?

Doug hailed from a dairy farm outside Dungog in mid-northern NSW. According to the legend, when he was 14 years old he took out the tractor and trailer one day and dug up as many ants' nests as he could find, brought them back to the front of the house and prepared an antbed pitch. The exercise was to serve him well in his later cricketing life.

It was a bowler's pitch that the groundsman prepared for the Third Test at the Queen's Park Oval in Trinidad in the Caribbean back in 1973. Ian Chappell's worn and weary men were trying to keep West Indian hands off the Frank Worrell Trophy. This wasn't a pitch for all bowlers, mind you. Just one. Lance Gibbs.

Lance was the world's champion offspinner of the time, yet he more resembled a toothpick than a torturer. He had a razor-sharp mind and the supple, stretched fingers that a pianist would kill for. 'His' pitch was a greyish-brown colour, like the bottom of a dry creek bed in the Australian outback. Made to crumble, to turn to dust.

The sight of something like that can play havoc with a batsman's mind just as much as a hard, bouncy greentop can. Chappell had the good fortune to win the toss. It was a welcome change of luck for the skipper, whose Test warm-up had been spent in ice packs, healing a sprained ankle.

More misfortune was not long coming. One of the openers, Keith Stackpole, fooled by the marshmallow pace of the pitch, bunted a catch to square leg, and the first over wasn't even up.

'Stacky' was an opening batsman with the mindset and style of a Harold Goodwin, or a Mudgee Cranney. In the First Test, the West Indies had produced a mystery fast bowler named Dowe. So fierce was Stacky's early batting assault someone in the Jamaican crowd created that gem of cricket folklore, the one about cricket's 11th Commandment — 'Dowe shalt not bowl.'

Dowe was out of the side in Trinidad and Stacky surely regretted missing the opportunity to take his blazing bat to the new opening bowler — a batsman, named Clive Lloyd!

The West Indian selectors had been so heartened by the sight of the pitch they had brought in another spinner, Inshan Ali, in place of the new ball bowler Vanburn Holder. Lloyd would take the new ball, but only for as long as it took to make it old.

Gibbs was spinning them down among his trio of short legs long before the Queen's Park cooks had contemplated warming the curried goat for lunch. Ian Redpath, as physically scrawny as a plucked chook, but mentally tough, and Greg Chappell, elegant and enterprising, denied Gibbs, and dealt with him, until the second last ball before lunch — Chappell, caught at bat pad by Kallicharran.

The West Indies, who were later to make the tactic of four fast bowlers an artform, were intent in this Test on making four spinners an artform. As well as Gibbs and Ali, who bowled left-arm 'Chinamen', there was a second offspinner, a part-timer named Foster, and a young lad, Elquemedo Tonito Willett.

Willett was just 19 years old and his steady left-arm orthodox didn't match the eloquence of his name. This was only his second Test match and, like all of us who saw it, he was destined never to forget it.

Doug Walters went into bat immediately after lunch. In the moments before the umpires Sang Hue and Gosein went back on, he had been sitting in the shade of the small dressing room verandah. By that stage of the day the dressing room had become a broiling sauna.

Already, he had his baggy green cap firmly in place. He was enjoying whatever whisper of a cooling breeze there was, and satisfying his habit of a last smoke.

The umpires went, then Rohan Kanhai and his men, and that was the signal for Doug to gather his gloves from the seat beside him, and the Gray-Nicolls bat propped against it and, with that familiar measured gait, his face that mask of unflustered self-assurance under the baggy green, he walked with Redpath out into the stifling heat and humidity of Queen's Park.

When he scraped his guard with the sole of his boot the puff of dust it raised could only have brightened the gleam in Gibbs' eye. What goes through a batsman's mind when he's confronted by a pitch like that? A pitch that's allowing the bowler a lot of turn, with bounce that's inconsistent and a bit two-paced?

And, as he stands waiting for the delivery, how conscious is he of the short legs in at his hip, waiting for the catch that might come straight from the inside edge, or deflect via the pad.

Does he think 'soft hands' … does he try to use his feet, try to come down quickly to meet the pitch of the ball and kill the spin, or to drive … or, does he play back more, let the ball come to him rather than prod forward?

Any West Indian anticipation of a spinner's celebration was not misplaced because Gibbs' figures in the second innings, five for 102, were his best for five years. In that innings he bowled Ross Edwards — he had padded up to a ball that pitched outside the off stump and it hit his leg stump! And Greg Chappell, playing forward, had edged a big spinner into his pad and been caught, not by the bat-pad fielder, but by the bowler!

Gibbs' match figures were eight wickets for 181; in the first innings he bowled 38 overs, took three wickets and conceded 79 runs. That's water torture, torment. Watching Gibbs was like watching an orchestra conductor … *fortissimo*, big turn … *esspresivo*, big bounce … *poco*, less turn, *glissando*, a bit of skid, *legato*, a bit of drift.

How did Doug Walters, the dairy farmer's son, Harold Goodwin's squash mate, handle this challenge to his cricketing character? And, to his technique, which a few purists in England had decided was diabolical? Well, he scored a century between lunch and tea.

Only eight Australians have scored a century in a Test in that session, Bradman and Rich among them. Doug did it that day as if he was still playing on his antbed pitch at Dungog.

It wasn't slather and whack stuff, and nor was it slaughter, because that invites a mind picture of a batsman hacking away at bowlers. Doug's was a demolition job — like the expert who methodically sets the explosive charges in a skyscraper that has passed its use-by date, then reduces it to rubble, cleanly and clinically, by pressing the right buttons.

When the ball was short his front leg would snap back, and around towards backward square, the full weight of his body transferred at the moment the bat made impact on ball. The pull shot.

Once it went high over midwicket, over the high wire security fence and into the packed terraces. He hit 16 fours.

When confronted with an onside field packed to favour the offspin, Doug stepped back, to the line of the ball, off stump, then drew the top half of his body back towards square leg to give himself room to cut, or square-bat the ball through the relatively unprotected offside.

When the bowlers tried flight he skipped smartly down the pitch, reached the ball on the full or the half volley and drove with that unique come-to-attention style of his. At the same time he drove Kanhai, the West Indian captain, to distraction.

He short-circuited the promise in the career of young Willett, who bowled 19 overs for 62 runs, no wicket. Willett can reflect on the moment, and shouldn't be too concerned.

He was 'milked' by the master, and anyway, he came from the tiny island of Nevis, and was the first Leewards Islander to play for the West Indies — who knows how many more Test players from the Leewards his selection might have inspired.

One was his nephew, Stuart Williams, an opening bat in the '90s. Some other Leeward Islanders who followed Willett were more famous, Viv Richards, Richie Richardson, Curtly Ambrose and Andy Roberts.

Doug played one false shot in 150 minutes; he'd just passed his half-century and mishit a ball to the fielder at midwicket. But it was a no-ball anyway, and Doug was so quick he'd have known that.

'Another Bradman', Doug was tipped to be, but many might have forgotten that there was a young batsman tipped to be 'another Walters'. His name was Peter Toohey, a hot shotmaker who hailed from one of the coldest corners of New South Wales, Blayney.

As fate would have it, five years on from Doug's triumph I saw Peter Toohey also take guard at the Queen's Park Oval.

March 3, 1978

My heart cried for Peter Toohey today. Put out of the First Test by a climbing Andy Roberts' bumper that sliced open his forehead, Toohey bravely came back with it stitched to again face the fearsome West Indies pacemen on a brute of a wet pitch and in fading light.

Even the fiercely partisan West Indian crowd put down their trumpets and whistles and set up the spirited handclap they reserve for their own champions as the tiny New South Welshman strode back to the wicket, his forehead swathed with a sash of white plaster.

The ground went almost silent as six foot four inch Colin Croft, the destroyer of Australia, strode in … and, it sighed with relief as Toohey survived.

The 23 years old Toohey made his brave decision to return to the crease after talking to captain Bob Simpson and manager Fred Bennett and, after three doctors had swabbed and stitched that deep wound just above his right eye and nose.

"If 'Cose' (Gary Cosier) doesn't get out then I want to go in," Toohey told Simpson, even though the doctors had warned him he would be foolish to bat again.

When Joel Garner sent No.10 Wayne Clark's middle stump cartwheeling and the Australian score was eight for 76, in strode Toohey with that familiar short step, quick gait. Cosier came to meet him: "What about I try to take as much of them as I can for a while, mate?" he said.

But Toohey would have none of it. "I'll take them as they come, mate," he said, and promptly tucked Croft's second ball away through midwicket for two.

It had looked bad when Toohey, trying to hook, had taken the blow to his face from the fourth ball of Roberts' seventh over. Only an over before he had slammed a bouncer from Croft away to the boundary boards. "The one from Croft held up like most bouncers do, but the one from Andy seemed to skid and just kept coming at me," Toohey said.

As he crumpled to his knees Viv Richards abandoned his gully post to rush to Toohey, to lift him under his armpits then cradle his chin and, with right hand raised summon medical assistance.

Toohey murmured: "I'm all right, I'm all right. How's my eye … is my eye all right?" An ice-filled towel was pressed to the bloody gash.

He made his wonderful comeback 75 minutes later. Croft's third ball was a wicked bumper. Toohey ducked. He reached 20 before a yorker from big Joel Garner uprooted his middle stump.

Toohey didn't take the field again in the Test, nor in the next two Tests — unbeknown to us all, even before he'd been struck in the head, another lifter from Roberts had badly smashed his right thumb.

Modern day cricket fans might be puzzled — Doug Walters' Test career record shows he was more at ease against West Indian bowling attacks than he was facing those of England. It's not that puzzling, rather it is simply clear evidence of the game's cycles and its uncertain nature.

In the 1965–66 season the great West Indian fast bowler Wes Hall came to Australia, not with the West Indies but to play as a professional with the Randwick Club in Sydney Grade cricket.

It's possible that Wes, a hero of his time in the early '60s, was the catalyst for the era of Caribbean pace that stormed the world from the mid-'70s to the early '90s. Wes was the Jilt Factor in the West Indies love affair with spin — Ramadhin and Valentine, and Gibbs.

Wes was a magnificent sight, a big fellow, with a thundering run and a gold nugget in the form of a crucifix around his neck. With every pounding step of his run-in, the crucifix went swaying, and shimmering. His leaping delivery was all powerful, expending as much energy as an Olympian jave-lin-thrower, and his heart was as big as the smile that announced his sense of humour. Modern day cricketers, especially fast bowlers, appear to have undergone a sense-of-humour bypass, which may be an advertisement for professionalism but is a pity for cricket.

These days it's a miracle if 40 people turn up to watch a Grade cricket match in Sydney, but back in the '60s Cumberland had Rich and Doug and Harold in the batting line-up. When they faced Randwick and Wes, 4,000 people were at Merrylands Oval, spilling onto the cycle track, to watch. During the week preceding the match the local council top dressed the ground — with a few inches of sand ...

Randwick lost the toss ... and when Wes, the thoroughbred of fast bowlers, ran in he looked like a draught horse. It was as if he was running in a vat of treacle. Cumberland, the accidental cheats.

Doug? He hit 131 before tea.

December 13, 19652

By 6pm on a typically humid Brisbane evening Doug Walters, a dashing 119 not out, promised to be a health hazard to English cricketers for many a season ahead.

It was the First Test of the Ashes series and Walters, then 19 years old, and with mercurial footwork and wrists steeled by hours in the milking sheds, pummelled the cream of England's bowlers, the offspinners Titmus and Allen, for five and a half hours.

But three years later, at lunch on a just-as-typical drizzly, cold, murky England May day at Lord's, a tall slender England fast bowler with the forgettable name of Brown, had found a cure.

Doug's debut century, 155, went into the record books alongside greats like Archie Jackson, Neil Harvey and Bill Ponsford. Keith Miller called Walters "a right-handed Neil Harvey". Rich and Bill O'Reilly urged no such name change by cricket deed poll.

The English press, and some Australians, said he reminded them of Bradman; later, fickleness took over and they tagged him a flop, especially when he played in England. But they were more cautious when the venue was Australia, where innings like his 103 in Perth in 1974 revived the old fears — he reached his century on the last ball of the second day by pulling Willis for a mighty six. Another century in a session.

Bowler Brown was David Brown — D. J. Brown, Warwickshire, right-arm fast, Test bowling average against Australia 35.4, wickets taken 23. While

Walters blossomed in Brisbane's heavy humidity that December day in 1965, Brown had wilted, but not in vain. He had seen what he thought was chink in the armour that was Walters' flashing blade.

Bill O'Reilly, in the grandstand, might have seen it too: "I can remember only one false step on Walters' part and that was a wind-and-water shot outside the off stump when David Brown was using the second new ball," he wrote in *The Sydney Morning Herald.*

Barry Knight, the England allrounder now living in Sydney, was 12th man in Brisbane and was fielding in the deep gully at Lord's. He recalls that England had a theory.

We'd had some early discussions about Doug in 1968 before the Ashes Tests, but it wasn't until after he'd hit 80 or so in the First Test at Manchester that David mentioned his little plan.

He'd noticed that when the ball was moving, to anywhere from six inches to a foot outside the off stump, Doug seemed to *have* to play — it almost seemed like an obsession, as if someone had over-coached him, 'Make sure you're across … and *play straight'*.

We felt he was trying too hard to get behind the ball and as a result he'd play balls back to the bowler that he should have guided to the off.

In effect he was angling his bat across the moving ball. So for the Second Test at Lord's we decided on the two gullies and off-theory. One gully was deep, one shorter.

I was a spectator at Lord's that day and I can still see Knight, the deeper and finer of the two gullies, diving and in mid-air grasping a sensational two-handed catch in a pose not unlike that of a rugby winger flying for the try line.

Knight remembers it, too: "We always had two gullies after that. The beauty of the ploy was that on the seaming English pitches Doug could never quite be sure when to let the ball go. It might duck back at him. And we did get him leg before a couple of times in that series. But what really amazes me is he never really conquered the weakness. That flaw in technique got him on the grassy South African pitches, too."

Well, I'd disagree with Barry. Doug did address the weakness, often having teammates throw short ones, bouncing around off stump to him in net practice. But in the end I suspect he found it disrupted his natural approach to the game. And, when we look at his career record, it surely seems like it was a minor weakness.

Cricket is a game for enjoyment, as well as resolve. Doug, in failure or success, only once appeared not to be enjoying the game. That was during his bumpy stretch against the first-class pace of Mike Procter, John Snow and Peter Pollock. And, he wasn't on his own, there.

After his Test debut in 1965, Doug gave a truckload of enjoyment to millions. We all love him for his courageous comebacks, for the gems of innings. Only a fickle few rubbish him for the relatively unimportant stat that he never scored a Test century in England.

Doug Walters in Tests					
Opponents	Matches	Runs	H'Score	50/100	Ave
England	37	1981	155	13/4	35.38
India	10	756	102	7/1	63.00
New Zealand	11	901	250	4/3	64.36
Pakistan	4	265	107	1/1	33.13
Sth Africa	4	258	74	3/0	32.25
West Indies	9	1196	242	5/6	92.00
Career	75	5357	250	33/15	48.26
In England	18	745	88	6/0	25.69

Doug spent some time in the Army, called into National Service during the Vietnam War, and that possibly took some of the edge off his cricket at a vital time. But it didn't rob him of the unaffected, natural style that won him friends aplenty, nor did it diminish the accolade, 'another Bradman'.

BRADMAN

On the first Saturday in September, 1976, there was a cricket event at Bowral in the southern highlands of NSW. Among those present were Sir Donald Bradman and Bill O'Reilly. It's been said there was bad blood between the two but, if that was the case, would there not have been a hint of it that day?

The great 'Tiger' O'Reilly made a match eve prediction that he would "castle 'The Don'". And it might have been realised if he hadn't decided to take off his coat, because on this day Bradman was in a benevolent mood, and there are bowlers around the world, and spectators, who can remember Bradman only as cold-bloodedly murderous.

It was a few minutes after 1.30pm that September Saturday, just before the official re-opening of Bowral's Bradman Oval, the highlight of which was to be a first ball bowled by O'Reilly to Bradman, a much-awaited moment.

The sight of The Boy From Bowral back on his home turf was reason enough for great happiness among those present, but there was absolute joy when, as he prepared for his tilt with The Tiger, he took time out to recall another cricket celebration, the Johnny Taylor-Arthur Mailey Testimonial which had been played at the SCG 20 years before.

Mailey, in civvies, had been called on to bowl one ball, too — to Taylor.

"In came Mailey and over went the stumps — all three," Bradman said. "Arthur, who at times during his career had built up a reputation of being expensive, came off and immediately told us all that he'd discovered something he wished he'd known a long time before. 'I should have always bowled with my coat on'!"

But the tip was lost on The Tiger. Resplendent in Irish green flat cap and green jumper, tie, grey trousers and reefer jacket, Tiger escorted the pin-stripe-suited Bradman towards the centre, and demanded, "Which end are you going to bat?"

"The far end — the boundary is shorter!" laughed The Don, quick as a flash. So Tiger, ignoring Mailey's Successful Bowling Tips For Spinners, took off his coat. He licked his spinning fingers … and wheeled down a long hop, wide of the leg stump. That Saturday in 1976 a chuckling Bradman missed it; in 1926 he sent such gifts whizzing through the gum trees ringing the same ground.

At a civic reception the night before, O'Reilly had taken us all back to that particular Bradman blitz. O'Reilly's memory was sharp, and his humour good.

"Tomorrow will be my second appearance at this ground," he said. "My first was fifty years ago when it was the council ground, unfenced, sloping and with a concrete pitch covered by coir mats, and a log to change on.

"I was coming down on the morning train from Sydney and at Wingello (O'Reilly's home town, 50 kilometres from Bowral) I heard a station announcement calling, 'Mr O'Reilly! Would Mr O'Reilly please come to the station master's office.'

"So I rushed along to see what it was about and the station master told me that Wingello were playing Bowral and I was in the side. I protested that I had no 'togs'. 'Oh, that's all right,' said the station master. 'We've been down to see your mother — here you are!' he said, handing me a brown paper parcel.

"Well, I got up to Bowral to find we'd lost the toss and were in the field. I was given the new ball and knocked some bloke over in the first over. I must say I had some pretty strong ideas about myself around this time — a, well … sort of Australian gift to world sport …" By this time O'Reilly had his tongue wedged firmly in his cheek.

"The next batsman dealt me, and my reputation, a mortal blow. A little bloke. Quite frankly, I thought I had a lot of early bad luck … but my God, you should have seen the bad luck I had later!" roared The Tiger.

"Bradman got 234 not out that first day and I spent all week worrying about it; next week, on my home ground at Wingello, I got him first ball. I'm going to do the same tomorrow."

According to Sir Donald that weekend, O'Reilly was the greatest spin bowler he saw or played against … "And you saw plenty of him. You couldn't get the ball off him." The funniest spinner? That night Sir Donald left those at Bowral with no doubts — it was Arthur Mailey.

"The Australian team was on the boat on its way to England," Bradman recounted, "And all one day, Arthur had been practising on deck with a rope ball. That night the team attended the dance and Arthur chose to foxtrot with a charming young English lass. She had noticed Arthur's exhaustive practice routine, and asked: 'Do you enjoy being on your feet, Mr Mailey?'

Arthur: Yes, I do.

She: Well, would you mind getting off mine?

Arthur: Oh, I am sorry but I'm a little stiff from bowling.

She: I don't care where you're from, just get off my feet!"

It was one of many delightful memories revived and related by The Boy From Bowral. He had moved there with his family in 1911, when he was just three and they had lived just across from the Oval in Glebe Street. He was 11 years old when he played his first game of cricket — for Bowral school against Mittagong.

In his second game he hit his first century. Later, when he played with Bowral club, his talents were such that opponents, when confirming the match, would optimistically demand, "Don't bring that Bradman kid."

He was 17 years old when he took the 234 from O'Reilly and Co. and followed it with 300 in the final against Moss Vale. Next season Moss Vale made the final again and Bradman made 320 not out.

Later, the mighty Sydney club St George secured him and, on December 17, 1927 he began his first-class career with a century for NSW against South Australia in Adelaide. And the legend began.

It was Jack Fingleton who once said, "Wherever cricket is played he will be discussed, dissected and decried, but never forgotten."

Bowral didn't forget. Friday night's reception and the cricket match on Saturday, Chegwyn's XI versus Southern, were full houses.

At the reception, Sir Donald and Lady Jessie welcomed guests at the door. Later, in his address, Sir Donald quipped, "I never knew I had so many relatives I couldn't remember."

He offered the point that, "some are remembered ... some aren't," and recalled that in 1948 he used to get about 600 letters a day. "It's fallen away a bit," he laughed. "But I received one the other day from India ... from a nine year old boy, who wrote, 'I have admired you since I was young.'

"But I should draw your attention to C. T. B. Turner, the man they called The Terror ... I heard Bill O'Reilly was a little miffed he had to settle for Tiger!

"On his first tour to England, Turner took 283 wickets at 11, his second tour 178 at 14 and on his third 148 at 13. A measure of his greatness is that no-one has taken 100 wickets on an Ashes tour since 1948.

"Twenty eight years after his death they discovered Turner's ashes in a cardboard box in a Sydney mortuary. If anything untoward should happen to me I hope it's not twenty-eight years before my remains are scattered over Bradman Oval."

And so it was, a weekend of happy, charming, even sad memories of the greatest game recalled by its greatest player. There is one more memory ...

The great Doug Walters, a country boy like Bradman, was fittingly captain of Chegwyn's XI. Not only Doug's cricketing reputation had preceded him. As he waited in the new dressing shed for his turn to bat, a local lad with a rough voice, and freckled face beaming mischievously, asked the doorman, "Are Doug Walters playin' cards in there?"

When Doug batted a three metre high hedge in Glebe Street arrested the flight of a mighty Walters' sixer as it flew straight and true for the front yard of the old Bradman cottage!

The critics once acclaimed Walters 'another Bradman'; perhaps that hedge was a symbolic rebuff to those that live in hope.

There can never be another Bradman.

Chegwyn's XI matches were the result of one man's lifelong love for the game. His name was Jack Chegwyn. The matches Jack organised were generally up country and helped perpetuate one of the truly great strengths of Australian cricket — the bush connection.

CHEGGY

I've been everywhere man ... crossed the desert sands man
... of travel I've had my share man, I've been everywhere ...
Armidale, Ashford, Atherton, Boggabilla, Blayney,
Cessnock, Dubbo, Lismore, Mudgee, Maitland, Taree,
Wagga Wagga ... I've been everywhere.

Long before the Australian pop singer of the '60s Lucky Starr devised his 'I've been everywhere' chorus, one of cricket's real gentlemen, Jack Chegwyn, had performed the lyrics. 'Cheggy' to his cricketing friends, Jack was best known nationally as a NSW selector for 22 seasons, from the '50s to the '70s.

Before then the sunlovers who sauntered to the beach, past Sydney's balmy Coogee Oval at weekends, would stop to watch the cricketers. Sometimes, a cricketer might even stop to watch a shapely sunlover.

But Jack, a chunky right-handed batsman crunched 11,943 career runs (20 centuries) for Randwick, so it's a fair bet he kept his mind on the game.

When Jack died in the winter of 1992, he left behind rolled gold memories of his 'Cheggy Trips'; the most lasting memorial is that he gave an early opportunity to some of Australian cricket's favourite sons, most notably Doug Walters and the mystery spinner, John Gleeson.

But 'Cheggy Trips' also offered the most isolated cricket fans the opportunity to see in action the big name players, whose deeds they might otherwise have only 'seen' via the radio.

It all began simply enough; in 1938, Jack had been on a private cricket tour to the central-western NSW country town of Mudgee, courtesy of John Darvell-Hunt, a dentist with a sweet tooth for cricket. Hunt regularly organised pre-season and end-of-season trips to country centres and Lou, while he was posted at Koorawatha, had played at Cowra for a combined district team against one of Darvell-Hunt's teams.

The trip to Mudgee was Darvell-Hunt's last — he retired. The very next year Jack Chegwyn took his first team away, to Canberra. The photo of that team remained forever on the study wall in Jack's Sydney cottage; among the faces was that of Tim Caldwell, who went on to become a chairman of the Australian Cricket Board.

Tim, impish and ruddy faced, was a comfortably proportioned but sharp-minded cricket supremo; in the photo he was fresh faced, curly haired and as slim as a greyhound as he rubbed shoulders with the greats, Bill O'Reilly and Stan McCabe.

Jack worked to a formula — names and entertainment — and advised his hosts that "on the field we give our best, off it we accept your hospitality". The locals knew they were in for a good time, sometimes even a wild old time. "Everyone wanted my team," Jack once said. It wasn't a boast, just the plain truth.

Over the years there were 150 Cheggy Trips, and the players who turned out were never less than the best, or they had what Jack always called 'promise' ... Keith Miller, Neil Harvey, Alan Davidson, Jim Burke, Colin McCool, Rich, Ray Flockton, Arthur Morris, Jim De Courcy, Don Tallon, Sid Carroll, Bill Alley, Norm O'Neill, Sid Barnes. I was a NSW Colts player when I went on my first.

Jack remembered the trips as "wonderful days", with a chuckle, but not without a hint of nostalgia. "It's a little different nowadays ... the entertainers are scarce." Jack wasn't talking about a six straight driven over the sightscreen, rather he was talking about the old soft shoe shuffle.

"In those early days the boys would entertain off the field as well as on it. Jimmy Burke was a great pianist ... once, he kept pace with the best ivory tickler in the town, matched him tune for tune, until the bloke went behind the piano, opened it up, and played God Save The Queen with his car keys!

"Jim De Courcy ... he was only a strip of a youngster, you know, but he had an amazing weightlifting act; Warren Saunders, 'The Little Favourite' Johnny Martin, and Sid Carroll ... they were magnificent harmonists — their signature tune was 'I'm Forever Blowing Bubbles', which they used to sing backwards ... 'Bubbles blowing forever m'I ... air the in bubbles pretty' ... try it. They never missed a beat!"

Cheggy referred to his cricketers as "my pioneers". The enormous impact of Cheggy's Trips, as well as their popularity, was reflected in the Air Board's wartime request to Jack to take a team to Mareeba, up in the far north of Queensland, to entertain the forces involved in the Battle of the Coral Sea.

Bill O'Reilly was in the team. He got up the morning after the most hospitable official welcome, still fully dressed, looked in the mirror and asked his roommate, "What rank am I?" The night before the troops had pinned their badges all over him!

The Air Board was so delighted with the morale boost the cricket provided they asked Cheggy if he would mind taking the team on to New Guinea.

"There had been an outbreak of smallpox, but the boys weren't all that worried about going there until a rumour started running that the Air Board had issued an order that the team would need to have more needles.

"As you can imagine, in those days, we'd already had plenty. The rumour turned out to be true. Bill O'Reilly came up and demanded, 'what's all this extra needle business, Jack? — You know what you can do with your needles!' Then up came Clarrie Grimmett. He was pleading with me, 'Please Jack, no more needles!' We didn't go on."

A Chegwyn's XI played a match at Iron Range up near the northernmost tip of the country — on the airport tarmac, on canvas matting. They flew into Mount Isa in the baking heat of central Queensland — the only green visible from the plane was the cricket field and bowling green. They once played a game at Cooma to entertain the workers on the Snowy Mountains hydro scheme.

"I once got an invite to take a team to Croppa Creek (north-west NSW, near Moree). We played on a private property on a private ground — on Good Friday. After we'd won the match one of the locals ordered the jackaroo to 'get the tomahawks!'.

"That started me wondering ... but in those days the hospitality was beer casks with steel rings and the tomahawk did the job."

Cheggy's team always won, as befitted its make-up, but a match in Cairns remained in Jack's memory as if it had been played yesterday. The locals batted and got 150. The Chegwyn XI batted and were four for nine — Morris, Carroll, Burke and De Courcy were all gone. "All leg before, too," said Cheggy.

"I got the message across to the boys not to get hit in the pads and when we were 4 for 151 — saved by a couple of young colts named Alan Davidson and Richie Benaud — I'll swear I saw the umpire walk over to the local captain and shrug his shoulders."

Davidson and Rich were not the last colts given a chance in top company by Cheggy; when he was in Scone as a NSW selector watching a country trial he saw Johnny Gleeson wheeling down his mystery spinners.

The very next season Cheggy's first trip was to Gunnedah and he made sure that Gleeson was in his opposition. Benaud, Davidson and Neil Harvey confirmed the judgment he'd made at Scone — each was mightily impressed, if confused by Gleeson's finger-flicking spin.

Doug Walters was just a kid when he impressed a Cheggy XI that visited Maitland.

Photos of his pioneers lined the walls of Jack's home, young faces grown old, and many passed on, but all of them smiling. To Jack they were all great, "... but I have a soft spot for O'Reilly and McCabe. McCabe was all class, a personality, a real great."

November 29, 1966

We're playing at the MCG in a match billed as 'a NSW XI' versus 'a Victorian XI'. It's not a Sheffield Shield match, nor is it designated 2nd XI status, but it promises to be a riveting game for one reason — a head-to-head contest that in those days was as compelling as is Warne versus Lara today.

The name A. P. Sheahan is in the Victorian line-up. An elegant player, Paul Sheahan has already made his Sheffield Shield debut the previous season against NSW, making 62. He is still only 20 years old, tall, dark and handsome and the game's bush telegraph has anointed him a dynamic batsman and the coming champion. Geelong College educated, he is even then being touted as a future Australian captain.

Sir Robert Menzies, the 'cricketing Prime Minister', has taken a particular interest in his fortunes. In other words a fair bit is expected of him, and in the NSW camp this has made us very keen to have a crack at him.

In the NSW line-up is the man expected to be his *bete noir* — the name, J. Gleeson. Untried at this level, he is 28 years old, the son of a railway worker, born in Kyogle, northern NSW, a little bit up the road from North Casino.

He's said to have played lawn bowls as a kid, and to have played his early cricket as a wicketkeeper, but now he's being called a mystery bowler, someone who has learned his bent-finger spin bowling trade by looking at pictures in a sporting magazine, then putting it into practice by propelling a tennis ball.

What a prospect, Sheahan against Gleeson — but, the cavernous concrete stands of the MCG are as good as empty. Pity, because Gleeson takes five for 28 from 24.5 overs and wipes out Victoria's first innings. Although Sheahan is not one of his victims, two of his wickets are off successive balls and two are leg before playing for a legspinner that was an offspinner.

By the summer's end he is in the NSW team and, at the start of the next season he's playing a Test against India. In the end he played 29 Tests and took 93 wickets. It may never have happened if Jack Chegwyn's team hadn't gone to Gunnedah and, soon after, the Balmain club hadn't invited Gleeson to play in Sydney.

Bush cricket has been the starting point for many of Australia's best cricketers — about a third of NSW players have come from the country. Most of them come to the 'big smoke' for a bit of polish but their character remains constant ... tough, especially in adversity.

THE GENERAL

The photo raised goosebumps — Rick McCosker, his jaw broken and grotesquely swollen, wired, and head swathed in a supporting bandage, going out to bat in the second innings of the famous Centenary Test of 1977 at the MCG. He was a bush boy.

"Style as I understand it may be good, bad or indifferent ... I am prepared to contend that style always tells. Generally speaking I believe it to be true that the cricketer who has a good style achieves something more than the cricketer who has indifferent style." — RICHARD BINNS, *THE CRICKETER*, 1940.

It was back in 1954 when cricket buff J. S. (Jim) White gazed out at the cattle grazing on his Boggabilla property in northern NSW, frowned slightly at the attendant emus, and unconsciously thrust Rick McCosker into the revered status he was later to command on the world's cricket stage.

McCosker was only nine years old, then; seven years later, as a gangling teenager, he stepped into Jim White's dream.

White and a Tamworth local, Ike Rowland, dreamed of a cricket carnival that would develop the game in the area. Every year there was to be a round robin with teams from Hunter Valley, North-West, Tablelands and Coast. It would last three days.

At its conclusion a combined side, Northern NSW Colts, was to be chosen. Every alternate year the side would visit New Zealand. A sweet dream ...

A decade or so later, they decided to call the Northern NSW Colts 'The Emus', after the birds roaming Jim White's property. Rick McCosker had made his carnival debut in 1961 with Tablelands. By 1967 he had played with The Emus three or four times and that year travelled to NZ with them.

A friend of McCosker's, Ken Falkenmire, recalled, "He was quiet, hardly said a thing, unassuming and very hard working. He always looked slow to move, but somehow his feet were always there in position, right on. I can still see him in those games, picture him as a bloke that played everything to the offside."

Ken wasn't alone in that assessment. Much later, at the start of 1973, McCosker's Sydney club played against Gordon, whose captain was Dick Guy, a wily legspin bowler with a knack of thinking a batsman out. He was also a State selector and later became an Australian selector.

Says Guy: "I had regarded McCosker as something of a plodder, slowish in his movements and completely restricted in his legside play. We determined to bowl there. He pelted us everywhere."

McCosker hit 126, a classical innings that earned him his first NSW cap. He was 27 years old.

McCosker was the classic late developer. After the Emus' tour to NZ in 1967 McCosker, 21st birthday celebrated, had decided to leave the antbed pitches around Inverell to try his luck with the vagaries of the Jubilee Oval pitch, home of the Sydney club.

He chose Sydney because he was friends with the captain Ian Fisher, whose sister had been his doubles partner on the tennis court back home. He had a reputation as a smart tennis player.

"But I had decided to concentrate on cricket," McCosker said. "I wanted to gain Grade cricket status. I was a little dubious in my own mind ... I really had no idea of the ladders I would have to climb." He began in Third grade and in round two went to Brookvale Oval where he carted the Manly attack for an unbeaten 148. He was promoted — and got a duck! After three more matches he was promoted to First grade.

These were his figures after his debut in 1967; at first glance they constitute a record as average as that of any Saturday afternoon Grade batsman who never made it to the top.

Year	Inn	NO	HS	Agg	Ave
1967	7	0	36	115	16.4
1968	18	1	57	466	27.4
1969	15	1	100	393	28.7
1970	17	1	108	320	20.2
1971	18	2	125	486	30.4
1972	18	4	108	565	40.3
1973	11	2	126	483	53.6
1974	8	2	74	266	44.3

But it's the trend, and the centuries that catch the eye. From 1970 to 1973 his average and aggregate progressed rapidly. So did his style — from a player obsessed with offside strokeplay to the one that whipped that 126 off Dick Guy's Gordon team.

McCosker once said of his style:

"I wouldn't say I have a lot going for me in the way of natural ability. I can't get out there and just blast away. I'm a patient type. I set myself a goal in every innings — to stay there. I'm in the team to score runs. I knew my knowledge of the game was limited so I had to widen my scope. Even now I'm learning. I'm a learner.

"I learned a lot from watching Greg Chappell. Distribution of weight in my shots. I was tending to hit my cover drives a bit like I muck up my golf shots — with all my weight on the back foot. Just a little thing to many people but really very important. I began to move forward and follow through with my weight right forward."

He loved batting with Doug Walters. "He never gets flustered Doug, never chats the bowlers. Maybe we're very similar types in nature, maybe that's part of it. I find I can actually draw on his coolness."

From October 19 to 22, 1973, NSW played Queensland at the 'Gabba. Rick McCosker, on the strength of his 126 against Gordon, was in the team, but named 12th man. NSW performed dismally. McCosker was dropped from the team for the southern tour — how do selectors do something like that? The new face was Ian Davis, certainly more stylish than McCosker.

"I'm not sure how I felt. Probably I was very disappointed, I must have been I suppose. But I remember thinking I'd just have to get my head down and get so many runs they couldn't leave me out."

He came back into the NSW team in November against South Australia. State selector Jack Chegwyn: "He was the solid type, gritty. We thought he could bolster the middle order. We decided to give him a chance." McCosker made only 13, but then hit an unbeaten 71 against Western Australia and then, in the last match of the season, 50 and 54 against Queensland, mature, fighting middle order performances that set the ailing NSW side up for wins.

Ken Falkenmire bought him a drink after the Queensland match: "You've made the grade." He was excited. McCosker was quiet: "Oh, I don't know. No, not yet," he mused. The Emus had no doubt. They gave him a trophy at their annual dinner. It was inscribed Emu Of The Year.

McCosker reflected on his start to the 1974–75 season: "I failed twice in the first match against Queensland. I got one and eight. I wasn't sure about myself. Then, the Western Australian game in Sydney ... it had the biggest influence on my career. I could do it, I could score hundreds in Shield cricket. Mentally, I was right."

Against Western Australia he made 138 and 136 not out; then 164 against Victoria, and 125. Four consecutive hundreds, innings that pushed him higher in the batting order, to the responsible No.3 spot ... innings that eventually won him a Test spot on the 1975 Ashes tour as an opening batsman. So commanding was his batting teammates had accorded him the sobriquet, 'The General'.

On that tour he hit twin centuries against Sussex, 111 and 115; then 120 against Leicester; then ... in the Fourth Test at The Oval, 127 against England ... "My greatest moment ... I'd made it, then I knew I'd made it."

And so Rick McCosker, for all his ungainly style, went on to become one of Australia's finest opening batsmen; he had that intangible, 'temperament'. And, he had a knack of making centuries — but that was evident in the progression of his Grade career. In his first-class career the ratio of centuries to half-centuries was 26 to 43, high.

And, we should never forget that he was the captain of NSW when it won the Sheffield Shield in the 1982–83 season, leading them out of a 17-year losing trough.

We shouldn't be too critical of the selectors who took so long to choose him. Richard Binns never would have.

NSW won the Sheffield Shield a dozen times in 16 seasons, from 1950 to 1966. They won nine times in succession ... heady days, indeed. Then, in the changeover of a generation, they started to lose. They were rough times.

POVERTY

I was a NSW captain in the losing times. I stood in for
Brian Taber, who had replaced Doug Walters, who had
resigned — or, was he given the push? I was sacked,
Brian Taber came back, then later I replaced Taber.
It was selection chaos.

Lou once said, "People young, old or in between always referred to me as 'Richie Benaud's father'." Therefore, I suppose it was only natural that I would be 'Richie Benaud's brother'. Neither Lou, nor I minded the compliment.

Twenty-two years after I'd played my last first-class game of cricket (courtesy of Keith Stackpole's misfortune, a broken thumb), the Fifth Test against the West Indies at Port Of Spain, Trinidad in 1973, I was at the Gilgandra races in central NSW.

I was there to watch a racehorse named Saloon Star, in which I had a third share, run in the Royal Hotel Star Of The Turf Handicap. After breaking free of its strapper pre-race and doing a few smart circuits of the car park it came out and won first up at eight to one.

As jockey Greg Ryan brought it back to the winner's circle the announcement came over the course loud speakers ... "Saloon Star, a black or brown two-year-old gelding by Celestial Bounty out of Drawing Room, trained by John Denison of Dubbo, owned by Mr J McQueen, Mrs J Macadam and J Benaud" ... and an old cow cocky standing beside me leaned over to his mate, and drawled, "John Benaud, eh — full brother to Richie you know."

July 16, 1996

Rich is as revered in England, where he commentates for the BBC, as he is in Gilgandra, or anywhere else in Australia. I'm at the Teddington ground, outside London, where the Australian Old Collegians are playing the London Club Cricket Conference.

If the batsman on strike at the southern end can hit a six in the direction of cow corner he will scatter a herd of deer grazing contentedly beneath the old oak trees.

On the other hand, if the batsman at the northern end belts a low, skimming six beyond midwicket there is a good chance it will scoot through the doorway of the hospitality tent, where a good amount of *bon vive* is still being enjoyed.

Lunch has been magnificent — smoked salmon, spinach and cheese ragout, ghame pie, wine, cheeses, fruit, port — prompting one Old Collegian, Shane Carlton, who hails from the far north of Queensland, to announce, "I don't think it'll get much better than this 'JB', unless those two waitresses go topless."

After lunch, in my role as team reserve scorer, I retire to the scorebox near long leg, and from there watch with interest as a gentleman of mature years emerges from the hospitality tent away to my left.

His features are Spanish Costa Brava tanned, his wispy hair a whitish mop. He is wearing a green and black striped blazer and fashionably crumpled linen slacks, the colour of which match his hair.

As he nears the scorebox my sizeable nose rather than my eyes, detect that he is smoking a cigar. A very large cigar.

Then, he is at my window, peering in at me through spectacles that resemble the bottoms of those famous soft drink bottles. In one hand I can see he has a nearly empty glass of red wine and, clutched in the other hand is the bottle, similarly full.

My fellow scorer, Viv, a middle aged lady cricket enthusiast, introduces us ... "This is Richie Benaud's brother" ... which brings forth the comment, in a well modulated, accented, pucker voice: "I knew someone who did his dry cleaning on the 1953 Ashes tour ... right cocky sod he said your brother was."

Stunning opening, that.

Generally in England they refer to Rich as sitting somewhere on the right-hand of God, so I make a mental note that my new friend in the green and black striped blazer might have things mixed up.

When I see him again it is out of the corner of my eye; it is many more runs later in the afternoon and I have swapped my bench in the scorer's box for a deck chair in the sun, but handy enough to the doorway of the hospitality tent to address any sudden case of overheating.

My friend in the blazer comes from my right, slowly with measured steps, the glass and bottle abandoned, the cigar in need of rekindling. He slumps into the deck chair beside me.

Initially, he fails to recognise me. I know this because his opening conversation gambit is, "What generation New Zealander are you?" I tell him I'm an Australian and, as he peers intently at me, I can see recognition suddenly writ large upon his face:

"Ah, yes ... what's it like being married to Richie?" he asks.

Did I get the NSW captaincy in the 1969–70 season only because I was Richie Benaud's brother? I had made my Sheffield Shield debut in 1966–67, played three games, then the following season played four games, got married, played two more, then hopped on a slow boat to England in January 1968.

What sort of credentials are they to be in the running for one of cricket's plum jobs? And, during all my cricket career my experience in captaincy had been neither extensive, nor very successful.

I apparently once organised my Parramatta High School First grade team so badly in the eyes of the sports master, an Englishman, he held my tactics up to ridicule at the next day's full school assembly.

I did better in an Under-16 end-of-season Combined City versus Country Boys rep match at the SCG where there was a gale blowing straight down the pitch, a gale so strong the umpires pocketed the bails. I bowled a very, very slow left-arm orthodox spinner named Ray Parker into it and he took nine for 23.

It was all Lou's work — the night before he told me about A. O. Gray, and had impressed upon me that the country boys were unlikely to have seen much spin bowling.

I butchered the Cumberland Under-21 team one day against St George. We were sent in to bat on a wet pitch and with the scoreboard showing Cumberland six for 19, I declared. It was a well-intentioned decision. "I have a theory ..." I explained to my bowlers.

They accepted it with open mouths. The plan was to get St George in on the pitch while it was still crook, dismiss them cheaply too, say for 50, then bat again when the pitch was improving, set them a target and bowl them out again and win outright. St George declared at one for 149 and we had collapsed to a dangerous seven for 125 in our second innings when bad light ended it.

Yet, after 18 months away from Australia, during which time I'd had tougher moments handling London club cricket than I'd had pacifying a platoon of East German border guards intent on tearing apart my Mini Moke at the Berlin Wall, the rumour was I'd get the NSW captaincy upon my return.

Why? Well, the chairman of the State selection panel, Stan Sismey, was reported to have said at a State training session, "We want another Benaud as captain." I was 25 years old.

Anyone privy to Stan's pronouncement might have suggested, "Excuse me, but don't you mean you want the best captain?"

There was great expectation in cricket circles that I should be able to do what Rich did. Captains fielded me in the gully and, if Rich had taken seven for 18 for NSW I was expected to take seven for 18 in my match the next weekend ... or was it all in my own muddled mind? Was I bringing the pressure to bear on myself?

Playing in a famous relative's shadow can be a frustrating experience. There was a 14-year gap between Rich and me, almost a father and son situation. Initially you hang on his every move, imagining that one day you might have the same good fortune in the game.

As you mature you read your own publicity, cut it out and paste it in a scrapbook, trying hard not to believe it, but hoping it's right.

Finally, when you make the grade, you strive to match him, whilst at the same time telling yourself it doesn't really matter if you don't. A sort of quitter's state of mind, I suppose.

I was never a quitter, but there were more than a few times when I had to remind myself of Lou's very good advice: "Son, in cricket as in life, you rise and fall as yourself, John Benaud."

Without a sense of humour in the game of cricket, you're dead. Arthur Mailey returned four for 362 against Victoria — that's serious stuff! — and observed, "I was just finding my length when the innings finished."

And, what about Trevor Chappell? He might be entitled to curse when people remind him over and over of his brother Greg's demand that he bowl the last ball underarm in that World Series match. Should he tell people to nick off? Publicly though he steadfastly remains well mannered, and good humoured about the incident that must have left him fairly numb.

He answers persistent queries by relating how Greg said to him: "How's your underarm bowling?" Trevor: "I don't know." Greg: "Well, you're about to find out."

A humour device in cricket is the 'nickname'. Some are straight abbreviations ... you hear 'Heals' shout "Bowled 'Warnie'," to Shane Warne in a Test match. Those simple, matey expressions are inspirational tools. Team bonding.

Warne's first nickname though was 'Hollywood', which was in keeping with the gelled blond hair, the smart dress, the twinkling eyes and the diamond stud in the ear. It was a nickname based on his personality.

Sometimes the nickname might be a famous name link: Geoff 'Henry' Lawson and Neil 'Harpo' Marks. Sometimes it might be the way a player's style appeals to his teammates: Graham 'Tonker' Thomas. Greg Matthews once copped 'Misere'.

It might be a play on words: 'Tugga' Waugh. It might be a physical idiosyncracy: Billy 'Blinks' Watson, Mark 'Tubby' Taylor. It might be a nickname Mark II: the NSW spin bowler Johnny Martin was 'Little Favourite' shortened to 'Little Fav', and the NSW fast bowler Johnny Martin, who followed him, was 'Big Fav'.

Or, the nickname might simply be a hand-down from another era: Rich was 'Benords' and so was I. Not much imagination from my teammates there! It wasn't always so.

Peter Philpott, the mischievous legspinner with a mind as busy and as inquiring as Professor Julius Sumner Miller's, came up with a nickname for me that might have been the most appropriate.

'Poverty' — little Rich.

The brothers who have played for Australia are: the Archers, Ken and Ron; the Bannermans, Alex and Charles; the Benauds, Richie and John; the Chappells, Ian, Greg and Trevor; the Giffens, George and Walter; the Gregorys, Dave and Ted; the Harveys, Merv and Neil; the McLeods, Charles and Robert; the Trotts, Albert and George; the Trumbles, Hugh and John; the Waughs, Steve and Mark.

The Benauds were the third set of brothers to captain NSW, after Ned and Dave Gregory and 'Gar' and 'Mick' Waddy.

*Rich captained NSW 32 times for 28 wins,
I captained them 11 times for three wins. But,
the selectors did get 'another Benaud' — in the
'loss' column. We both suffered six.*

CAPTAINS

Bill O'Reilly: "I have never placed great importance on the choice of a captain. There is nothing in the job more than the skill to write down the batting order legibly and to walk in front of the team as it takes the field. The rest is rule-of-thumb stuff that any well-trained collie dog can perform."

Bill, a stirrer as well as a spinner, might have had a twinkle in his eye and a mischievous grin when he penned that. After all, he'd have known it was going to screw up a few egos, and provoke a few second thoughts about captaincy's hall of fame.

And, as time has gone on it has been the iron bar with which the media have belted a few disappointing captains, even the odd successful one. Bill did have a point — cricket tactics have been handed down from captain to captain over a couple of centuries, and been well tested and refined.

Mind you, we can't be too sure which tactician handed down to Arjuna Ranatunga the Sri Lankan's 1996 theory for the One-day game — that slow-running, unfit batsmen be allowed a runner every time they run out of puff.

But otherwise it's pretty straightforward stuff — knowing what to do upon winning the toss, knowing where to place the field for batsmen with certain styles and certain strengths and weaknesses, knowing which way the wind's blowing, knowing which end certain bowlers should come from, and so on.

As with any other aspect of the game, captains have their own way of doing things. Because no list of Australian captains would be complete without Bradman in it, the tables opposite are based on a minimum 24 Tests, the number Bradman captained.

What can we make of all that? A stack of figures that show Bradman was Australia's most successful captain and Kim Hughes the worst. But Hughes' supporters are entitled to point out that his captaincy career was subjected to unusual, if not unique pressures, and not the least of which was the backwash of the World Series Cricket/Establishment split.

Captain	Matches	W	L	D	Win%
Benaud	28	12	4	11	42.86
Border	93	32	22	38	34.41
Bradman	24	15	3	6	62.50
Chappell G	48	21	13	14	43.75
Chappell I	30	15	5	10	50.00
Hassett	24	14	4	6	58.33
Hughes	28	4	13	11	14.29
Lawry	25	9	8	8	36.00
Simpson	39	12	12	15	30.77
Taylor	33	18	10	5	54.54
Woodfull	25	14	7	4	56.00

	Record at Home			Record Away		
Captain	M	Win	Win%	M	Win	Win%
Benaud	16	7	43.75	12	5	41.67
Border	51	19	37.25	42	13	30.95
Bradman	15	10	66.67	9	5	55.56
Chappell G	33	18	54.55	15	3	20.00
Chappell I	13	9	69.23	17	6	35.29
Hassett	14	10	71.43	10	4	40.00
Hughes	8	3	37.50	20	1	25.00
Lawry	12	5	41.67	13	4	30.77
Simpson	15	7	46.67	24	5	20.83
Taylor	16	11	68.75	17	7	41.17
Woodfull	15	10	66.67	10	4	40.00

Hughes often had to share the job with Greg Chappell, who elected not to tour overseas on occasions — when you consider Hughes' Away record note also Greg Chappell's Away to Home ratio of Tests captained.

And, Hughes' fans can offer this: if he was such a poor captain how did he lead Western Australia to two Sheffield Shields? Still, a more dispassionate view might be that Kim's captaincy too often suffered from the same affliction as his batting career — taking too many rash options.

On stats, Lindsay Hassett and Bill Woodfull might be the most underrated captains when comparisons are being made. Hassett followed Bradman, when Australia were rebuilding, while Woodfull regained The Ashes twice, the only captain to do that, and he had to survive Bodyline to do it. Woodfull's record is strikingly similar to Mark Taylor's.

Possibly a better way to judge success when it comes to captains is by their series results:

Captain	Ser	Won	Lost	Drawn	Win%
Taylor	9	8	I	–	88.88
Benaud	6	5	–	I	83.33
Woodfull	5	4	I	–	80.00
Bradman	5	4	–	I	80.00
Chappell I	7	5	–	2	71.42
Chappell G	16	8	3	5	50.00

Some say a captain is only as good as his team, but there's no doubt that a poor captain can stuff up a good team. The great captain will, at some time, be all of the following:

- Hell bent on winning — but not to the detriment of the game;
- A sportsman — someone who respects the spirit of cricket and its traditions;
- An entertainer — spectators have to want to come to the next match;
- A psychoanalyst — good man manager who knows how to get the best out of every one of his players, and who can manage himself;
- A leader by example — high rating personal performance;
- A prophet — able to 'read' the game, anticipate outcomes;
- Lucky — more times than not he'll beat adverse odds.

When you think about it, it's not often they all fall into place.

February 18, 1973

Doug Walters still remembers the the third day of the First Test between Australia and the West Indies in Jamaica. Doug worked for Rothmans at the time and, the night before he had to attend their ball, in the hills above Kingston.

I got back to the team hotel rather late, about 9.30 ... or something like that (an afterthought accompanied by a telltale chuckle!). I set the radio alarm clock, organised an early morning call, ordered breakfast for nine o'clock ... all three failed.

Five minutes before play was due to start I got a telephone call from 'TJ' (Terry Jenner) who said, 'Where are you, the game's about to start?'

I got a cab to the ground. The driver spent more time on the footpath than the road. When I got to the ground I'd missed the first three overs. I changed in a flash then stood at the gate, waving ... 'Fellas, I'm here.'

The whole lot of them ignored me, for another three overs. I charged on to the field to be greeted by that very polite captain, Ian Chappell. 'Fine leg you.'" Next over, 'Third man you ... fine leg ... third man ... fine leg' ... until lunch arrived.

I'm coming from right down the other end and the others were long gone from the field. Except the captain. He happened to be waiting at the gate to greet me. 'It won't __ ing happen again, will it Doug!

As a captain Ian Chappell had the knack of managing his men, even if 'the problem' happened to be one of his best mates.

How do some of Australia's captains rate against their overseas counterparts? And, can we really compare captains from eras that are far apart? For instance, what influence might a particular player, a champion of his era, have on a captain's record — Botham on Brearley's, Hadlee on Howarth's, Alderman on Border's, Warne on Taylor's?

The performances of Botham and Hadlee, listed here when they played under the captains in question, indicate they had some considerable impact on the outcome of matches.

M	Runs	HS	Ave	Wkts	Best	Ave
Botham for Brearley						
26	1489	149*	41.36	150	8/34	18.77
Hadlee for Howarth						
30	1221	103	30.53	152	6/51	19.80

And, if we regard Alderman's outstanding 1989 Ashes series in which he took 41 wickets as the winning difference between the two teams then it's possible he saved Border's captaincy.

Border's record stood at seven wins in 39 matches (13 losses, 18 draws and a tie) before that series. To have again lost The Ashes would surely have tested the selectors' patience, if not the Cricket Board's. Of course, the question that raises is: who could have taken over? Geoff Marsh?

Greg Chappell had a rampant Dennis Lillee at his command. Ian Chappell had Lillee and Jeff Thomson as a pair.

M	Wkts	S/rate	Ave	5W/i	10W/m
Lillee for Greg Chappell					
38	199	47.99	23.63	15	5
Alderman for Border					
20	91	54.88	23.33	9	1
Lillee for Ian Chappell					
20	92	58.48	23.52	4	1
Thomson for Ian Chappell					
10	49	53.14	23.65	3	–

Lillee was certainly a major player for the Chappells, and Ian was blessed with Thommo as well. Still, the captain has to have the right tactic in place to get the best results, even from a champion.

And, those statistics tend to take the adage, bowlers win matches, a step further — it's probably why we had Bodyline and why the West Indies perpetuated their line of fast bowlers. Pace bowlers win more matches, maybe because they scar batsmen's minds more. The above are all aggressive, and either fast, or good swingers of the ball.

Of course spin bowlers influence a captain's results, too — consider Rich's impact on his own record or Shane Warne on Mark Taylor's. But mostly the spinner will have smart pace support. Rich once conceded, "'Davo' (Alan Davidson) got me a lot of my wickets." Glenn McGrath, Craig McDermott and Merv Hughes surely contributed something to Warne's success rate.

Warne's performance is similar under both Taylor and Border, and his strike rate as impressive (around five wickets a match) as any of the fast bowlers.

M	Wkts	Best	5/10	Ave
Warne for Taylor				
31	148	8/71	6/2	23.9
Warne for Border				
26	116	7/52	5/1	23.9

Trying to compare captains from different eras creates exactly the same problems as comparing players. It's interesting, but fallible. In the era of uncovered pitches captains were faced with unique problems — precise judgments on how a wet pitch, or a drying one, might play, whether to bat or to bowl, the timing of a declaration to maximise any advantage in the changing conditions.

Clive Lloyd and Viv Richards were captains of Test teams with great records and, it's probable that we will be well into the next century before another cricketing nation even comes close to matching the West Indian record of 29 successive series without losing.

Computer buffs like to match Bradman's 1948 'Invincibles' with Lloyd's West Indians but never mind changed conditions, even the laws of the game were different. If we had a Time Machine what should we do, transport Lloyd's heroes back to the ways of the cricket world just after World War II?

Or, should we imagine how much better Bradman and Co. might have been given modern day fitness trends, covered pitches, hi-tech gear, and so on? An imbroglio. And, those modern day captains who would seek to compare their teams with Bradman's forget one thing — the '48 team had Bradman!

It is easy to underrate the captaincy talent of Lloyd and Richards who had to organise themselves into a batting order of Greenidge, Haynes, Kallicharran, Richardson, Gomes, Logie and Dujon. And then choose the best time to bowl any of Holding, Croft, Garner, Roberts, Marshall, Ambrose and Walsh.

It could be argued that there was no great inspiration involved in deciding when to hand the ball on from Holding to Croft or Ambrose to Walsh, or from Roberts to Garner or Marshall. Cynics likened their challenge to an Olympic relay race — captaincy by baton change.

And, how should we compare such a challenge with Mark Taylor's job of deciding when to share the ball between McGrath, Gillespie, Warne or Bevan? And still come up a winner.

In the 1969–70 season the name of the NSW captain was announced one week before the selectors named the rest of the team. It was a move unprecedented in NSW cricket history.

Dick Tucker wrote in the *Daily Mirror*, "The early appointment of John Benaud, younger brother of Richie, former Australian skipper, reflects the selectors' determination to pull NSW out of the depressing slide of last year."

So, as well as defying history, or tradition, an unrealistic expectation was being created: NSW was about to be blessed with the same sort of winning leadership practised by Rich a decade before.

Let's face it, naming captains even before a team is picked is wonky stuff. It was particularly so in my case because I'd been out of the country on business for nearly one and a half seasons.

A modern-day example of a pre-team captaincy announcement going awry followed Victoria's decision in 1995–96 to relieve Dean Jones of the captaincy of the Sheffield Shield team for the next season.

They appointed Shane Warne. Nothing wrong with that because Warne appealed as a smart young cricketer and, in maturity, a prospective Australian captain, but … at the same time, they appointed as vice-captain Tony Dodemaide, the medium pace swing and seam bowler.

Tony is a solid, sensible cricketer, but it's more likely Victoria named him to stifle any suggestion that Jones might be revived as captain when Warne was on Australian duty.

The Vics had to play their first match of the 1996–97 season on an SCG pitch apparently relocated from a funeral parlour. As such, it was hardly any good for Tony's talents.

Result: the vice-captain, whose appointment had received so much publicity before the summer had even warmed up, was made 12th man! Worse was to follow. Before the Vics' next match, for which Warne was unavailable because of Test duty, Dodemaide broke a finger. Out.

The captain? Jones.

In 1970, Rich wrote in the *Daily Mirror*: "Last year when a State selector told me John Benaud might captain NSW this season my reply was, that if asked I would tell John to think long and hard about it and then decline in view of what had happened to Doug Walters."

Walters, shortly before, had been asked to declare publicly that the captaincy was affecting his batting, and he would like to be relieved of the responsibility.

Walters is a slightly more cynical man today, now that he has realised the cricket politics that were behind his original appointment.

I probably did ask Rich for advice about accepting the NSW captaincy, I can't remember. Chances are I considered his advice, then ignored it.

Think of it this way: the offer of the captaincy of your State is an honour that very few young cricketers would knock back, even on reflection, or even on the very best of advice.

'I can do it', would be the overwhelming feeling. There would be a spurt of adrenalin. That is human nature. And anyway, in my case it was to be only for one season while the regular captain, Brian Taber, was away with the Australian team in South Africa.

It was the stuff of dreams, but it became a nightmare.

What is now the traditional Boxing Day Test at the MCG used to be a willing Sheffield Shield stoush between NSW and Victoria. In that 1969–70 season the match result was one of the closest in Shield history — Victoria won by one wicket.

VICS

NSW, captained by me, lost their first two matches …
"Benaud On Carpet" said the headline over a story about
the selectors being unhappy, too. But cricket has a lovely
bite-back clause and, if you can negotiate it, it will
drag you up off any carpet.

Christmas, 1969

It's late in the day, the third day of the Boxing Day match of 1969 and the sun is going down on the Vics; they're losing the unloseable game. The strange thing is they'd had it won from the very first ball on the first day, when 'The Mule' (Bruce Francis) nicked 'Froggy' (Alan Thomson) to slip — "You bloody beauty, one for none," squealed the Vics.

After another 31.2 overs it was all over. We'd capitulated to some bouncy stuff around the off stump from Froggy, the Vics' fair-haired, square-shouldered, wrong-footed pace bowler.

He had a strange double-arm action at the delivery, in its beginning like The Wave, at its release like the spinning tail rotor of a helicopter.

And, we'd been bamboozled by some cheeky 'Chinamen' from a left-arm spinner whose name, Blair Campbell, would have looked more in place among the credits at the local playhouse. We NSW boys, average age 24, were all out 131.

We'd been going for our shots. The Vics went for theirs too, big time, and after seven overs from 'Big Shine' (Dave Renneberg) and 'Big Fav' (Johnny Martin) the openers, those phlegmatic left-handers Ken Eastwood and Bob Cowper, had put on 56 — big indeed! And, in no time at all, they were none for 130 — "Bloody hell," gasped the NSW boys.

Enter 'Skull' (Kerry O'Keeffe) and exit the Vics. His pacey legspin accounts for four of them and at the other end 'The Fox' (Dave Colley) gets another four with his cutters. The game's only a day and a bit old — "We're back in this," exclaim the NSW boys.

Just look at that scoreboard! The Vics are now nine for 220. There's an old, hand-me-down tactic among cricket captains: when you've got the last pair in you don't change the bowling that's got you to that point, especially if they've got you there quickly!

So, Skull and The Fox carried on against the Vics last wicket pair — who just happened to be Froggy and Blair Campbell! The buggers must still have been under the influence of adrenalin. Or, possibly the NSW bowlers were stuffed, or maybe the captain of the NSW boys went to sleep … the old, 'eight-out, all-out' syndrome.

Whatever, Froggy and Blair slogged hugely and in no time at all the Vics' 89-run lead had turned into 147. Fifty-eight runs off 63 balls! — "(Expletive deleted) it!" chorused the NSW boys as they slowly trudged off, up the players' race, and into the bowels of a featureless, somewhat sombre in mood, dressing room. They padded up again.

It was a lovely sunny afternoon in 'Bleak City' (Melbourne). What more could the early NSW batting line-up of The Mule, 'Fitteran' (Alan Turner), 'Sticks' (Ross Collins), 'Hatch' (Geoff Davies) and 'Jack' (John Wilson) have wished for? Well, a less groggy second innings scoreboard would have been nice — one for 49, two for 59, three for 72 and … it's another Froggy benefit!

The NSW boys might have wished for a little more luck, too … Froggy makes it four in a row when Jack tries to avoid a bouncer and falls into his stumps. It's like a scene from a Whelan The Wrecker building site.

Enter me and, apparently at my right shoulder, God, and furthermore it turns out he's smiling. I am to face Robert Rowan, a young man whose Nordic features suggest he should be into cross country skiing. Instead, he is a smart baseballer of the time, who on this occasion is bowling left-arm quicks, which he can either slant across me or bend back in, sharply.

I have made maybe four runs. It may have been a few more, but for sure it wasn't anywhere near enough to wipe out the deficit which was still about 60. I am playing my natural game, and I try to cover drive Robert's slanter, as Robert had hoped I would, and all I manage is a nick, and a loud one it is, to the 'keeper.

The umpire calls: "Not out."; I whisper: "Thanks God!"; the Vics, incredulous, screech: "Christ, he cover drove the bloody thing!" Someone even suggests I should 'walk'. Why didn't I? Well, Lou said … and, you'll see.

Up at the other end, next to the umpire, was Hatch, my little mate; we lived in the same suburb, played with the same club, and were 'roomies'. He watched this drama at first wide-eyed, then, when the umpire said 'not out', wide-mouthed. Into the last over of the day — it's still only the second day, remember — Hatch had reached 91, I'd passed my hundred and we'd put on 204, a lead of 133 runs.

Who could believe that … more to the point, who would believe what happened next? The previously unlucky Rowan was the man bowling that last over, and he bowled a bouncer which Hatch tried to hook.

It feathered his gloves on the way through to the 'keeper, and he was given out — "Why me? Jeez you're an arsy bastard Benords," he says to me as we plod off, despondent, downtrodden, etc.

Day three turns out to be an even more remarkable day of cricket than its predecessors, oozing fluctuating fortune. If you're a player you hold your pounding head, if you're a spectator you shake it.

It begins with Froggy taking three wickets in 10 balls, then another which gives him eight for the innings, 13 for the match, and 47 in his first-class career, which at that stage was just six matches old — "Pick him in the Test side right now!" screamed the Bleak City media.

So, the Vics need 181 to win and they've got the best part of two days to get them. Drama. The Vics' first innings batting hero, Eastwood (86), is out second ball for a duck, then Cowper goes not long after — "You're into the tail," shouts a wag from the outer, almost certainly a New South Welshman gone south for Christmas.

Yes-s-s …! and not long after we are! The Vics are mesmerised by the twin spin of Skull and Hatch. Heady legspinners, both of them, Skull the pacier of the two, a bit flatter in trajectory, Hatch slower and higher, more teasing. Skull has mostly bad luck, but Hatch has four wickets for bugger-all — "Gee, it's a great game, Benords," he tells me.

And indeed it is, for the scoreboard reads: Vics eight for 102. NSW are in a position to win the unwinnable game. But … it was the scheduled time for stumps, day three.

Still, not to worry. In that season the playing rules said that if, in the opinion of the umpires, a result could be achieved by a half hour extension to play then that extension should be granted to the captain of the team making the request.

Well, open and shut case, eh? Thirty-eight wickets had fallen in three days, and by even the roughest of mathematical applications that's an average of two an hour. On this particular day 13 wickets had fallen, so the odds would be on NSW clinching victory sooner rather than later — or would they? Maybe the umpires, Bill Smyth and Keith Butler, thought the number of wickets that had already fallen was over the odds. To my appeal for the extra half hour's play they said, "No way!" and off we all went.

There could be only one possible reason for Bill's and Keith's decision to 'walk' — they thought the Vics batting was strong enough to survive. And 'Beatle' (Graeme Watson), a recognised batsman, was still at the wicket. Batting with Beatle was Rowan, who had made a duck in the first innings, given out caught by the wicketkeeper, the irony of which would not have escaped him when his own appeal for caught behind against me had been given not out.

Was he not due for a luck change? And, the last man in was Froggy — a hero if ever there was one. In view of earlier proceedings what Victorian in his right mind would suggest that Froggy's status was about to change?

So, we NSW boys came back the next morning … and it was raining, a workhouse grey day in that huge grey concrete, soulless stadium, a grey film of water on the outfield that made the ball so greasy it hopelessly disadvantaged the two NSW bowlers who had made the Vics' batsmen such a bunch of novices the day before.

Our potential match winners, Skull and Hatch could only take one wicket between them that morning, Beatle stumped off Hatch when the Vics were 178. Three runs to win, one wicket in hand ∴ Rowan, facing Big Shine, gets them with a thick, outside edge — "We wuz robbed," growl the NSW boys.

Still, the game might never have reached such a wonderfully controversial point if the Vics had not been "robbed" of those hundred-plus runs I scored after being given not out caught behind. And, imagine if I'd 'walked' — I'd have ruined a perfectly good game of cricket.

Sometimes one result, even a loss, can turn a team around. That one did it for NSW that summer. We won our next two matches outright and only heavy rain cost us a third. None of it was enough to save the captain from the gallows, hung by his bootlaces.

THE BOOTS

It was tagged The Boots Affair, a silly little episode that exposed the Us versus Them psyche that often exists between administrators and players. "We'll see who comes out on top of this business in the end," said one administrator, darkly.

There were three of us sitting in the executive room at the SCG, me the player, and the administrators, Mr S. G. (Syd) Webb, Q.C., and Mr A. R. (Alan) Barnes. It was the second day of the return match between NSW and Victoria, a Sunday morning.

In an ideal cricket world, we three should have been saying a little prayer … "Dear Lord, please help NSW win this match outright and we'll be in with a rough chance of winning the Sheffield Shield for the first time in four seasons."

But we weren't contemplating that exciting prospect, instead we were discussing my cricket boots, and how many spikes they should have had in the heels. Incredible, but sad to say, true.

There was a mention, too, of my immaturity. On the latter point the others certainly had an edge — Mr Webb, Q.C. was 70 years old, Mr Barnes was 54 years old and I was 25 years old. An open and shut case? If I'd been given the chance I'd have denied immaturity, I might have pleaded guilty to 'headstrong'.

Judgment on the boots and the question of their suitability was less clear cut. Two days before this important Shield match the NSW Cricket Association executive had decreed (by letter) to its Sheffield Shield players that they had to wear a 'regulation' cricket boot — one that had three spikes in the heel and six in the sole and, just in case anyone was in any doubt, they introduced a new law to that effect.

They were said to be acting on advice from the selectors, Messrs Stan Sismey, Neil Harvey, Jack Chegwyn, Sid Carroll and Ern Laidler, all of them former players.

The problem with the new law was that all season (we had already played five matches) just about all the NSW team had been wearing a new style of comfortable, low-cut, lightweight cricket shoe with a rubber heel. This heel had sharply angled wedges for grip instead of spikes.

So, the Association decree meant that just before a must-win match most of the players had to revert either to a pair of old boots or, as was my predicament, go out and buy a new pair and run them in. My new boots were heavier, had leather uppers and soles, and of course the stipulated number of spikes. And, they were stiff as new leather shoes generally are.

I wonder how sport's modern day psychologists would rate that out of 10 for player motivation? This is an exaggerated example, but imagine an athlete at the Olympics being asked to switch to a heavier racing shoe on the eve of his race.

The decree came about because the administrators/selectors, in the privacy of their executive room in the SCG Members' grandstand, quarantined from any alternative views, became convinced that the new ripple heels made players drop catches, score fewer runs and take less wickets.

Publicly, the administrators stressed only the poor catching. It must have been fascinating to hear Webb Q.C. for the prosecution, establishing the case for a link between the heel of a cricket boot and an outbreak of butter-fingers.

It was true that players wearing the new boots, early in the season, had slipped in the field, but it happened at the end of a sprint after a ball hit into the outfield, at the moment when they braced their foot, heel down first, as a brake to stop their momentum. The slip interfered with the turn and throw, not so much the pick up.

That's not perfect cricket, but to leap from that point to a dropped catch in the slips, as the administrators did, was illogical. Where would it all end? It had the potential for high farce — how many strands of elastic should there be in a regulation jock strap?

And, imagine if these administrators had been around when Greg Chappell got all those ducks in the early '80s — would there have been a rule introduced about the weight of a regulation bat?

Sir Donald Bradman, wearing a neck brace to correct a long standing spinal complaint, speaking at a farewell to the South Australian captain Les Favell, was reported to have quipped, "I was wearing one of those conventional boots Mr Syd Webb says we should wear and fell over."

NSW upper house politician Joe Kelly pointed out, "Accumulated scientific knowledge decreed that the American astronauts wear ripple-soled boots for their moon landings. Apparently they are non-slip on the moon but not on the SCG."

The argument that I put to Messrs Webb and Barnes that Sunday morning was exactly the same as the one I had put to the NSW chairman of selectors, Stan Sismey, on the first morning of the match.

- The ban on the boots, so close to a vital match, was poorly timed.
- Our team had begun to win — why destabilise it?
- Please compromise — the executive had made no mention of the banned boots creating problems for batsmen, so why the total ban? Allow us to bat in the banned boots.
- We'll wear the regulation style on the southern tour, a fortnight away, which would allow us time to adapt to the change.

All this turned out to be a sign of my immaturity; Webb told me I was being "a silly boy".

A spot of counselling for the problem player, perhaps? Or, the administrators? Webb twice called me 'Richie'.

I was just naive, not silly. Another problem with the new pair of 'all-spikes' I had purchased was they were narrower than the banned ripple-heeled boots — it was a recipe for sore and blistered feet, and that was indeed the result after practising in them.

When I had spoken to the selection chairman in the dressing room on the first morning of the match, me perched on the edge of the long table in the viewing room, he standing in front of me, I told him that playing in the new, regulation boots would be difficult, so much so that I couldn't possibly give a 100 per cent effort for my team.

I explained that because of those misgivings I was determined to bat in the banned boots. I was heartened by what I perceived to be his positive reaction, that he considered it to be a sensible suggestion, and that he would take it up with the executive upon leaving me.

But it should be noted, Sismey never did use the words, "Go ahead and wear the banned boots when you bat, I'll fix it up with the executive." Rich was to offer me some advice later: "Never assume anything." If I had been 'silly' it was then.

But consider this: if Sismey, in our discussions before play on that first morning of the game, had felt even the slightest uneasiness about my stated intention to bat in the banned boots, had felt that I was merely being a half-smart opportunist wantonly defying the ban, would he not have immediately demanded full compliance and, if it was not received, then wouldn't he have asked the other selectors to drop me for disciplinary reasons?

Or, as chairman, wouldn't he have taken it upon himself to oust me from the team then and there and play the 12th man? I was so convinced Sismey believed my proposition to be sensible, so sure he was going to negotiate a compromise that I relayed my confidence to our in-form batsman, Tony Steele — "Stan's going to sort it out, there'll be no problem wearing the boots."

So, six of us batted in the banned boots in the first innings. The official reaction was swift — to them, I had openly defied the ban, and had led the team up the same path. Rebellion. That wasn't my perception because of my session with Stan Sismey.

When I met with Messrs Webb and Barnes that Sunday morning it was soon clear that if Stan Sismey had indeed been to see them the previous day then he had struck out. Webb's references to me as 'Richie' might have been a case of poor memory, but more likely bad memories.

Webb had managed the 1961 Australian team to England and had become frustrated, maybe even irritated, because he wasn't being accorded the profile he felt he should have been. So Webb 'gagged' the captain — who was Rich.

Now in 1970, Syd had his stout, comfortable, suede shoe on my throat. Could I get up? Well … the state of play at stumps on the Sunday was this: NSW 278, Victoria 183, and NSW, in again, looking for a solid score on the Monday to set up a declaration that would leave us plenty of time to dismiss the Vics.

That would be three outright victories in a row. Two of them would have been 100 per cent achieved in the controversial boots and the other with 60 per cent of the players batting in them, possibly compelling evidence to put before the administrators to have the ban relaxed, if not overturned.

But on the Monday, the third day, the first two sessions were lost to rain and that changed the NSW game plan — in whatever time was left some slogging was urgently needed to achieve a declaration target.

So, late in the day I promoted myself to No.3 from No.6 to do a bit of slogging; and, I wore the banned boots; and, when offered 'the light' by the umpires I decided not to come off, so we could stretch our lead.

From a purely cricket viewpoint you might think all three were sensible tactics, but to Webb and Barnes it must have seemed as if I was purposely baiting them.

To bat again in the banned boots was in direct defiance of the outcome of my meeting with them the day before, when they restated their determination to enforce the ban.

Does that make me 'silly' … trying to ensure I continued to give my best for the team? It's important to note here that no other batsman wore the banned boots in this innings, because I had made them aware of the negative outcome of the meeting with Webb and Barnes.

And, does that further reinforce my point about the relaxed, positive nature of my Saturday meeting with Sismey, when I believed compromise was certain?

To win, the Vics needed 310 runs on the last day. They were seven for 261 when bad light ended the game. Ironically, I once had a chance to catch Peter Bedford, the batsman who had held us at bay, but just failed to reach a skier ... I slipped, even though I was fielding in the regulation boots.

Back in the dressing room after the match, even before the roomie 'Big Siddie' had handed me my first beer, Alan Barnes was at the door, handing me two letters, which basically said this:

- You're sacked as captain;
- You're dropped from the team;
- You're barred from playing any cricket in NSW, indefinitely.

The first letter said in part:

Dear Mr Benaud,
I am directed by the executive committee of my Association to charge you as follows:
(a) That you violated by-law 45(a) ...
(b) That you disobeyed an instruction ...

The second letter said in part:

Dear Mr Benaud,
I am directed by the executive committee of my Association to inform you that pursuant to NSW Cricket Association by-law 38 you have been suspended from playing in any Sheffield Shield matches or in matches arranged or recognised by the NSW Cricket Association as and from 28th January, 1970.

What goes through your mind when you read stuff like that? It was like a sort of cricketing court-martial. Suddenly you've been sacked from the game you love, and over such a trivial thing — heels dug in over a pair of boots, because somebody old couldn't come to grips with something new and wanted to show the cricket world who's the boss. 'Violate' ...? Hang on, we are talking cricket here, aren't we?

Improper cricket apparel, 1970s style.

You look around the room at your teammates, all wrung out from their willing work over the previous four days, and one of them, Dave Renneberg, is talking about going on strike, thus proving that fast bowlers don't need a ball in their hand to propose a little aggro.

But what good would a strike do? It would merely offer the administrator an early chance to test his much-aired theory that "there are plenty more cricketers out there who'd love to take your place".

It was quickly agreed that a better option would be to dispense the aggro on the field — go on to win the Shield.

The press are milling around. "Will you appeal?" Why? I'd stated my case. I could only appeal the penalty. And anyway, the selectors had already picked the squad for the southern tour, the final two Sheffield Shield matches, and not even a successful appeal would change that.

I guess in the 1990s some smart alec lawyer, possibly even a Q.C., would have been talking Supreme Court writs, an odious trend in sport.

In the days that follow there are many inquests; Rich advises, "No matter how stupid the decision of a group of men may be in cricket … you never tell them. There's more to this game than going on to the field and being a crowd pleaser … a touch of cynicism is essential and a knowledge of the slightly frightening politics of the game just as important."

Someone else suggests I apologise.

Footnotes:

In Perth, in the match against Western Australia, NSW player John Rogers, chasing a ball in the regulation boots, turned to throw and his heel spikes caught in the grass, tearing ankle ligaments and forcing him out of the next match against South Australia.

In Adelaide, where South Australia beat NSW by 195 runs, 10 of the South Australian team wore the boots banned by NSW.

When the ban was lifted I was permitted to play in a Grade cricket match — in the ripple-heeled boots, because the ban only applied to first-class matches.

The following season the Association amended the controversial by-law to read: "It is not the intention of this by-law to prescribe the type of sole and/ or heel or the number of spikes that might be worn in generally approved footwear."

And finally, this is how the Association reported the matter in its annual report:

The Association found it necessary to introduce a new By-law (45a) covering the wearing of proper cricket apparel in matches. Unfortunately the operation of the By-law in its original form led to disciplinary action involving the suspension of a State representative player from being considered for selection in the NSW team's last two Sheffield Shield matches and in other matches played under the Association's auspices over a period of four weeks. The suspension of the player was lifted on 19 February and subsequently an amendment was made to the By-law in respect of the section which motivated the incident.

You will notice the word 'boots' fails to get a mention, nor 'captain' nor the name of the player, and nor does the phrase 'we were wrong'. Funny that.

There was one great irony in The Boots affair and it was this: the captain who was appointed in my place, Tony Steele, went on to create one of the most successful sporting goods' agencies in Australia — and its strength was Adidas, the manufacturer of the banned ripple-soled cricket boots!

MIKE

Tony Steele might have matched Bradman when it came to business nous. Others who made a dollar out of the sporting goods business and who, by coincidence, played in the season of 'the boots' were Mike Pawley and Greg Chappell.

Declarations have drifted out of the game, which is a pity because they add a dimension to the play, and to viewing, and they can announce a player's character. Today's captains are less willing to take a risk trying to win, in case they lose.

Another reason is the generally ideal conditions under which matches are played these days. Once, turf pitches were not covered. A captain confronted with a saturated pitch would bat upon winning the toss.

The surface, although slow, was easy to bat on and, what's more, the wet outfield ensured the opposing bowlers had to contend with a slippery ball — no grip, no swing or cut.

Then as the pock-marked pitch began to dry and a crust formed on the surface, causing the ball to rear awkwardly, the batting captain could plan a declaration that would favour his bowlers. And they'd have a dry ball, too. Sometimes getting the timing of a declaration right could be as dicey as reading the behaviour of the pitch.

Tony Steele was Australia's premier batsman in the 1969–70 season, with 677 runs — all but about 250 wearing the suspect ripple-heeled boots — in 12 innings, average 67.70, a rush of runs that won him a place in the Australian 2nd XI that toured New Zealand.

His batting style was textbook precise, cool and calculating, and worth watching. His captaincy was a little more like his business style — the millionaire in him shone through.

On a fine, sunny Sydney morning, if one team gets another team out for 29 in its first innings, then the outright victory should be a foregone conclusion … yes? Balmain, Tony Steele's club, were playing Manly at a seaside ground, Manly Oval.

Some oldtimers in Sydney cricket reckon that the tide can have a major influence on matches played at grounds near the sea, that before high noon the ball will swing much more, and do more off the pitch.

Manly batted first and made 29, not because of tidal movement, but because the pitch was underprepared. It held no terrors for the Balmain boys. Skipper Steele called in his openers when they had made 36.

Of course, Steele did have another option: he could have batted on, hoped for say another 100 runs, thus substantially increasing Manly's deficit and, at the same time, blotting them out of the game. And the wicket might be worse, too.

But why do that? Why not take advantage of Manly's mental insecurity? After all, his bowlers had taken just 16.2 overs to dismiss Manly in the first innings. So, why risk it?

He'd only had to use two bowlers, too — by coincidence they were brothers, the Fitzgeralds, Chris and John, and they both bowled left-arm — and they certainly weren't tired.

Go for the jugular! Why put at risk a certain 10 points for the outright by batting on? Whereas five Manly batsmen had failed to score in their first innings, in the second only one of them, Mike Pawley, got a duck, which gave him a pair. But, Manly scored an impressive 136.

Pawley then provided some proof to all and sundry that cricket has great levelling qualities — he bowled 7.7 overs and took six for 14. Balmain were beaten outright; in their second innings they made only 87.

A characteristic of Mike Pawley's calling was refelected in his face — twinkling blue eyes ablaze in a forest of merging freckles; a quick smile, cheeky and dazzling white; unruly hair, a red shaggy carpet.

The mischievous countenance of a spin bowler. Like Tony Steele he enjoyed the challenge of captaincy, and wonders about the attitude of some players today. "They never think of cricket as an adventure. They're always thinking about their batting average and their bowling average, not 'what have I got to do to try to win this game?' or how they might change things to try to control the game instead of letting the game control them."

Mike Pawley's Sheffield Shield career with NSW was like a game of snakes and ladders. In a career covering five seasons he played 10 matches, and seven of those were in his first season! He didn't play at all in two, and bowled just two overs in another.

Was this a case of dithering selectors, or was it lack of patience with a young man striving to perfect the spinner's art? Or, maybe Mike just didn't have 'it' — the mysterious, intangible something that separates the champions from the other starters.

He wishes he'd been in less of a rush at the start of his career, wishes his self-confidence had matched his talent, wishes he'd known early what later brought him great success in Grade cricket.

Mike had the desire and, amongst the thousands upon thousands of letters that Sir Donald Bradman received there was one from Mike ... "Dear Sir Donald ..." It was a plea from the heart. "I am a left-arm orthodox spin bowler, could you please give me some advice ..."

Generously, Sir Donald replied. It was in a philosophical vein — that on hard bouncy Australian pitches it was better to try to perfect wrist spin. Mike considered the advice, tried over-the-wrist, but never pursued it.

Obviously, that was another regret — Mike later raced three greyhounds and named them Ima Googly, Flighted Googly and Another Googly, in honour of the wrist-spinner's mystery ball!

Mike had a lovely, gliding run-in, a wheeling left arm and a strong shoulder action that brought with it flight and spin. A backyard-coached boy, by a father who had been a rugby league footballer, a father whose home turf was sure to bring a glow to any bowler's nose.

Lionel Pawley rolled out a strip of kikuyu, the roughest and toughest of grasses, about 18 metres long and, to ensure it maintained durability, he regularly top-dressed it — with chicken manure.

Mike made his Sheffield Shield debut for NSW against Western Australia in 1969–70, the season of 'the boots'. He wasn't chosen in 1970–71, nor in 1971–72. Bradman's words haunted him ... the main spinner was the leggie, Kerry O'Keeffe. David Hourn, the left-arm wristy, was also being encouraged.

Before the 1972–73 season Ian Chappell's Ashes tourists came home with a tied series behind them, and greater glory ahead. But first they did their best for charity in a match at Sydney's Drummoyne Oval to support the spastic children of NSW. Mike showed the Ashes heroes no charity.

He finished with six for 90 on a typical early season Grade pitch, slow and gripping. *The Sydney Morning Herald* reported: "It would have been tough to name a player of the match but there would have been little dissension if Manly's left-arm orthodox spinner Mike Pawley had been the one."

Among his victims were the Chappells, Ian and Greg. Such a wonderful start to a season, even if it was for charity — yet he played only one Sheffield Shield match, the very last of the season. The scorecard shows he bowled two overs and got one for four. Why is it always the spinners who are offered a lonely over, or two before a break?

The NSW selectors chose him for the first match of the next summer, against Queensland on a 'Gabba shirtfront. "It's great to be back," he said, then bowled to Greg Chappell, who at the time was using a three pound

Gray-Nicolls and getting the same results with it that the world's militia men were getting with bazookas. Mike's Sheffield Shield career died instantly. Yet in the decade that followed their diverse careers in cricket were to be fleetingly intertwined via the most extraordinary events — each dabbled in the wiles of underarm bowling.

February 1, 1981

Greg Chappell, now the Australian captain, orders his brother Trevor to bowl the last ball of a World Series Final underarm so the Kiwis can't hit a winning six.

What makes a captain go that far? What sort of pressures must he be under to plumb such unsporting depths to deprive an opponent of so much as a sniff of victory?

Greg might have been nervous because a couple of summers before, during the Packer World Series breakaway, Australia had lost a limited-overs match at the death to the West Indies. The West Indian No.11, Wayne Daniel, had slogged a match-winning six off the last ball by Australia's Mick Malone. Greg's brother Ian was the Australian captain.

But the odds must have been astronomical that it would happen again, that another No.11 hacker named Brian McKechnie, whose batting strike rate in limited-overs internationals was a shocker, 41 runs for every 100 balls faced, would slog for six on the big MCG a smart bowler like Trevor Chappell, who on average conceded four runs an over.

It's more likely the pressure of a long, hot summer finally got to Greg. He was out in the middle of an MCG packed as tight as a sheep truck. The best-of-five series was all square, 1–1. The capacity crowd was wailing, fence-banging, demanding — "C'mon Aussies, c'mon …"

At that moment, Greg made winning everything, to the detriment of the spirit of the game. In the heat of the moment he forgot to ask himself the simple question, "What if …?"

What if McKechnie had hit the six? Could the disapprobation that Greg had to wear over such a thrilling loss have been as long lasting as that which he, and brother Trevor, have had to bear over the underarm, ever since?

Still, it wasn't a completely new theory. Arthur Mailey (in *10 For 66 And All That*):

> Hobbs and Sutcliffe had batted all day and promised to keep us out
> there for the following day, too. We sat in the Windsor Hotel until two
> in the morning evolving attacking schemes … and even our captain,
> Collins, a man with a rich appreciation of the manly old game, lowered

his ideals to such a state that he suggested in all seriousness an ordinary, underarm, grubber. This goes to show how desperate one becomes in such hopeless circumstances.

January 22, 1977

A few summers before Trevor Chappell's there was another underarm incident, but one more funny than foul. At Drummoyne Oval, the home team, Balmain, were sliding to defeat and feeling squeamish despite the prospect of a mouth-watering afternoon tea — the scoreboard read eight for 130.

Although it was getting late in the game the pitch was still quite tacky, trying to dry out after one of Sydney's typical overnight thunderstorms. Balmain's opponents, Manly, had enjoyed perfect conditions the Saturday before and had scored 290.

Balmain's No.10 batsman was Donald Renneberg, the younger brother of Dave Renneberg. Donald, like Dave, was better at bowling bumpers than scoring runs. His highest score in Grade cricket was recorded as 37, his career batting average a meagre 9.83.

With the casual, don't-fuss-me stride of a true Renneberg, Donald had gone out to the crease to join Michael Murfin, a lad whose stubble of fairy fluff confirmed he'd barely finished school. Michael was tall, and his forte was bowling very slow, loopy right-arm legspinners.

He batted left-hand and he too seemed to be in his rightful place low in the order — highest score 32, average 15.00. On that Saturday he had still not scored when Renneberg joined him.

The Manly bowling attack included Mike Pawley, then its captain. A tacky pitch … a massive deficit … the second last pair in, batting 'donkeys' both of them … the result was a foregone conclusion, Manly to win.

Yet, the lip-licking anticipation of early celebration drinks dissipated as the unlikely batting heroes soldiered on. And on. Murfin waged war by thrusting his padded right leg far down the pitch and allowing Mike's well flighted deliveries to hit it.

In fact, in one eight ball over Murfin did it five consecutive times. After the fifth ball had been padded away, and before the sixth, the umpire at the bowler's end, Rocky Harris, received a stunning request: "Left-arm under, thanks ump'."

The ever-alert Renneberg immediately warned striker Murfin, "Watch the bias!" So, Mike strolled in and bowled what was very probably Sydney Grade cricket's first underarm delivery since the overarm style was recognised.

"I thought I had him," said Mike later. "It was a gentle little slider, right along the ground. Actually, it would have hit the stumps but he got an outside edge on it … although, thinking about it again perhaps it didn't have enough pace on it to remove the bails.

"The next one … well I was frustrated, wasn't I? In the heat of the moment it was badly directed and went down the legside."

Mike bowled the last ball of the over overarm. Donald Renneberg and Michael Murfin went on to add an unbeaten 134, which was a new Balmain record for the ninth wicket.

Neither team got any points in the competition — NSW Cricket considers draws to have no merit. And few of them do, but occasionally for a selector they can mirror a cricketer's character.

In 1973, the season that the NSW selectors tell Mike Pawley his services are no longer required he responds by taking 62 wickets in Sydney Grade, at 8.71. It was a rare performance, and usually found only after names like Bill O'Reilly, Alan Davidson and M. A. Noble.

Asked to explain this success Mike nominates a broken spinning finger and the greyhound, Ima Googly. How can a combination as ridiculous as that advance a bowling career? A broken finger should be an impediment.

But in this case, its stiffness allowed Mike to slide a freakish arm ball off it, one that was just about impossible for a batsman to pick. One that curved gracefully in the air, like a Ray Lindwall inswinger, and zipped in further off the seam.

Amazing. What sort of a fickle god can it be who watches over the spin fraternity, permitting one of them to develop his most potent weapon in adversity, and just as the selectors say sayonara?

And, the greyhound … well, Mike ran with Ima Googly every afternoon after work, up and down the fairways on Long Reef golf course, and on the nearby sand dunes. Physically Mike was never fitter.

Mentally he was sharper, too — he knew absolutely nothing about training a greyhound so this was learn-as-you-go, full-on initiative. For instance — how to train a greyhound to come out of a starting box?

Mike hired a couple of starting boxes and put them in his backyard. He cooked pieces of steak and attached them, one at a time, to a long piece of string.

Then, he placed Ima Googly in a box, offered it the 'scent' then gave the end of the string to Jeanine, his daughter. "Run," shouted Mike, and off she'd go, this seven year old moppet, down the side of the house, the steak on the string bouncing around behind her.

Then, Mike would trigger the spring-release lid on the box and out would bound Ima Googly. Perfect. Then tragedy — suddenly Ima Googly lost interest and stayed in the box. It was the same day Mike lost his grip on the lid release and the lid suddenly, and forcefully retracted, kayoing the dog.

When its lid-phobia receded Mike took Ima Googly to Wentworth Park, the big time, Sydney's main track. The SCG of dog racing. There was a big crowd in, with Mike in the middle, palms sweating, wallet a little lighter, waiting. Ima Googly was slow to start, but then railed beautifully … until it got Mike's 'scent'. It jumped the fence, and zig-zagged through the crowd to his side.

Mike loved the greyhounds almost as much as he loved spin bowling. And he had as much luck. He took Flighted Googly to chilly Lithgow for a race and they stayed in a first-class motel — the dog got the double bed, Mike got the sofa. In the race the dog pulled up lame after 50 metres.

He trained Another Googly by giving it the run of Manly Oval, Mike's home ground. Manly was like a sweet dream for a finger spinner. Every weekend there was a nor'easter or a sou'easter. A good'un like Mike could float the ball like a trout fisherman casts his fly.

After practice, it was Mike's habit to spin yarns with his mates over a beer at The Steyne hotel, while the dog waited in the car. Well trained. One evening Another Googly took off from Manly Oval on its own, and up to The Steyne looking for Mike. It only found the bumper of a fast moving car. What might have been … the story of Mike's cricketing life.

Ima Googly never got to run at the only greyhound track in Australia that encircled a first-class cricket ground — Brisbane's 'Gabba. The track was still under construction when NSW played Queensland in the opening Sheffield Shield match of 1971.

THE ASHES

Most young cricketers' dreams are romantic, limitless:
wear the baggy green, score a century on Test debut in
front of 70,000 at the MCG, go on the Ashes tour ...
Missing an Ashes tour, when you're on the brink, takes
you down a peg, or two.

Even though the greyhound track no longer encircles the 'Gabba, it once provided inspiration for the television commentator Tony Greig who chose to remind cricket fans just how dicey the pitch had once been: "The difference now is that the cricket pitch is better than the greyhound track."

How incongruous that a sport as gloomy as greyhounds should have shared memories with a sport as glorious as cricket.

October, 1971
The 'Gabba looked like an abandoned building site. Torrential rain in the first week had held up final work on the greyhound track and, with play about to begin in the Sheffield Shield match between NSW and Queensland, the 'Gabba landscape was blotted with light poles of thin piping, planks and scaffolding, grey Besser bricks and piles of brown sand.

The picket fence and piles of sawdust, cricket's traditional props, were an afterthought. The sky was black. Doug Walters was in good form — "Bad light starts play," he quipped.

Sharp as a pin, Doug. We once shared a NSW teammate who, five innings in a row came off and hurled his bat into the dressing room wall — "I was robbed," he said of three catches to the 'keeper and two leg befores. In the sixth innings, he was bowled. As we watched him coming back to the dressing room, Doug said: "Bet it was a no-ball."

The pitch in the middle of the 'Gabba was a grey colour, a splash of green here and there, and greasy. The practice pitches were soft and wet, and unuseable. Probably dangerous. So, some of us went across to the malthoid pitch adjacent and took it in turns tossing at each other, short ones rising quickly up into the chest — we'd lost the toss and we expected a blitz from Tony Dell.

Tony was a big lump of a bloke who'd have looked comfortable packed into the front row of a rugby scrum, but he'd made his sporting mark as a left-arm fast bowler. His new ball partner was Bill Albury, who was later to become a household name in baseball. His cricket nickname was 'Wild Bill', a good call.

Bill was a red head with a chest puffed by exercise not ego, and his strong, wide shoulders carried a wiry body. He'd have brushed up okay as the lead role in any mini-series about a tough stockman challenging the Queensland outback.

There was a hint of Andy Bichel about him, but his action was rougher around the edges — less coached maybe. He bowled at sharpish pace with a bit of outswing, and he made the ball skid on a bit. He had a good offcutter that in favourable conditions could snake back at you, real quick. Wild Bill's attitude to the job of fast bowling matched the forboding darkness of his red hair.

He bowls, I aim a hook at a flying offcutter, get the wedge on the back of the bat on it, and it goes for six — over first slip! Bill, snarly, bowls another flying offcutter but it pitches further up, I scramble a back defence, the ball jams the first finger of my bottom hand against the bat handle …

I come off at lunch with Alan Turner, discussing the difference in pace and bounce between malthoid and greasy turf, and take a few minutes to get my batting glove off, my hand has swollen so much. It's pointless not to keep batting after lunch because it's obviously broken.

That was the bad news. The good news was I made 87. The really bad news was, that in Australia, there is a certain cricketing folklore attached to the number 87 — they say it's rare that anything good ever comes of it.

Hard-nosed cricketers rubbish the '87 is bad' theory by pointing out that of the 8,700-plus Australian Test dismissals only eleven have occurred on 87. But hang on … what about 87 elsewhere on the scoreboard — a partnership total, a bowler's runs-conceded statistic or, a batsman out in his 87th innings, the 87th over of an innings … and, don't forget that 13 is 87 from 100. Of course it's bad luck!

That season, 1971–72, had promised to be one of the most interesting in Australian cricket history. Australia would play South Africa in a five-Test series, a series that was sure to have quite an edge to it.

The South Africans were a champion team. Led by the Pollock brothers, Peter and Graeme, Barry Richards and Mike Procter, they had whipped Bill Lawry's Australians 4–0 barely 18 months before. And, at the end of the series the selectors, Neil Harvey, Sam Loxton and Phil Ridings would choose the 1972 Ashes squad. A lot of cricketers would be on 'the edge'.

South Africa never arrived. The Australian Board cancelled the tour at the last minute, saying,

Whilst there was substantial evidence that many Australians felt the tour should go on, the Board was equally made aware of the widespread disapproval of the South African Government's racial policy which restricted selection of South Africa's team.

There could be no doubt the tour would set up internal bitterness between rival groups and demonstrations on a large scale would be inevitable.

The Board decided to advise the South African Cricket Association with great regret that in the present atmosphere the invitation to tour must be withdrawn.

Instead, a Rest Of The World team toured. The captain was Garfield Sobers and on paper it had a formidable look about it ... the Pollock brothers, Bishen Bedi, Sunil Gavaskar, Tony Greig were some who toured.

Australia's most recent Test record had been indifferent — nine won, nine lost, nine drawn. Among the losses, The Ashes. No cricketing nation is likely to accept a record like that, nor any selection panel. In this series the selectors tried 19 players in five 'Tests'. I was one of them.

Where were you when Garfield Sobers made his 254 at the MCG? Think of the New Year, 1972, January 3rd and 5th. I was out in the middle, appreciating a ringside view of the champion West Indian's batsmanship, a heavyweight performance later described by Bradman in this way: "I believe Sobers' innings was probably the greatest exhibition of batting seen in Australia. I have seen nothing to equal it in this country. Overseas, I still believe Stan McCabe's 232 at Nottingham was in some respects better."

This Melbourne match was the third in the series and the World XI were one down, sunk by Lillee's eight for 29 in Perth.

Now, in the first innings here Sobers had made a duck, one of Lillee's five victims. Lillee was on his way to greatness, the World XI was seemingly heading for another loss.

So, when Sobers came to the crease in the second innings not only was he on a pair, but his team were gasping for life, three wickets down and only 45 runs ahead of Australia.

When he left, the World XI were 400 ahead. I clearly remember two of his scoring shots, both boundaries. One was from the bowling of Bob Massie, who was swinging the ball late, offering up a sample of what was to come at Lord's in a few months time — 16 wickets in his debut Test there.

Sobers had his eye well and truly in by this time, but Massie 'did' him. The left-handed Sobers picked the ball as an away-swinger to him, and raised his bat high, it seemed in preparation to pad up. The ball was an in-swinger.

In a flash the bat came down, the wrists rolled, and the ball sped between Terry Jenner at midwicket and me, at mid on. No surgeon could have been more precise. TJ and I looked at one another, then I fetched it.

And, when Lillee was coming on strong with the second new ball, and bowled him a scorching yorker, Sobers did the impossible. The ball seemed to be perfectly pitched in the blockhole, aimed at the off stump, maybe just a fraction outside. It was all the room Sobers needed.

He square drove it. Kerry O'Keeffe was out on the boundary, behind point, about where the old practice pitches used to be at the MCG. The ball hit the gutter at point, and rebounded a few metres. O'Keeffe had hardly taken a step, so fast did it travel.

There are a host of statistics: he hit two sixes, off successive balls from O'Keeffe; he hit 33 boundaries; he and Peter Pollock put on 186 for the eighth wicket — and Sobers made 129 of them. But consider this: he averaged 79 runs per 100 balls received.

Rapid batting like that can turn a match. It allowed the World XI nine hours to dismiss Australia. It is impossible to argue against the theory that bowlers win matches. But they need time to do it.

In his compliment to Sobers, Bradman mentioned McCabe's double-century in 1938. On that occasion Bradman invited the rest of the team to "come and watch this, you may never see its like ever again."

At the MCG, Sobers' exact scoring rate was 78.63 runs per 100 balls. McCabe beat that, his rate being 84.06. There are five double-centurions ahead of them:

Player	Opponent	Score	Rate
Botham	India	208	92.04
Greenidge	England	214	88.80
Bradman	England	244	88.09
Richards	Aust	208	84.90
Hammond	N Zealand	336	84.42

Was it good luck or bad that I was on the field when Sobers played maybe his greatest innings? How do you rate luck? Rich once cursed his luck because he'd never had the chance to bowl against Bradman. Keith Miller replied: "Don't worry Richie, every one of us has some good luck in life."

What about getting out for 99? Unlucky or unthinking? That happened to me in the last 'Test' of that series against the World XI. What should a batsman on 99 do? Push a single, or play the ball on its merits? The bowler was Intikhab Alam, the chubby figure who in more recent times filled out the tracksuit of the Pakistan Cricket Manager.

'Inti' bowled clever legspinners and wrong'uns but at that moment in 1971 he bowled me a long hop. My reflex said, "Pull shot!" Not only that, it was such an inviting long hop that a six into Adelaide's George Giffen Stand seemed like a good idea at the time.

I got halfway into the shot and thought, "Hang on … 99. Push a single."

I bunted it to Gavaskar at midwicket. Inti got me again in the second innings. That made five times in six innings in the series.

I was Inti's 'bunny', and the selectors would not have been impressed. "This bloke doesn't learn from his mistakes," would have been a fair judgment. On the bowlers and bunnies scale 80 per cent is carelessly high.

Over the years some top Test bowlers have puzzled some top Test batsmen:

Bowler	Wickets	'Bunny'	Times out	Out%
Bedser	236	Morris	18	7.63
Grimmett	216	Tate	11	5.09
Bedser	236	Harvey N	12	5.08
Snow	202	Chappell I	10	4.95
Holding	249	Gavaskar	11	4.42

Of course, the stat tells a lie because it covers the players' overall career dismissals; if we take Ian Chappell versus John Snow and focus on the four series when they squared off (1968, 1970–71, 1972 and 1975) then it shows Snow got his man 10 times in 38 innings, or 26.31 per cent of the time.

In those days there was no more nerve-jangling moment for a young cricketer than listening to the radio for the Ashes team announcement. I was propped on a kitchen bench. It was read out in alphabetical order, after the team leaders — "Ian Chappell, captain, Keith Stackpole, vice-captain …" When your name starts with 'B' the rest means little if the next name out is Greg Chappell's.

Missing the Ashes tour cuts you up a bit, maybe more so when just a few weeks before the selectors have had you in the top 12, and you've scored 99. But, no tears, or anything sentimental like that, no shock. And, no counselling required, which is one of the quaint suggestions doing the rounds these days for disappointed cricketers.

You feel just a brief, stunned emptiness and, after a while, ask yourself the question: Why?

Simple enough, really. I hadn't scored enough runs to beat Paul Sheahan, John Inverarity was a bit of an allrounder, Bruce Francis was an opener, and Graeme Watson, 'Beatle' from the Boxing Day Battle of 1969 was an allrounder. On the basis of balance I wasn't in the running.

Beatle could bat anywhere in the order, even open as he eventually did in the final Test of that 1972 series. And he could bowl sharpish pace. Moreover, he'd had the experience of previous tours to South Africa and New Zealand. I wasn't the only 'name' missing — so were Ian Redpath and Graham McKenzie.

It's a potent cocktail — the magic of the Ashes and a disappointed cricketer — and in the eyes of that particular player's supporters there is only ever one scapegoat, the selector, sitting at his table behind the closed doors of a backroom somewhere, pushing and pulling players this way and that, perhaps altering their lives forever. It's a tough job.

In 1972 I was a 'victim', in 1989 I was a 'villain' — a member of the selection panel that couldn't find a spot in the Ashes touring squad for the popular NSW left-arm fast bowler Mike Whitney.

'Whit' had just played in the final Test of the series against the mighty West Indies in Adelaide, and had taken seven for 89 and two for 60.

The bowlers who were chosen for the Ashes tour were: Terry Alderman, Greg Campbell, Geoff Lawson, Merv Hughes and Carl Rackemann. In my view Alderman, Lawson and Hughes picked themselves, although there was a great deal of anti-Hughes feeling among the public, at least in NSW.

The word 'joke' was often used around Merv, but that was more a reflection on the cricket ignorance of some in the media than it was on the man himself. In any comparison with Whitney the two 'bolters' could only be the rookie Greg Campbell and the veteran Carl Rackemann. Rackemann hadn't played a Test all summer, nor was his Sheffield Shield season an outstanding one — 24 wickets in eight matches. Whitney had taken 58 wickets in 13 matches, more than any other bowler in the summer.

But was Campbell really that much of a bolter? The media made much of the fact that he was a Tasmanian, but the selectors don't look at the map while they're choosing a Test team.

The important thing to the selectors was Campbell's consistent ability to move the ball away from the batsman at sharp pace, and to maintain his line over long periods.

Terry Alderman was 33 years old. We were looking for a bowler to carry on the Alderman tradition and our early choice, Tony Dodemaide, had had a lean summer. Campbell had the potential. It would have been irresponsible of the selectors to pass up an ideal opportunity to groom his successor, particularly when the maestro himself was on hand to do the coaching.

But, so much for philosophy, potential and forward planning … I knew the theory was in big trouble early in the tour. Television pictures beamed back to Australia showed young Campbell in the dressing room during a rain break in a Test, holding up a placard addressed to his sweetheart in Tasmania — "Marry me," it said.

A few summers on and Campbell was only playing Grade cricket in Brisbane, having married and left the chill of Tasmania to raise a family in the sunshine on Queensland's Gold Coast. He played four Tests and took 13 wickets at 38.

Whit played 12 Tests between 1981 and 1993 — one a year when you think about it — taking 39 wickets at 34. His Test career may have been unfairly hobbled by expectation because early on he was tagged 'another Alan Davidson', a gross exaggeration because 'Davo' was a champion allrounder.

Nor could Whit swing the ball anything like Davo, and that tempered judgment on him at the selection table, too. Bruce Reid, when fit, was preferred.

*If missing an Ashes tour is the ultimate downer
then being dropped from a Test team is not far behind;
but what about being dropped from the Test team
when the match still has a couple of days to go?
And, into the bargain, you're 'not out' as well?
Now that's an experience.*

CHAPPELLI

Ian Chappell told his teams, "My door's always open,"
confirmation that he was heavily into man management.
Some cheerfully took Chappelli at his word, even as late
as 3am. He had another good captaincy trait —
leading by example on the field.

When he was captain of Australia Ian Chappell once said, "I have never really been concerned about gaining the respect of the press, administrators or the cricket-watching public. That sort of respect never bothered me because of my theory that half the people like you and the other half don't, and it's useless to try to change those figures. The most important objective in my cricket life was to win the respect of the players in my team."

At the time, I wondered why Ian thought that only half the people might hate him. After all, he was never big on understatement and the headlines of the time suggested the whole world was against him.

- In a Test during the 1974 New Zealand tour: "Kiwi cricketers claimed today that Ian Chappell told their champion opening batsman Glenn Turner, 'Keep your __ ing nose out of this, you __ ing little __ , or I'll do you too'."
- In England in 1975: "His image in English cricket has been consistently bad, to the point that he almost qualifies as the 'ugly Australian'."
- An un-named administrator commenting on Chappell's retirement as captain of Australia: "I'm glad the bastard has gone. He's a bloody rebel."
- On charges of misconduct: "An angry Ian Chappell bowled two overs of medium paced 'beam' balls to NSW batsmen as a protest against the Sheffield Shield bonus points system which he says is unfair."
- And, charged with misconduct over the dropping of his trousers while batting: "I would have thought the normal thing to do when your protective equipment has come undone is to adjust it, and the only way I know of doing that is to undo your pants."
- And, in baseball: "South Australian catcher Ian Chappell was today benched as a disciplinary measure in the Claxton Shield against Victoria."

Come to think of all that, maybe Chappelli was right about the fifty-fifty reaction. For every hang-him reaction to the above you'd be sure to get a reasonable defence.

- Who really cares that he 'gobbed' Turner? He didn't hit him with a cricket bat, he just told him to mind his own business, colourfully. And, anyway, whatever happened to cricket's once acknowledged golden rule — what's on the field stays on the field?
- If his behaviour was so bad in England in 1975 why did *Wisden* name him one of its five cricketers of the year?
- 'Glad he was gone' … a year before, the administration had acknowledged that Chappelli's enterprising and thrilling captaincy had captured the imagination of the Australian public, lifting crowds.
- The 'beam balls' incident was extreme — but we should all be thankful that the bonus points system has disappeared from Shield cricket.
- The busted jock strap incident. Maybe he was expected to leave the field for five minutes? Maybe there should have been an emergency screen on hand. Or should all the players have gathered around?
- He did offer an excuse to the baseball coach — he was visiting his wife in hospital.

When we get it all into perspective it's hard not to raise an eyebrow, shrug our shoulders and ask, "Was that really major stuff?" And, Chappelli's teammates … well, he achieved his objective there. They were forever volunteering to walk on water for him.

It's a strange fact of cricketing life that some players do better at particular grounds, and it's not always on their home turf. Take Matthew Hayden, for instance. Just before he made his Test comeback against the West Indies in Adelaide in 1997 his statistical order of favourite grounds read like this: Adelaide, average 84.75 per innings, Bellerive, 80.30, 'Gabba 65.88.

The MCG, the SCG and the WACA weren't in the picture. Why was it so? Was it the batting surfaces, the 'seeing' conditions? Maybe the shape of the grounds suited his style? Or, was it to do with the standard of the opposition bowlers in Hayden's era?

Some players' best memories are of the MCG. I made my NSW 2nd XI debut there, and 'froze'. My Sheffield Shield debut, a tough Boxing Day encounter, was memorable for the Victorian umpires calling a feast of NSW no-balls. The NSW opening batsman, Lyn Marks, got into the spirit of things by singing, to the tune of 'Noel', "The first no-ball the umpires did call … was hit by Ken Eastwood right over the wall … no-ball, no ball …"

My 'Test' debut there — 'unofficial', because it was against The Rest Of The World XI — was memorable, too. On match eve my captain Ian Chappell took me to the screen adaptation of Boccaccio's *The Decameron*, which was fairly raunchy stuff for the times. I guessed this was a sort of extension of his 'my door's always open' philosophy. A nerve settler for the new boy.

In Australia's second innings, after Sobers had made his classical 254, I was batting with Chappelli, and we were battling to try to save the game. I pushed a ball just wide of the fieldsman at midwicket, Intikhab Alam, and called, "One!"

Ian responded, uttering the very same words that many years later got him into trouble as a television show host, "Jesus __ ing Christ!"

He was run out by a yard, and not happy. And reasonably so — why would I call such a risky single when we were trying to save the game, not win it? Dumb cricket.

The MCG, December 29, 1972

Australia are playing Pakistan at the MCG in the second Test of a three Test series. There's a heatwave. The players are frying, trapped inside that imposing concrete bowl, like eggs in a frypan. It turns out to be a red hot game.

Australia bat on paradise, and Ian Chappell declares midway through the first session of the second day — ask yourself, how many Test captains do that these days? In perfect batting conditions? The scoreline is Australia five for 441.

Here's a date to remember — December 30, 1972. There's about half an hour to the best lunch in Australian cricket, steak and salad at the MCG, when Jeff Thomson — *the* Jeff Thomson, 'Thommo' — makes his Test bowling debut. In the Pakistan first innings he bowls 17 overs and takes no wickets. The Pakistan batsmen belt an even century off his bowling. A debut to forget.

I'm puzzled; this is false advertising because I've played with him in Sheffield Shield cricket and I know he can break batsmen's stumps, their bones even. When the Test is over Thommo confides to me that one of his feet is " __ ing killing" him. An x-ray a couple of days later shows he has bowled in the Test with a broken foot.

December 31 is a rest day. On day three, New Year's Day, Pakistan declare at eight for 574. How often do you hear that in a modern Test? Both captains declaring their first innings within the first three days? The Pakistan lead is 133 runs with two days to go. Handy.

Australia begin their second innings about half an hour before stumps.

A strange thing happens. Ian Chappell revises his batting order. He moves himself out of No.3, where he has established himself as Australia's premier batsman, to No.4.

He moves me from No.5 — where I've got a formsheet as poor as Ima Googly's — to No.3, where I've been doing fine for NSW. Why? This is a Test match, and Australia are in the red. At the end of the day I am 11 not out … I might as well have been 13, 87 from one hundred, because that night I get bad news.

I've been dropped for the next Test. Happy New Year! There's no doubt about it, getting dropped in the middle of a Test match, especially when you're not out, has a way of sharpening your focus.

What should a cricketer do? Expect his captain to ring up the chairman of selectors and threaten to go on strike? Or, should the player confront the selectors himself and offer something in the way of abuse? Go out and get pissed, maybe? Call Lifeline?

Lou often made the point that a cricketer's best ally when he's up to his knees in 'it' is 'fierce determination'. I remember hitting the first ball of the next morning, a half volley, off my toes out to deep, deep midwicket and thinking how good it felt off the bat.

And, there were cover drives into gaps, one after another. All off the middle of the bat. My partner, Paul Sheahan, came down after one and said, "How do you do that?"

Who knows? I just got lucky. It was one of those perfect days, and any cricketer will tell you they do happen. Our 233 run partnership was a record that lived for a decade, but remember, Pakistan were a fledgling Test nation, then.

Australia makes 425. Pakistan's win target is 293, and five and a half hours to get them. Detecting a nervousness in one of his players Chappelli announces, "How many teams ever get 300 to win on the last day of a Test?" That Pakistan team turned out not to be one of them — they made 200.

Who knows why Chappelli changed the batting order? Did he do it for me, or was he out of sorts? This captain certainly didn't send me in as a nightwatchman for himself. Mind you, I once did see a captain send in a nightwatchman for himself in a Test — 40 minutes before stumps, and in bright sunshine!

And, Chappelli wasn't making some sort of gesture towards me, because he'd have known that I'd been dropped from the next Test. He would never compromise the team to massage any individual's ego.

Maybe it was a mental thing. In light of my indifferent form down the order, Chappelli might have reasoned that I'd be better value to the team at

No.3, more comfortable, and that I'd play more confidently. He certainly wouldn't have been concerned about his handling of No.4.

Whatever the reason, the captain showed confidence in me when I was struggling. He gave me a chance to score a century — going from 94 to 100 with a six off Intikhab! — that got me into the Australian team to the West Indies in 1973. It was one of Australian cricket's finest tours.

The Queen's Park ground in Port Of Spain, Trinidad can be one of the prettiest. Lift your glance from the browned off pitch and straw outfield, up and into the distance, and it's an oasis of rolling green hills, lightly masked in a heat haze of misty blue chiffon, and above it all, flitting clouds of cottonwool.

The tennis courts are less attractive. Cement, in a box of wire. The day before the Third Test in 1973, after a centre-wicket practice watched by the equivalent of a first day Sheffield Shield crowd, Chappelli, Ross Edwards, Ian Redpath and I played tennis.

Chappelli was a fierce competitor. Not a net shark, but an interceptor with total faith in his own judgment. He'd try to chase down anything. If he was in the backhand court it was a safe bet he'd encroach into the forehand court.

Well into the match he anticipated my cross court return, but was wrong-footed when it turned out to be a sliced shot down the line, off the wood.

He sprained his ankle. Badly. There was no physiotherapist with the team, an oversight critics of the Cricket Board can reasonably query.

In those days such a luxury was generally only available on the longer tours, like The Ashes. The length of the tour, rather than its toughness appeared to be the governing factor. How quaint.

The start of the Test was less than 24 hours away. Chappelli got to his feet, running … like a broken down trotter trying to break its hobbles. And, he was shouting, "Ice! Get some __ ing ice! Get a bucket of the stuff." Around and around the 'tramlines' he hobbled, while we went to the Members' Bar of the Queen's Park Club seeking ice, a bucket of the stuff.

At first, Chappelli had been white with pain, by the time he jammed his foot into the bucket of ice his face had reddened through the sheer exertion of his limping marathon, trying the beat the pain barrier. Even after the local physio had strapped the ankle Chappelli could hardly walk.

The next morning he made it out to the toss with barely a sign of a limp so tightly was he strapped. His opposite, Rohan Kanhai, might have been inclined to disbelieve the local physio's story of Chappelli's plight — until the batting order went up — at No.6, I. Chappell.

He was caught and bowled by the chinaman bowler Inshan Ali, for eight, creasebound, unable to properly dance to the pitch of the ball like he normally would.

His dismissal, score and method, prompts a useful discussion about player fitness and selection — and the risk factor. The top cricketers often play through an injury, particularly batsmen and wicketkeepers, both of whom are prone to finger injuries.

But a leg injury can be another matter entirely. Chappelli, and the other tour selectors Keith Stackpole and Rod Marsh, had to consider this:

1. **if Chappelli didn't play his replacement could only be me — total experience two Tests, current tour form inconsistent. No question about it, Ian Chappell on one and a half legs was the value bet;**

2. **all Test matches are vital, but this was the Test on which the West Indies hoped to turn the series — Chappelli's toughness, his experience, his captaincy, his first slip expertise, his player motivation all outweighed any suggestion he should step down;**

3. **how bad was the sprain or, to be more precise, for how much of the match would he be inconvenienced?**

4. **how would team morale be affected if he didn't play?**

Now consider this. In the second innings Chappelli batted at No.3. He came in when the score was 31. He left, a tick under four hours later, when the score was 231. He was the seventh out. He had scored 97.

Consider the courage of that innings. The humidity was dreadful, mentally and physically sapping. He was only 75 per cent fit and that restricted his footwork in conditions where it was sorely needed — facing three spinners, Lance Gibbs, Inshan Ali and Elquemedo Willett on a 'turner'. The trio bowled 94 overs between them of the 107 the West Indies bowled in the second innings. Wickets were falling at the other end.

The term 'captain's innings' is often abused. This was a captain's innings … as surely as Crocodile Dundee said "This is a knife."

Chappelli's innings inspired a Test win, one of the greatest in Australian history. The West Indies needed 334 in the last innings of the match to win. At lunch on the final day they were four for 268. Deadset winners, only 66 needed.

So, there we were, in that dogbox of a dressing shed, a cement floor, a few green wooden bench seats at the perimeter, a table in the middle stacked with plates of curried goat and rice that nobody wanted.

Everybody is in the room. Dennis Lillee is there in his street clothes, because his back is busted; Keith Stackpole is in tracksuit pants and a T-shirt, because he's taken a sweep shot to the face that has sliced open his cheekbone and filled his left eye socket with blood. Bob Massie looks sickly and has been.

Max Walker has a bottle of friar's balsam and occasionally he plunges the second finger of his bowling hand deep into it. It stops him talking — to grit his teeth. There's a large hole been worn in the end of the finger from cutting it across the seam of the ball. So far in the match he's bowled 50 overs.

The captain, who has as good as busted a leg the day before the Test, then absolutely played his guts out, sternly reminds his team about character, which he says is flagging, but he didn't put it quite that mildly.

Then he lies on his back on one of the bench seats. His arms are crossed over his chest. His baggy green cap is across his face, blocking out the light.

His team looks around, each at the other, now and again at Chappelli. What is this — inspiration or desperation? Then, the umpires knock, and go. Chappelli gets up, and we're ready to go. He clamps the baggy green onto his head, tugs at the peak, and the message is simple: "This'd be a great Test match to win."

First ball after lunch Kallicharran edges Walker to Marsh and Australia go on to win the unwinnable Test by 46 runs.

Ian Chappell's team went through the tour undefeated. They remained the last international cricket team to beat the West Indies in a series on their home turf until Mark Taylor's team won in the Caribbean in 1995.

The team was a strange mix of characters, some marginally eccentric, and they blossomed under Chappell's freestyle captaincy. He encouraged each team member to be himself, with one important proviso — nothing should compromise the team performance.

On the first leg of the tour, the local brewery, Red Stripe, offered a two-gallon keg (full) to the team as a public relations gesture. It was fixed to the railing of the verandah of the room occupied by Doug Walters and Terry Jenner.

I doubt that such sponsorship generosity would be tolerated by a team management in the professional nineties.

But a lot of the camaraderie that inspired the team to extraordinary highs of performance later in the tour, particularly in the Trinidad Test, was developed at the informal team meetings around the keg(s) — one was never going to be enough.

The camaraderie in that cricket team is not easily explained. Ian Redpath once offered: "It was a team of desperates, and the only thing they liked more than having a good time was winning."

And, Ross Edwards tried, musically. He composed a team calypso, the chorus of which was: "We may hit, and we may miss — but no-one can say we're 'c'n'ope-less." But it was Kerry O'Keeffe who nailed it, nearly 20 years later, in an after-dinner talk at the Adelaide Oval.

The occasion was a charity cricket match and 1973 team reunion dinner. Its purpose was to raise funds for the Adelaide City Mission. Here's Kerry:

> If I stay away with this lot any longer I'll be a customer of the Mission rather than a fundraiser.
>
> My recollection is that I just don't know how we won.
>
> We got liquored up at the pool every day.
>
> We slogged their medium pacers every game. I bowled them out which was a total shock to everybody.
>
> We had a captain who thought P and R were two letters late in the alphabet.
>
> We had two openers, Stackpole and Redpath who looked like Laurel and Hardy — and played like them.
>
> Greg Chappell, two weeks into the tour, could have played for either side with his golliwog hair.
>
> We had a middle-order player in Walters who was nicotine-riddled and alcoholic.
>
> We had a poofy middle-order player in Edwards who strummed a guitar and wrote sort of gay songs.
>
> We had a wicketkeeper (Rod Marsh) who was eight hamburgers over par.
>
> Jeff Hammond was called crayfish because he was all arms and legs and had shit for brains.
>
> Dennis Lillee was our strike bowler. He was touted as a sex symbol — he's bald, with false teeth and an IQ about his Test bowling average.
>
> Who have I missed … ?
>
> Bob Massie was in hospital with food poisoning. He was discharged and found by a keg 12 hours later.
>
> And we won. I can't believe it.

He received a standing ovation, led by his fellow cricketers — whom he'd just taken the piss out of, mercilessly!

The next speaker was Terry Jenner who, for many summers had jousted with O'Keeffe for the Australian legspin spot.

"It's probably one of the funniest talks I've ever heard in my life … but it sort of goes with his bowling action doesn't it?"

The last word on the team, and Ian Chappell, was from the late Alan McGilvray, who covered the tour for ABC Radio:

> I travelled with teams from Bradman on, and never saw a team that had more discipline, more unity, more desire. They were real Australians those fellows and when they played that match at Trinidad I've never seen a better display of fielding.
>
> Why did they do that? You see, you've got to look at the reasons when you're trying to explain what's happening (on radio). Chappell's leadership … was something I'd admired. He seemed to be able to get something out of people that others could not.
>
> Lots of things I didn't agree with him on. We've had lots of discussions about that … he's a very stubborn fellow. But Chappell knew where he was going. I have a great regard for Ian.

In November 1973 there was a unique moment in cricket. Brothers Ian and Trevor Chappell played for South Australia in a Sheffield Shield match against Queensland, which was captained by the other brother Greg. The manager of the South Australian team was Martin Chappell, the father of the three brothers, and watching in the stand was Jean, their mother.

Ian Chappell was a blue heeler of a cricketer; he got respect from his teams, and not just on the field. Even in social moments, over a beer or during a game of golf, the skill of maintaining the edge on his opponents was practised, and perfected.

BACCHUS

The only bet most cricket fans connect with Rod Marsh is the joke one where he and Dennis Lillee ripped a few hundred quid off the bookies by backing England at 500 to one to beat Australia in a Test. I once saw Rod Marsh win $5 off Ian Chappell at golf — but, they might have been playing for a sheep station!

January 6, 1976

Ian Chappell and Rod Marsh perused pro golfer Ted Ball's bright red shirt. On the left sleeve, in white lettering, was printed 'Tournament Pro Model — Ted Ball'. Probably worth a bit of money those few words, the cricketing duo mused.

How would a few small words look on a cricket shirt sleeve …? Advertising tended to run through cricketers' minds in those days. The World Series Cricket revolution was still one long summer away.

Chappell and Marsh were possibly the most outspoken of Australian cricketers when it came to professionalism. So it was somewhat incongruous that the two were amateurs on the rest day of Sydney's Fourth Test against Clive Lloyd's West Indians.

They were contesting a pro-am golf tournament at the Liverpool course, an undulating, wind-swept, watery hazard about 40 kilometres south-west of Sydney. Austere cricket officials would have blanched — the two were adverts from eyeballs to golf balls.

Heavens! They had on sunglasses — probably some well known brand. And Chappell was advertising ducks of all things — his light brown shirt was covered in them, all with cricket ball red beaks. Marsh's shirt was all horses and buggies — big-hitting Rod, the slow coach!

And, they had on those modern shoes with logos along the outside and the instep to identify the manufacturer — Chappell's were orange with three black stripes, Marsh preferred red ones with a blue flash. Very nifty. And so were their golf balls — they had American Express imprinted in black on a blue square.

Marsh was accompanied by Frank Phillips (twice Australian Open champion) and an American trick shot exponent, Wedgy Winchester, came along, too, just for fun. Marsh was soon doing his best for the sponsors — off the first tee his American Express ball fairly flew into the galleries.

"Bit worried about the wind, Rodney," laughed Chappell as the ball scudded along, decapitating grass shoots. It was a laugh with an edge to it, pure Chappelli gamesmanship ... some early niggle from the master of niggle.

Perhaps predictably, Marsh had a bogey. Chappell, partnered by the professional Billy Dunk and urged on by Dunk's large gallery, arrived safely at the first green.

"How many am I? What's par?" The adrenalin was fairly surging. Then ... "I'm here in regulation," announced Chappell, as if it was the most natural thing in the world for him to reach a golf green in regulation.

He is nine metres from the pin. For Chappell, this prospect generates a totally uncharacteristic reassessment of the situation, bordering on the negative: "This is where the problems start," he confesses to the gallery at large. Chappelli in doubt!

Then the real Ian Chappell, the psyche we see every moment on the cricket field, super confident: "Take the pin out," he demands of Warwick, the schoolboy caddie.

The putt rolls to a stop for a tap in. And the 60-strong gallery is still applauding as it rushes to watch Marsh drive off the next tee. He hits it into the long grass on the right, behind a wire fence.

"Big gallery make you nervous, Rodney?" asks Chappelli. Marsh turns on him, points the grip of his two-wood, and 'fires' from the hip. He laughs, but there's a glint in his eye, and you know he sort of wishes he had live ammo.

Then it's Chappell's turn and the gallery oohs and aaahs "nice shot" as he drives straight and long. Unmoved is Billy Dunk's caddie, his son Ian, aged 10: "Gee, Mr Chappell hits his tee a long way," he remarks to his Dad.

Another Marsh bogey, another Chappell par. But by the fifth Marsh has won a fan. Wedgy Winchester is uttering encouragement such as, "outa sight", "beyoodiful pardner", "don't you love it, you just love it", and "mmmmmm!".

But then there is a choked "arrghhh!" as a Marsh eight iron discovers a tributary of the Georges River that curls around the course.

At the next there is a lake with three spouting fountains between the tee and green. Before they play their tee shots Chappell, level with par, announces he wants to raise the ante; he challenges the less fortunate Marsh to increase their side-bet to $5.

Marsh slogs a wood and leaves himself with a birdie putt, then offers Chappell some advice: "Don't forget the water, Chappelli!"

"Wot water?" growls Chappell.

Chappell hits onto GUR (ground under repair) and takes a drop. His drop rolls down an incline and into a bad lie. Chappell shows self control the cricket public mightn't think he possesses when his next shot splashes into the water. Advantage Marsh.

But, he nearly lets it escape. On the eighth, after a superb drive, he has to carry a lake to the green.

"Dummy," he screeches as the ball biblically walks for a metre or two, then sinks, never to be seen again. "Anyone got a ball, I've run out," he laments. A spectator obliges. "Wait a minute, maybe Wedgy can show me the water trick shot …" A lost ball, but Rodney's still got his sense of humour. Wedgy surveys the ever-expanding ripple.

"Any sharks around here?" he asks. Only Rod Marsh! He recovered and shot a great 79 to Chappelli's 81 — and he won the visitor's trophy and Chappell's $5.

When they arrived at the 19th hole Marsh tugged on Chappell's shark's tooth necklet and laughed, "False advertising, Chappelli …"

At a testimonial dinner for Dennis Lillee, Ian Chappell mentioned the contribution made to the great fast bowler's record by Rod Marsh, a great wicketkeeper. Chappelli obviously thought his mate 'Bacchus' should have captained Australia … "They gave Kim Hughes the goldmine and Rodney the shaft," he said.

But Australian selectors have never been keen on offering wicketkeepers the captaincy. In 120 years we've only had one, J. McC. Blackham (eight Tests). Barry Jarman's one appearance, as stand-in for an injured Bill Lawry, should be discounted.

Bradman made the point:

A wicketkeeper suffers from the disability that he must minutely concentrate on every ball, even from the moment the bowler's run commences.

Adding to that burden the task of captaincy is really too much. It does not matter in fixtures of lesser importance, but I think it is an unfair responsibility in the international field.

Statistics possibly support his argument. There have been only 16 'keeper-captains in Test match history, and their win percentage is only 21. Gerry Alexander, who captained the West Indies in 18 Tests for seven wins, equalled the record for dismissals in a series against England in 1959–60, but lost the rubber. And, lost the captaincy to Frank Worrell for the next series.

I'd add another point to Bradman's. Captains are expected to leave their stamp on the game, a signature. Traditionally, it's been mostly a broad or flashing bat, occasionally some wizardry with the ball.

The problem for the 'keeper-captain might not be so much performance as perception.

The 'keeper is rarely perceived to be leading from the front. His profile tends to be business-like, almost mundane, reactive rather than proactive, more rearguard than frontline. The cricketing public is unlikely to warm to a 'keeper's six-catch haul as it would to a legspinner's six-wicket haul or a batsman's blazing century.

Anyone inclined to point to Hughes' indifferent record as a captain, then announce Marsh could have done better, is a victim of hindsight, never an option in cricket selection.

How should a selector judge wicketkeeping talent? Soft hands, anticipation, good feet movement, a sparky motivator for the rest of the team in the field, and how highly should his batting rate? Well, all that comes into it, but maybe just ahead of anything technical, toughness is the real test of the best.

Not long into Rod Marsh's Test career the media had tagged him 'Iron Gloves'. They got the instruments of his trade mixed up with his character. When he first played for Western Australia he announced his arrival with a fearless century — and his hooking and driving off Charlie Griffith, Wes Hall's partner in pace, showed scant regard for the fast bowler's demoniac reputation.

Marsh played his cricket — indeed, often approached life — as if he were in a perpetual tennis tie-breaker. Although a 'slogger', he once rescued Western Australia from a hole by using his right pad as he might normally his bat.

As Marsh came off, heading for the dressing shed, an unimpressed spectator chided him, "Why don't you use your bat?" Marsh turned on him, with "If you don't pipe down I'll use it in a way you wouldn't believe!" Advantage Marsh.

An Australian selector, travelling nationwide and watching Sheffield Shield matches, can always be sure of one thing — being collared by well-meaning officials offering advice about their own local heroes.

Queensland had one particular senior administrator who was always pushing the case for a wicketkeeper named Peter Anderson. "I can't understand why you're not picking Peter," he would say. "You've only got to watch him to see he's the best in the land."

Naturally, I'd always give his remarks respectful consideration and then respond … "If that's so, why do you keep picking Ian Healy in front of him?"

It was bizarre. Ian Healy was the Australian 'keeper at the time, and here was a Queensland official advocating his understudy as his replacement. The history of the Queensland wicketkeeping spot at the time was that Anderson had pulled out with a broken finger and been replaced by Healy, who had been chosen for Australia and never looked back.

The official, clearly a strong supporter of Anderson in the initial selection process, appeared to be letting sentiment get in the way of his judgment. Commonsense dictated his request was impractical, if not impossible. Sentiment has no place in the selection process. Any selector who wears his heart on his sleeve should quit. His judgment has been compromised.

Should size influence the choice of a wicketkeeper? Surely not, yet how often do you see a tall, lean wicketkeeper? Don Tallon. It's hard to know why tall 'keepers are unfashionable. Someone might have a cute theory about them having trouble reaching down to their ankles.

In 1994 the Australian selectors chose Mark Atkinson from Tasmania in an Australian XI match. Atkinson was so small he'd have looked more at home in silks on the favourite at the Mowbray races.

No trouble touching his ankles, but the theorists on height disadvantage must surely concede that the very short 'keeper might have problems stretching wide to either side, and upwards. Might he not spend more time diving, and watching wayward returns pass over his head?

They are the extremes. Generally 'keepers are about five foot eight inches tall, solid build. Maybe this stereotyping has something to do with junior cricket — the coaches always seem to put the smallest, toughest, most rascally boy behind the stumps.

How do Australia's 'keepers rate? When we consider the record hauls of modern-day wicketkeepers surely we should take into account the fashion in gloves today — that pouch of leather between the thumb and index finger transforms each glove into a baseball mitt. Old style gloves had no such 'safety valve'. The device is particularly useful when diving low and wide to those edges that fall in front of the first slip, and scooping up the catch. Using 50 'Tests played' as the marker these are the top 'keepers:

Player	M	Inns kept	Dism	Ct/st	Per inn
Healy	94	166	329	307/22	1.98
Marsh	97	181	355	343/12	1.96
Grout	51	97	187	163/24	1.92
Oldfield	54	100	130	78/52	1.30

In your assessment, as well as allowing for modern refinements to equipment, remember also that the covered pitch surfaces of today promote truer bounce and pace.

You might also like to consider that in Oldfield's era it was still accepted 'keeping practice to stand up on the stumps to the faster bowlers, not only the spinners. That's not to say that percentage-wise it was a smart tactic, rather a qualification on form.

On Marsh versus Healy many rate Healy best on the basis of his talent to the prodigious spin of Warne and remind us that Marsh was only a 'standback' 'keeper.

But who is to say Marsh would not have coped with Warne just as well as Healy has? Suffice to say both deserve champion status.

A 'keeper's best mate might be first slip, but it's more likely to be a bowler, even though for most of the game they are anything from 40 metres to 20 apart. One of the most famous pairings was Davidson and Grout, another Lillee and Marsh.

LILLEE

Was Dennis Lillee the greatest fast bowler of all time?
Statistics can drop us a hint, but the proof of it might be
in the legacy he leaves the game. Today he criss-crosses
Australia, even goes as far afield as India, ensuring that
his craft lives on.

When Greg Matthews was chosen for his first Test, against Pakistan, Boxing Day 1983, he mentioned that it meant he would be putting his kit down next to the great Dennis Lillee's.

Dennis's Test career spanned 13 summers and 70 Tests, so there were plenty of Australian cricketers, 67 in all, who were able to appreciate the same magic moment. I was another 'Cumbo' who once found his kit next to Dennis's. It was against Pakistan at the Adelaide Oval in 1972, on the practice day.

Dennis was two summers and an Ashes tour on the way to greatness by then and a sponsor had presented him with one of those big, plastic, green coffin-like kit bags that seemed likely, if the occasion should arise, to hold at least half the stock of any good sports store.

My kit, though, was a small, brown leather, ex-bowls bag Lou had handed down to me, along with his slightly oversize, baggy batting creams. By coincidence, 16 years later I sat on the Australian selection panel with Jim Higgs, whose nickname was 'Glad' — because he too carried a gladstone bag as his kit bag.

Quite a few cricketers used to smoke in 1972, cigarettes mostly, but in the case of Ross Edwards a pipe, and after practice we all sat around the room chatting about Mushtaq Mohammad, Sadiq and Saleem, Ali and Altaf, and so on. I lit up with a match from a book of matches.

You had to be careful with those book matches because sometimes the combination of sudden flare and a suddenly bent cardboard stem resulted in a singed thumb and forefinger.

I tossed it to the floor after light up, and aimed the sole of my cricket shoe at it. Maybe the raised spikes made my stubbing gesture futile because about five minutes later, a moderately deep discussion about Sarfraz Nawaz's straight-backed bowling action — would 'Steel Spine' be a suitable nickname? asked Rod Marsh — was interrupted by another, more urgent question: "What the __ 's that smell?!"

Lillee, after flaring his nostrils to test the air, lowered his eyes to the floor and shouted, "It's my __ ing new cricket bag, that's what!" And, noticing my half-smoked fag, added, "I'll __ ing kill you, Benaud!"

Total damage done was to one end of a cricket bag, one pair of creams (right leg), one shirt (left arm), one sock (right). It was not my earliest memory of the great man, but it remains my most vivid.

Dennis Lillee, and reputation, came to the SCG in 1969. They were the days of The Beatles and The Rolling Stones but Dennis's only concession to the fashionable hairstyle stakes was a set of sidelevers, and they were trimmed as neat and as sharp as the shape they matched, twin meat cleavers.

He had a ball in his hand and a glint in his eye, visible even at 40 paces, the distance between me and the start of his even then fluid run-in.

Dennis was a bit of a tearaway in those days, a locomotive careering down a hill. The bumpers came about one an over and I recall him landing on the full at least once up on the wide concrete expanse that used to front the old Sheridan Stand.

I felt the sting of his tongue and the stare of those deep, dark eyes. Typically, I was using the edge of the bat with great purpose and Dennis, who was bowling his heart out, stood at the end of his follow-through, hands on hips in exasperation, and with just a hint of gamesmanship announced, "Richie must have been a __ of a coach."

Twenty-eight years and a few months later, in mid-March 1997, Dennis is back at the SCG. He's a couple of months away from his 48th birthday but he looks strong enough to be still playing a form of the game much more serious than his most publicised annual outing, which is for the Australian Cricket Board Chairman's XI.

The chairman likes Dennis to take the new ball against touring teams when they play their opening game at Lilac Hill, in Perth. So far, Dennis has played against the West Indies, England, New Zealand and Pakistan. Notable victims have been Richie Richardson, Phil Simmons, Chris Cairns, Martin Crowe, Mike Atherton and Graeme Hick. More notable than all that is the fact that Dennis smiles a lot. At his peak he offered very few batsmen even the semblance of a smile.

At the SCG, he's out the back in the practice area. The first chill of autumn is in the air and the Sydney Swans football team are training on the main arena. Dennis is at one of his old stamping grounds to offer advice to young fast bowlers. This is Pace Australia.

The fact that Dennis looks as fit as any of the Sydney Swans is important. He is a role model. A big name is one thing, but tips on how to be a great fast bowler somehow don't seem as forceful if they are coming from the lips of a coach with as many bulges as the Michelin tyre man. Respect goes out the door.

Dennis still has a rigid fitness regime. A knee operation in 1996 put an end to five kilometre runs, now it's quick-walking or a stint on the exercise bike; he swims 1500 metres a day — 500 metres, two minute break; 5 x 100 metres, with 30 seconds between, then a two minute break; 10 x 50 metres, with 15 seconds between. Plus, he does light weights.

"If I had my career over again I'd have trained differently, done more weights, maintained a much more varied program," he says. He's impressed by some of the modern training aids. This day, Dennis is in shorts, smart runners and white socks. The legs remain well-muscled, an advertisement: "When I talk about fitness, and how to achieve it, you can believe me." Dennis's pupils can see for themselves — he still trains hard.

He stands back among them, where they start their run-ins, and watches them bowl either at a batsman or a single stump. In the batsman-drill he asks each young bowler, "Where have you got your field?" He wants them to think. He is relaxed, selectively chatty, a ball in one hand, offering one-on-one advice.

"The wrist should be a little more like this," he tells one lad. Physical gestures accompany the words of advice — a high arm, a cocked wrist, a swivel of the hips, a raised leg. In his pomp, Dennis's 'delivery' was fast, fierce, fiery, pure confrontation. His coaching 'delivery' is measured, watchful, all encouragement. And, so he captivated them.

"Bit more acceleration in the run-up … you tend to drop off a bit. Make it a gradual build-up." And, "You don't have any trouble with no-balls, do you? You were a mile over then." And, "See what I mean about keeping the forward momentum going? Be aware of it." And, "When you get tired that's when you're not doing this …"

What does he look for in a fast bowler? "It's a 'feel' thing," he says. He's alluding to that sixth sense, the selector's instinct. He likes his prospects to be 'athletic-looking', to have rhythm when they move, to have endurance. He likes a strong frame and some height, about five-ten is good. The eye-catcher will be the prospect with the fast-twitch, the sharp explosive action that translates into pace and aggression.

His mobile phone chirps. "Hello." Every coach needs one. And a video.

At the end of the day the young bowlers sit in the No.1 dressing room, the Australian dressing room. Inspirational. They watch play-backs of their endeavours.

Once, the video scampers from the grass to the sky and back again, not a budding fast bowler in sight. "Nice work, Cecil," says Dennis, a gently cynical reference to the video man's skills compared with those of the great Cecil B de Mille. Dennis always had a sharpness about him.

There is a soft silence about the youngsters as they watch, a concentrated alertness. Lillee stands at the back of the room, a leg up on a benchseat, chin resting in the palm of his hand, thoughtfully watching, occasionally pinpointing faults ... "Pull yourself through a bit more." Or, highlighting the best points ... "He's got a good, explosive front foot." But always encouraging ... "That's better, much better." And, "That's terrific!"

When the video ends, he addresses them. "I'm happy. There's nothing much else I can do. Changing something you've done all your life is hard work. If you've got any problems write them down.

"Remember when you're trying to remedy a problem, walk it. Do it slowly. I used to walk down the corridor at home in front of a mirror to make sure I was doing everything right.

"If you have to make changes you've got to drill yourself. It worked for me."

How did this happen? In 1985 a New Zealand motor car company had sponsored Dennis to coach young Kiwi fast bowlers; word spread as fast as a Lillee outswinger and the flow-on was a letter to Dennis from, not Australia as you might expect, but India.

From Syed Kirmani, the Indian wicketkeeper. Soon, Dennis met with a young Indian businessman, Ravi Mammen, of the Madras Rubber Factory. Ravi had a vision for Indian cricket — that when their teams went to faraway places they would no longer struggle because they had no fast bowlers.

The MRF Pace Foundation was born. Two graduates are Prasad and Srinath, India's 'fast bowling life after Kapil Dev'. The Foundation is open to fast bowlers from any country around the world.

Of the Test playing nations only the West Indies and Pakistan haven't bothered. Australia sends. "It's invaluable cross-pollination," says Lillee. "A chance for the players to get used to the pitches, the heat, the food, the lifestyle in a strange country. When the time comes to tour India it's not culture shock like it used to be."

Lillee makes three visits a year to the Foundation. When he's not there the coach in charge is T. A. Sekar — "He is as good a coach as I've seen. I'm happy because he's prepared to teach my methods."

When he was playing Dennis was a nick on the clean-shaven face of Australian cricket officialdom. Not quite the ever-present angry young man, but just occasionally he was inclined to allow the aggressiveness of his on-field job get in the way of his better judgment.

Any pen picture about Dennis will mention the aluminium bat incident, the betting incident with Rod Marsh and the Miandad incident. Each made a sour headline, but in the passing of time even some of his toughest judges will probably offer him parole, and be inclined to adopt the philosophy of the spin bowler Arthur Mailey when they reflect on Dennis.

It was Mailey's view that "Cricket would lose much of its adventure and robustness without the rich blood of the rebel. We have seen the result of its anaemic tendencies over the years and while, in other walks of life, organised rebellion may cause much inconvenience, a solitary rebel here and there in cricket, to me anyhow, is like champagne after lemonade."

April, 1997

Dennis, can you tell us of all your 355 Test wickets, which three stick most in your mind?

"No.1 — Brian Luckhurst at Lord's, 1972. He played the 'wrong colour', played the Bakerloo line (brown) and the ball was on the blue (Picaddilly). It pitched middle and leg and went up the slope instead of down. Best ball I've ever bowled.

"No.2 — Boycott at the MCG, 1980. The pitch had nothing in it so I shortened my run to concentrate on cutting the ball. I gave him a series of leg-cutters. He kept shouldering arms. I gave him an off-cutter that came back about three to six inches and he shouldered arms and lost his off 'dolly'. He walked down and patted the pitch before walking off.

"No.3 — Viv (Richards) at the MCG, 1981. 'Claggy' (Kim Hughes) made that great hundred (batting No.5, an even 100 not out in 198 on a dicey pitch against Holding, Roberts, Garner and Croft) and then we had them four for 10 at stumps. It was just an off-cutter, and he played it on. Not a great ball but a great result. Last ball of the day. It took the stuffing out of them."

Other fast bowlers have taken more Test wickets than Lillee's 355, among them Richard Hadlee, who was knighted for his contribution to the game. This is how they compare, using as the starting point the end of the innings in which they took their 355th.

Player	M	Wkts	Ave	5 wk/i	10 wk/m	Best	S/rate
Lillee	70	355	23.92	23	7	7/83	52.01
Hadlee	70	355	22.46	29	7	9/52	50.96
Kapil	101	357	28.93	21	2	9/83	59.58
Imran	88	362	22.81	23	6	8/58	53.75
Marshall	76	356	20.88	22	4	7/53	46.49
Botham	85	357	27.05	26	4	8/34	54.20

There is a picked seam between Lillee and Hadlee. People talk of sportsmen with 'iron constitutions' — it's possible Kapil Dev did indeed have one, for India can be unforgiving on a fast bowler. Malcolm Marshall has the strike rate, but he also had three other support fast bowlers around him. One thing is certain — they were all great.

Lillee is generating a new thicket of fast bowlers, refining actions and techniques using orthodox coaching methods. But, what might he have done with his great fast bowling partner, Jeff Thomson, if he had been called on to coach him in his youth?

MAGIC

Barbados is only a tiny island in the Caribbean, but it produced cricket's greatest allrounder, Sobers, and a battery of great fast bowlers — Martindale, Hall, Marshall and Garner. But one memorable afternoon it was a 'blow-in' from Australia who set feet stamping.

March 17, 1978

It's late in the day at the Barbados Test ground, Kensington Oval, in the capitol Bridgetown, the first day of the Second Test between Clive Lloyd's men and Bob Simpson's young Australian team. Bob's boys (the selectors' best of the rest after Packer's World Series had taken 'the best') have been bowled out for 250 in 65 overs in their first innings.

In its beginning, Graeme Wood has hooked and cut for 69, done a job on the great fast bowler Andy Roberts. Such perfectly clean shot-making, a scalpel job.

And, at its end, Bruce Yardley has smashed 74, kaleidoscopic slogging — swishing cover drives, happy hoicks over midwicket, a hooked six and, finally, an eye-widening square cut for six that made the target of his assault, the giant Joel Garner, apoplectic. But all this was mild fare to what Jeff Thomson, Australia's fast bowler, served up.

The West Indian batsmen who took guard to 'Thommo' in that sun-bathed late afternoon were Gordon Greenidge, Desmond Haynes, Viv Richards and Alvin Kallicharran. The formidable four. Each may deny until the day they die that Thommo's pace, his deadly line and lift, startled them, upset them, unbalanced them, but I saw it.

Greenidge faced and Thommo was instantly at his fastest, his line perfect, a touch outside off stump — his lethal stock ball, landing not so very short, but steepling and slanting back in towards the batsman's rib cage. Sometimes it came at his throat, sometimes the chin depending on Thommo's rhythm. The pace was always searing.

Greenidge, head protected only by the cloth of his country's cap, mimicked a boxer as he bent his body away from danger. And when Australia's wicketkeeper Steve Rixon moved to take the ball it was as if he was climbing a step-ladder, and even then it was with gloves raised above his head. He was standing another pitch length back.

Vintage Thommo — a raised two fingers to those critics who had announced he'd slowed down since his accident, the on-field collision with his teammate Alan Turner three years before.

In Thommo's first over a ball 'thunked' into Greenidge's gloves as he arched backwards, body shaped like a crescent moon in a desperate manoeuvre to avoid the climber; from the gloves, the ball ricocheted up into his shoulder and flew to Craig Serjeant fielding in the gully.

Greenidge rubbed only his shoulder and the umpire's decision was 'not out'. Later that evening, over a beer, Thommo smiled when he recalled the moment: "Yeah, that took a bit of courage to rub his shoulder, 'cos his busted hand must have been hurting like hell."

In his third over Thommo got Greenidge exactly that way, via the gloves via the chest, caught by Gary Cosier in the slips cordon. The dismissal lit the touch paper on one of the game's most gloriously explosive passages of play, one that remains forever in the mind.

Memorable for its sheer depth of purpose, for its head-on collision of pure, natural talent, for its suspense.

Viv Richards came out to bat. He was not yet The Master Blaster, more a rising superstar, a 'reputation'. Thwack! Thommo immediately fired one through him, cannoning it into the left pad, and Richards spent no short time hobbling around his crease. Genuine pain, or a ploy to waste a little time late in the day? Pain.

In that same over, before he'd even scored, before he'd adjusted to the conditions, Richards went for his favourite pull shot. He miscued it from high on the bat, beaten for pace, the ball ballooning, spinning and swirling in front of square leg. Trevor Laughlin had to run from behind square but he dropped the catch he should surely have held.

The shot raised an immediate question: was this Viv playing what we all came to applaud later as his natural, compulsive, arrogant, attacking game … or, was he so stirred by that first ball of such tremendous pace and, what he'd seen of Greenidge's discomfort, that he was mentally unsettled?

And, later we all wondered if it was that shot, and its faulty execution that spurred Thommo to such incredible heights that late afternoon. Maybe it was the time of day — Thommo knew his spell would be short, why not make it sharp, too? Maybe he just wanted Richards' wicket, badly. Maybe he was annoyed because Australia's tailender Jim Higgs had been bounced. Maybe captain Bob Simpson's dressing room oratory had been gladiatorial.

The next ball hammered into Viv's right wrist, a brute of a lifter that you'd say 'came from nowhere', except you knew it was from Thommo and it could only have come from what the text books describe as 'just short of a good length' — when a batsmen's instinct might be to play forward.

How do you define fear? It's certainly not 'gutlessness'. It's a condition of the mind, anxiety, which presents itself in a physical form as panic. The game plan is suddenly out of control. Greg Norman losing the Masters to Faldo.

Did that happen to Viv, or was he employing the tactic that made Jack Dempsey the heavyweight champion of the boxing world? — kill the other guy before he kills you.

Thommo's fifth over lasted nine balls, including no-balls. He was eager, and on the scent, straining for even greater pace, greater lift. Richards took a single off the first, then Haynes hit a four, then a single. Thommo to Richards, two men out for the hook — Wayne Clark behind square on the boundary board, Laughlin now forward of square, right out too.

Richards hooked the fifth ball between them for four, but it wasn't a good shot because he got a thick edge and it flew in the air for a long way. The sixth was a bouncer too.

Richards stepped quickly, a lithe body movement, right foot back. Shoulder muscles rippled, and biceps threatened to burst the seams of the pure white shirt, immaculate and buttoned at the wrists. He hit a flat-bat pull — the finest I've ever seen — right in the middle of his heavyweight bat with its jumbo trademark.

Crack! It went over midwicket and, it never got much higher than about nine metres, but it was always going up, up …

Its progress was momentarily halted by the red tin roof of the grandstand at midwicket, the one sponsored by Berger paints. Thunk! The ball hit about the first 'R' in Berger, then it hopped over the top, and out of the ground, much as a golfer might hop a seven iron into the bank about a green, and on for a putt.

Thommo said later, and there was awe in his voice, "Was that a hit, or was that a hit!" In a strange way his pure honesty about that bad luck confirmed that Greenidge had certainly received the benefit of no doubt earlier in proceedings. The over was now costing 16 runs.

Next, Thommo held one back, a change of pace that deceived Richards completely. The result flashed me back to the SCG in 1961 when Ian Meckiff beat Sobers with a slower one. Sobers, committed to his forward shot, changed his mind, rocked back and hit the ball back over Meckiff's left shoulder for six.

Richards' back foot hit bounced once into the concrete sighting wall behind the bowler. Clonk! It was a shot that had 'him or me' inscribed on it. This was a moment in time … Thommo, hands on hips, looked spent; Richards, contemptuous prods of the bat at imaginary rubble on the pitch, looked like a winner.

The ninth ball … Thommo summoned one final effort, the last desperate sling, one more bouncer. Richards hooked, but was late on it. He got the top edge. The ball corkscrewed high and out towards square leg, a bit behind, and both Clark and Laughlin began to converge. A skied, swirling catch … from where I was, in the press box, Clark's catch!

But suddenly Clark hesitated … Laughlin, a beefy blond, was coming from his left. Then Clark started again, then stopped, and so did just about every heart in the ground.

Then he came on again, and dived full length forward, the backs of his hands scraping the rock hard ground, and he held the catch aloft in two hands like a prizefighter might raise his championship belt. Thommo was the champion.

Thommo bowled the final over of that first day. The second last ball was to Kallicharran. It pitched about the line of the little left-hander's legs, just short of a good length, then snaked up and across his body, threatening his chest. Or, if it climbed a bit more, his life.

'Kalli's' reflex sent down an urgent message to his hands — 'Get the bat up, quick!' Like a boxer who can see the knockout punch coming and who starts to raise his guard … the ball cannoned from his gloves to Bruce Yardley at backward leg. The unplayable ball.

The umpires called it a day. Thommo had bowled just 6.5 overs. There was a maiden, 40 runs, and three wickets. The next day his final analysis was six wickets for 77 — the best figures by an Australian bowler in a Barbados Test.

Thommo was a champion, more a freak than a thoroughbred some said. But his strange action was really quite pure, mechanically. His success begs a simple question: why doesn't the coaching manual show youngsters how to bowl like Thommo?

THOMMO

"Bankstown-Canterbury have lost the services of highly promising speedster Ian King to Queensland but have found an adequate replacement in schoolboy Geoff Thompson [sic] who captured six wickets in the first round"
— *Sydney Grade cricket item, mid-1960s.*

The Sydney Grade club St George is rich in tradition. In the 1990s their players have resisted the surge for change and still wear the red and white candy striped caps as worn by Don Bradman, Bill O'Reilly, Arthur Morris, Norm O'Neill and Brian Booth, some of their champions.

Their home ground is still Hurstville Oval, where the scoreboard once registered, D. G. Bradman, most runs in a season, 1931–32 (785 in eight innings at 112.14), W. J. O'Reilly, most wickets in a season, 1943–44 (147 at 8.20). It's heartening to see some tradition preserved.

In the '60s St George had two fine, aggressive opening batsmen, Bill 'Blinks' Watson, who toured with Rich to the West Indies in 1955, and Warren 'Wacky' Saunders. Saunders was a particularly good player of the hook shot, sending bouncers skidding away across the kikuyu turf, over the green-painted wooden boards masking the long jump sandpit just forward of square, and up onto the whitewashed bike track that circled the oval. It was there that Saunders faced Jeff Thomson.

Kerry O'Keeffe, the sharp-minded legspinner of the Ian Chappell era, was in the St George team and later recounted the events of that day in this way:

Thomson arrived an hour late to open the bowling ... for a Bankstown lad in those days, balmy Sundays were meant for sun, surf, and ... 'doing your best', if you pick up my drift. Anyway, Thommo strolled into the ground with a bleached blonde stunner blessed with the figure of a Paris model and, as it turned out, the IQ of a surfboard ...

Kerry saw the humour in the young Thommo's laidback approach to the day, but Saunders, a State selector at the time, saw something markedly different — a red blur.

He'd hardly made the first movement into his hook shot when the ball from Thommo hit him flush on the jaw, and he was taken off to hospital. Once the doctors got the jaw back into working order Saunders was straight on the phone to Neil Harvey, an Australian selector ... "You've got to come and see this bloke!" he told him. See, selectors are always on the look out for talent.

Jeff Thomson only got a couple of wickets on his Sheffield Shield debut, a Queensland duo with the country and western 'moniker' of Allen and Jones. It was late October, 1972. His second match was at Perth, a couple of weeks later and what a wild old time it was.

The NSW wicketkeeper was Brian Taber, who had done the job for Australia not so long before, but not even his years of experience, nor his agility, could cope with Thommo's waywardness.

In the Western Australian first innings third top score (28) was sundries, among them six wides and, of the dozen byes, at least half should have been called as wides.

As Taber's soccer goalie dives to the legside became more despairing and the sundries mounted the NSW brains trust had a flash of inspiration and introduced a widish leg slip — a second line of defence as it were.

Chosen for the task was the middle-order batsman Ron Crippin, whose nickname was 'Physical'. He was strong and fearless, no doubt a legacy of his involvement in rugby, the game in which the major stratagem seems to be to try to survive the mauling feet of a dozen or so rucking monsters.

Ron had just the right credentials for the task at hand — to take any of Thommo's off-target Exocets with his bare hands. Thommo was very quick, but raw.

A couple of years later on a Saturday afternoon in Sydney, the opening day of round 10 in the First grade competition got underway. Thommo only bowled 10 overs, but what overs! He took six wickets for 31.

The Mosman batsmen fell like this: 1–3, 2–6, (batsman Greg Bush retires hurt, face smashed), 3–6, 4–9, 5–9, 6–10, 7–16 (Thomson strains a groin muscle), 8–84, 9–94 (all out, Bush fails to resume). Thommo's career had been underway for quite a few summers, but that day was pivotal in shaping his reputation.

October 30, 1994
The England cricket team have just arrived in Australia. Their coach, or cricket manager Keith Fletcher announces he has in his bowling line-up "another Thommo, or two" and "another Fred Trueman".

That's about a 700-wicket reference. It gets sillier: Fletcher adds: "You can compare my quicks with Thommo for sheer speed."

An England bowler as fast as Thommo? Possibly that will worry those Australian fans who constantly long for 'another Bradman', because now is one of those rare times when we're being told we don't have another runmaking superman on the horizon.

The jury is still out on which England bowler on this 1994–95 tour is as fast as Thommo but preliminary evidence suggests, at least in the case of Martin McCague, that Keith may have got 'pace off the bat' confused with 'pace onto the bat'.

Of course, Keith is simply engaging in some good, old-fashioned psyche when he says, "You can compare my quicks with Thommo for sheer speed." His message is for the backs of Aussie batsmen's minds: in 1994, we've got some bomb-throwers, not the pie-throwers that Rod Marsh said were in action during most of Australia's 1993 Ashes demolition job on England.

Keith is one of those well-intentioned, old cricketers who rejects the pasture option in favour of working with today's cricketers; but, sometimes they forget their reaction times decrease as fast as their birthdays increase.

They stand around practice nets, watching their charges, thinking, "Gee, they hit harder than they did in my day. Bowl a lot faster, too."

Keith celebrated the big 'five-O' back in May. Twenty years ago, about this time, he was a batsman who had come Down Under with Mike Denness's team, hearing the first whispers from the Australian media about a "terror called Thomson".

Then, as now, reality was just around the corner in the shape of the First Test of the Ashes series, at the 'Gabba. Thommo got nine wickets (six for 46 in the second innings) and the England batsmen John Edrich and Dennis Amiss got fractured hands.

Tony Greig was also a member of that England team, and even today he well remembers the atmosphere in the England dressing sheds at the 'Gabba after their first taste of Thommo. "It was clear there were some batsmen in a very nervous frame of mind," says Tony.

Anybody who played with, or against, Thommo has no argument: there will never be another like him. Keith Fletcher is the exception to the rule.

Speed and Thommo are the best of mates. He always fancied a fast car and, these days, he enjoys drag racing. In the late '60s he would hitch a fast boat to his fast car and take his mates on water-skiing jaunts on the Nepean River, near Penrith.

Later, when he'd burned his name into cricket history, a wide-eyed young lad stood before Thommo and, awestruck by the tales of his lightning fast

bowling, asked, "How did you do it, Mr Thomson?" — and probably anticipated a technical lesson in fast bowling.

Thommo replied: "Ahhh … I just ran up and went whang."

But there was more to Thommo's success than speed alone. He was a fast
learner, too. Steve Small, the former NSW opening batsman and a club-
mate at Bankstown, recalled that pivotal moment in Thommo's fast bowling
education.

> It was the 1973–74 season, in a game at Bankstown Oval against
> Mosman. It was a wet "deck" and there were no covers in those days.
> Scary …
>
> Thommo went whang and the ball climbed from a bit short of a
> length and hit a bloke called Greg Bush a terrible blow in the eye. The
> next bloke in was Dave Colley [who'd been on the 1972 Ashes tour with
> Ian Chappell's team]. Bush's blood was still on the pitch and when 'Fox'
> (Colley) got to the crease he must have seen it. I remember him adjust-
> ing his mouthguard. There were no helmets in those days. Scary …
>
> Thommo came in and went whang. You could see by the way Fox
> was shuffling his feet he was expecting a bouncer. It was a yorker. Took
> out the middle and leg stumps.

In the next season, 1974–75 Thommo played in the Ashes Tests and
that yorker was to become his trademark against England — 'the sandshoe
crusher', Thommo called it. It generally followed a few balls that steepled into
the rib cage, laughingly called 'rib-ticklers'.

For batsmen facing Thommo the problem was not just his speed. It was
that unconventional slinging action which inevitably confused a batsman's
sighting process.

The orthodox fast bowler is more predictable — the coaching manual
demands that the ball is shown, in the hand, wrist cocked, near to the chin,
prior to the arm sweeping down.

Thommo's hand action started down near the back of his knees, in the
middle of his strange sliding, crossover foot movement, and where it was hidden from the batsman's view. Surprise …!

Thommo's most terrifying talent was the 'throat ball'. He could make the
ball rear viciously from just short of the good length, and not just on a wettie
at Bankstown, but on a sun-baked belter in Bridgetown.

When facing Thommo, any batsman who applied the coaching tip 'when
in doubt, push out' risked a knockout.

Greg Chappell heard Keith's comment and this was his verdict: "Thommo
was three yards faster than any other bowler I faced." That covers some

talent: John Snow, Bob Willis, Michael Holding, Andy Roberts, Colin Croft, Joel Garner ...

Even before Australia's most recent Test batsmen passed judgement on the 1994 England pace attack, former Australian Test batsmen were predicting the only way Keith's 'quicks' could match Thommo for speed was to hitch a ride with him to the 'Gabba Test.

For the record this is how Keith's quicks, the only ones who could realistically be rated 'quick', performed on the 1994–95 tour to Australia. An England selector observing Gough would have experienced a tingle of anticipation, that he had the potential to turn a future Ashes series:

Bowler	M	Wkts	Ave
Gough	3	20	21.25
McCague	1	2	48.00
Malcolm	4	13	45.23

In the Ashes series 20 years earlier, Thommo took 33 wickets in five Tests, average 19.30. And let's not forget that all up he took 200 wickets in 51 Tests.

Thommo's Barbados blitz in 1978 was done in the name of 'official cricket'. In 1979 he was back in the Caribbean, but playing under Ian Chappell and for 'World Series Cricket', the Kerry Packer inspired breakaway. It was tough, too.

BRUCE

You won't find the name Bruce McDonald in any
Wisden, nor in any Who's Who of Cricket. But
those who played with the breakaway World Series
Cricket and, once 'peace' was negotiated, played in
the only game in town, will recall Bruce with
fondness — he was Mr Fixit.

What do we know of Arthur Mailey? Couldn't dance, if we take Bradman's word for it, although we should bear in mind there was a whiff of the old 'smoko' atmosphere during that special evening with Bradman in Bowral back in 1976.

Mailey could spin a ball, though, and he had a delightful way with words.

A few hours with his autobiography, *10 For 66 And All That*, is as satisfying as scoring your first single after a run of outs.

Arthur was born in 1886, and by the time he was a young man, thinking expansively about life, and how to influence the rest of it by playing cricket (and, almost certainly, how to influence his cricket by thinking expansively!) some stiff-collar atop a stuffed-shirt probably thought of him as dangerous.

Today, Arthur Mailey would be called a lateral thinker; he preferred the unorthodox, and he spent hours perfecting it, a man full of enterprise. In 1932 he took an Australian team to America, 12 men, a hundred quid each, 50 matches. It was then that The Don (Bradman) met Babe (Ruth) of baseball fame.

And Mailey had vision. He wrote this in 1958, in *10 For 66 And All That*, when discussing a possible drop-off in crowds once the game was televised:

Heavy charges (by Cricket Boards) for the right to televise will of course make up for (any) loss in gate money, but if the (Cricket Board's) charges are unreasonable it is quite possible that powerful television corporations will buy up Test teams lock, stock and barrel.

What Hollywood did with actors I suppose television can do with cricketers. One can paint a fantastic picture on the possibilities of Television v. Cricket Boards wrangles of the future.

How's that for foresight?

Kerry Packer did cricket on a grander scale than 'Cheggy'. But, when all the fab 'flab' — the new financial deal for players, the white ball, the lights, the coloured clothing, the game-in-a-day concept — was scraped from World Series Cricket, the bare bones that remained were not unlike the Jack Chegwyn concept.

Packer's cricketers were pioneers, too. They criss-crossed the length and breadth of the nation, from Bunbury in the west to Coffs Harbour in the east, via Cairns and Devonport — a troupe of cricketers satisfying public demand.

And Mailey's prediction was right — it was fantastic. Another 'Ma-l-ee' (John Maley) produced cricket pitches nurtured in concrete tubs in hot-houses, pitches which were then lifted by cranes and lowered into holes scooped out in the centre of football grounds.

Fantastic times, but fantastically tough, too. Early in 1979 World Series Cricket toured the West Indies to play five SuperTests and 10 One-day Internationals.

If that tour finally broke the spirit of 'official cricket' it just as much tested the spirit of the WSC players. And Bruce.

The following excerpts are from his diary of the tour:

Our tour left Australia for the West Indies on 15th February, 1979 and, after two aborted take-off attempts, we finally departed at 9.50pm.

February 19
I examined the whole of Sabina Park. It appears that 10,800 people, not including members, can fill the place. I have carefully examined the entry points, fences and entry procedures, and have found that whatever else may be ahead, all that can be done is being done. Questioned why seats in sun are more expensive than ones in shade — seems the latter are rained on daylong by peanut shells!

February 20, 21
A stand-by-stand count of Sabina Park showed that many more people were in attendance than were reported. Further problems with fence jumpers. The ground is a disaster.

February 22
Met new group employed to control crowd entry to Sabina Park SuperTest. The chief is a former assistant commissioner of police and really knows his work. Gates were checked, some were locked, some were nailed up. Every point of entry was checked. Tomorrow I feel we are in for a good day.

March 1
Our flight to St Lucia was full of events. Firstly it was put back 40 minutes

VIV JENKINS

PETER BARNES

ABOVE: Being named in the Test 12 for your country, even if it's happened a half-century of times before, is good reason to smile. Even a subsequent 'demotion' to 12th man shouldn't be all that bad, but for Dean Jones the 'drinks' job in the First Test against the West Indies in 1992 was the end of the world. Was he simply a victim of cricket's great uncertainty, or was his demotion a conspiracy?

LEFT: Michael Slater. Was he sacked because he enjoyed his batting too much, or because he was careless?

VIV JENKINS

RIGHT: Allan Border, 156 Tests, meets Wayne Phillips, one Test — in fact, his only one! The Phillips' case raised a number of perplexing selection issues, not the least of which was the usefulness, or otherwise, of having a Test captain on the panel.

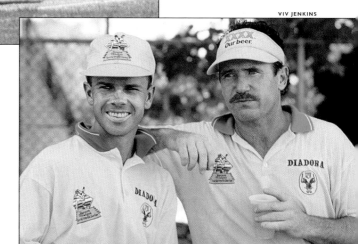

Captains courageous.

'Captain's innings' can be an over-used compliment, but it certainly applied in the Caribbean in 1973 when Ian Chappell, crippled with an ankle injury, but typically defiant and uncomplaining, played a hand of outstanding courage and commitment, one that very probably broke West Indian hearts and decided the fate of the Frank Worrell Trophy. Note the swirl of dust at his feet; this was the Trinidad pitch, deathly grey, on which Doug Walters made a famous century-in-a-session.

Look-alikes Bill Woodfull and
Mark Taylor captained their
country 65 years apart; by
coincidence, each had to
withstand a searching test of
his character, Woodfull by
'Bodyline', Taylor by 'Headline';
and by coincidence, they had
similar, intriguing records as
captains and players.

PATRICK EAGAR

ABOVE: Doug Walters was never, ever going to be another Bradman — no one is, in case you haven't investigated the 'Tests Played' column in the latest list of Top Ten Test run-getters — but he sure enjoyed offering the scribes the best evidence with which to prime their pens. Here he is on his way to a remarkable Test century, scored in a session against the West Indies at Port Of Spain, Trinidad in 1973. It was truly the greatest innings.

OPPOSITE: Some people like to perpetuate the line that 'The Don' and Bill O'Reilly were sworn enemies. If that was the case then they put on a memorable show of make-believe mates at Bowral in 1976, when Bill was the guest of honour at Don's party, the re-opening of Bradman Oval.

ROBERT PEARCE/FAIRFAX

The mentor.

RIGHT: Three generations of Benauds. Left to right, Rich, John, Lou and Richard Grainger Napoleon. It was 1953, and Rich was about to leave on his first Ashes tour.

OPPOSITE, FAR RIGHT & BELOW: The first legspinner in the Benaud family was Lou, who once took all 20 wickets in a match playing with Penrith Waratahs. He is seated, front right, in the Waratahs' 1922–23 premiership-winning team.

BELOW: Lou the schoolteacher, Flemington, Sydney in 1943. Tough times.

GREAT BOWLING

Ten Wickets in Each Innings

L. Benaud, of the Penrith Waratah Club, has been responsible for a remarkable bowling performance. In the Nepean District B Grade competition against St. Marys. He captured 10 wickets for 30 in the first innings, and 10 for 35 in the second innings.

Benaud, who is only 19 years of age, has captured many wickets this season for Parramatta High School in the Schools competition. In four matches with the club he had taken prior to this match 27 wickets for 162 runs, an average of 6. He has a batting average of 27.5, and is also a fine slip field.

L. Benaud.

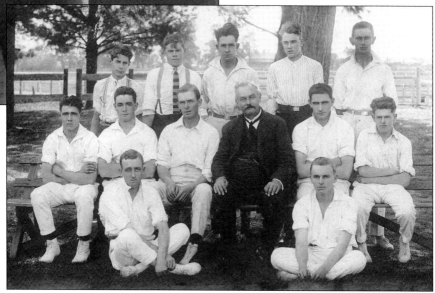

ABOVE: A boy in a bow-tie, and a bat. Rich at Jugiong about 1934, when his cricket was showing signs of strong development.

OPPOSITE: Richie Benaud at the SCG in 1964, his last Test, going out to bat against South Africa.
ACP

FAIRFAX

John Benaud hits a six and goes from 94 to 100 in his second Test, against Pakistan at the MCG in 1973, the day after the selectors had dropped him for the next Test. The bowler was Intikhab Alam, the legspinner who, up until then, had made Benaud his 'bunny' whenever they squared off.

LEFT: The Boots ban was a silly moment in cricket history. It happened in 1970, and was a classic case of the dangers petty politics, pig-heads and hot-heads, and the generation gap, can temporarily present to the game of cricket. Two of the main players in this strange ball game were John Benaud, the NSW captain in 1969 and, on his left, Stan Sismey, the chairman of NSW selectors.

RIGHT: Also a player in The Boots was Neil Harvey (left), seen here with Rich as they headed off for the 1961 Ashes tour, which Rich captained. But arguably the main player in The Boots was Syd Webb (right), the team manager. A tangled web, indeed.

ABOVE & OPPOSITE: Cricket creates unique friendships, and one of the most lasting has been between Merv Hughes, one of Australia's roughest, toughest fast bowlers, and Merv Seres, a gentle man, a sort of a cricketers' handyman. It is a friendship based on like senses of humour, a clue to which is given in Merv Hughes' postscript in this pictorial greeting to his mate, the other Merv: "I'm the good looking one!!"

From out of the west.

VIV JENKINS

ABOVE & LEFT: The great Dennis Lillee, on the way in. For one selector, the most respected Laurie Sawle, who saw Lillee on the way up during a Grade game in Perth, it was love at first sight: "They don't come along too often," he said of the champion.

RIGHT & BELOW: Rod Marsh. Hugely talented, focused, uncompromising, tough, the niggly sort of sportsman opponents were most likely to call a 'bastard', but never to his face because they knew he had a heavy return of serve. He and Ian Chappell once squared off in a golf pro-am; it was a sporting version of *War and Peace*.

Blood and guts.

RIGHT: In the Caribbean, securing the best spot from which to watch a Test — this was the scene at Jamaica's Sabina Park in 1973 — was a challenge as dangerous as … well, playing.

LEFT: In 1978, Australia without the World Series Cricket players like the Chappells, Marsh and Lillee, faced up to a West Indian team with WSC players, like Holding, Roberts, Croft and Garner. On the first day of the First Test at Port Of Spain, Bob Simpson's young Australians made only 90 on a damp, under-prepared, unpredictable pitch. Peter Toohey was put out of the game not by this head injury, as you might expect, but by a broken thumb.

RIGHT: And, in 1973, in the famous Third Test at Port Of Spain, Ian Chappell's vice-captain, Keith Stackpole, was fielding at short leg when Alvin Kallicharran swept hard, and, with the spin of Kerry O'Keeffe, putting Stackpole out of the game.

BELOW: But anyone who saw this moment in Caribbean cricket — Kallicharran, caught Marsh bowled Walker, 91, first ball after lunch in that same Third Test — saw the moment that inspired one of the greatest Test wins in Australian cricket history. Ian Chappell's team came back from the dead and were on the way to winning the Frank Worrell Trophy.

PATRICK EAGAR

PATRICK EAGAR

Glitches and glory.

RIGHT: Every now and again something ugly happens in cricket, just to test its strength, its fabric. At the 'Gabba, in 1992, Ian Healy thought he'd stumped a disbelieving Brian Lara, and the umpire, Terry Prue, agreed. Both were terribly wrong. Television replays, unofficial because the value of a third umpire was still being debated, showed Healy had dropped the ball.

LEFT: In a World Series final at the SCG an unfit Sri Lankan captain Arjuna Ranatunga protested umpire Steve Randell's definition of unfair play.

RIGHT: In a Test against Pakistan at the WACA in 1981 Dennis Lillee and Javed Miandad went to extraordinary lengths to settle a personality clash.

VIV JENKINS

VIV JENKINS

Every one is a classic case of human nature hoist on the spur of the moment. Yet, if your faith in the great game should ever waver, it can take just one memory of one magic moment to restore it …

For nearly two decades, winning back the Frank Worrell Trophy became an Australian obsession, and when it finally happened, in 1995, the absolute joy of a nation was reflected in a tickertape parade in Sydney for Mark Taylor's team. Note the arm reaching out, just to touch the Australian cricket captain.

Cricket's 'fab-four'.

How would you rate them, the styles of these legspin bowlers Shane Warne, Richie Benaud, Bill O'Reilly and Clarrie Grimmett? Grimmett has the stats to say he was the best, but …

ABOVE: O'Reilly.

LEFT: Warne.

ABOVE: Grimmett.

LEFT: Rich.

RIGHT: Warne, in the first flush of Test glory, seven for 52 against the West Indies at the MCG in 1992.

BELOW: Grimmett in a match situation. Note the point of delivery, from behind the crease, an old trick to deceive a batsman keen on front foot attack.

Some wild, old times.

This is good advice for young players — when you go on a cricket tour make sure you pack your sense of humour.

The Bunny flies with 'The Geese'; John Benaud with dairy farmer Tom Morris and his wife Tara, the creators of a cricketing heaven in Somerset, England.

ABOVE: Not every Australian cricketer can boast that he flew a figure-of-eight over Victoria Falls, one of the world's seven wonders, in a World War II Dakota. Fast bowler Denis Hickey, who toured Zimbabwe with Mark Taylor's Australia B in 1991, can.

LEFT: Shane Warne in Zimbabwe in 1991. The Daktari Suit he was wearing had been worn by all other team members and had attached to it a certain stigma that suggested, at best, failure, at worst, stupidity. Some survived the 'daktari experience' better than others.

ABRIAN MURRELL/ALL SPORT

Night cricket at the SCG, and it's when thoughts invariably turn to Kerry Packer and the World Series Cricket breakaway, white balls, lights, cameras and action, even the occasional quirky run equation. Some might even think of Disneyland, for these cricket jousts sometimes do have that certain aura about them.

Anyone who was among the overflow crowd at the SCG on the night of November 28, 1978, when the lights were first turned on for a WSC match between Australia and the West Indies, knew they were 'experiencing the way of the future'.

VIV JENKINS

RUNS B HO FOW   RUNS WKT

SOUTH AFRICA TO WIN

NEED 22 RUNS OFF 1 BALL

Bruce McDonald was there that night of nights … helping Kerry Packer man the turnstiles! And, when WSC toured the Caribbean, Bruce was caught in the middle of the riot that stopped the SuperTest in Guyana. Bruce is a 'Mr Fix-it', one of those behind-the-scenes cricket people who are generally summoned when the going gets less than smooth.

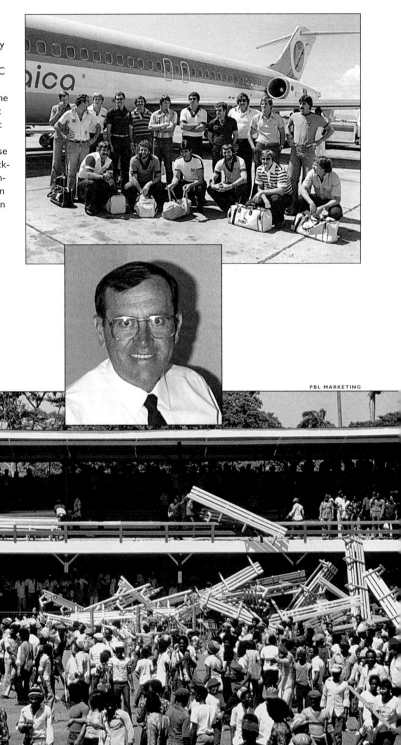

PBL MARKETING

VIV JENKINS

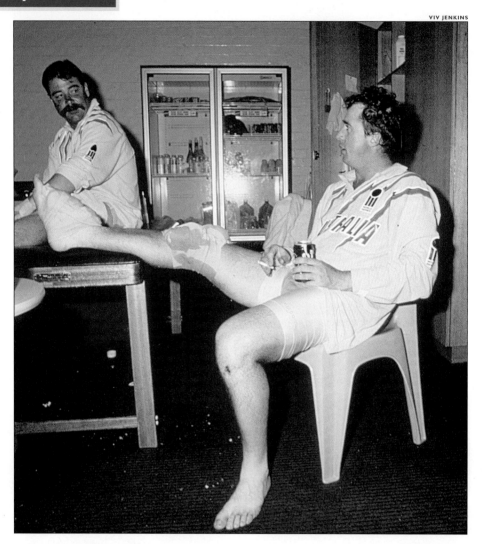

Offspin bowling, it's a fact, has none of
the glamour of wrist-spin bowling and one
of its better exponents, Tim May, often a
little the worse for wear, hardly seemed
likely to erase what might be termed as
the historical 'grass stain' on any offie's
character. That is, until a 'night to forget'
at the SCG led to a 'day to remember'
at the Adelaide Oval.

When Greg Matthews scored 128 in an Ashes Test at the SCG in 1991 he did more than drive the 12th man Merv Hughes mad with his constant requests for comfort level adjustments. His fourth Test century raised the spectre that the selectors might have got it quite wrong when they sat in judgment on Greg as a bowling all-rounder, rather than as a batsman who could dabble in offspin bowling, if required.

RIGHT & BELOW: You've got to have a thick skin to survive and thrive in Sydney grade cricket. Manly's Mike Pawley was a frustrated spin bowler but he so loved his trade he named his racing greyhounds Ima Googly, Flighted Googly and Another Googly!

FAIRFAX

MICHAEL PAWLEY'S "Ima Googly"

LEFT: Ken and 'Choc' Hall were just a couple of cheeky kids. In maturity they were key players in a whole team of Halls which proudly accepted a cricket match challenge offered by the rest of the district — and won!

BELOW: Petersham's cricketers were *tout au contraire*, a cast of calm or cantankerous characters. Two were captains, Brian Riley (back row, far left), an incorrigible sledger with a drill sergeant's delivery, and Col Blackman (same row, 4th from left), punctilious. And, two were opening batsmen, 'Crazy' Cantwell, whose repartee was as sharp as an epee, and Max Benjamin (2nd back row, far left) as obdurate as an old brick wall. And, there was a champion spinner, Johnny Martin (seated row, 5th from left), the gentleman Test cricketer.

Terror.

ABOVE & RIGHT: When he started making a name in Sydney club cricket it was 'Geoff Thompson'; when he started to get 'it' right so did 'they' — "Jeff Thomson has arrived" announced the headline. Later, they tagged him simply 'Thommo'. Just a love-able larrikin, Thommo — unless he had a ball in his right hand and you only had a bat for protection.

Gordon Greenidge, and other great
West Indian batsmen, faced Thommo
one evening in Barbados. Test cricket
may never have witnessed such electric
moments. Thommo maintains to this day
that Greenidge, given not out here, was
out caught off the glove — and that the
damning evidence was the flash of
Gordon's teeth, gritted in pain.

RIGHT: Harold 'Mudgee' Cranney was a young opening batsman who took to opposing fast bowling attacks like a cane cutter harvests sugar sticks.

BELOW: He played with NSW, and notable among his 1923 teammates (Mudgee is seated, second from right) were the relaxed Arthur Mailey (seated, second from left), the captain Charlie Macartney (seated, centre) and W. A. Oldfield (standing, second from left).

JOHN CRANNEY

CRICKET NSW

RIGHT: Mudgee's methodology lived on in the flashing blade of the fearless Harold Goodwin. They played in different eras for Sydney's Cumberland club, the 'breeding' ground for seven Test cricketers — among them Doug Walters and Greg Matthews — and, where all the Benauds enjoyed the game of cricket.

LEFT: F. A. Iredale, Cumberland's first Test cricketer, and an Australian selector.

LEFT: W. P. Howell. On his maiden tour to England in 1899, in his first match against Surrey, he took all 10 first innings wickets for 28 runs.

LEFT: G. R. Hazlitt, a swerve bowler, came from Victoria to Cumberland from where he won a spot on the 1912 Ashes tour.

Bush boys.

RIGHT & BELOW: Jack Chegwyn, 'Cheggy' to all who knew and respected him, was a city slicker who spread the glory of cricket into the bush for as far and as wide as any crows might fly. He even took a team to Mareeba, Coral Sea battle territory, in 1944, to entertain World War II troops. You'd possibly recognise some faces, certainly some names — (standing) 7th from left, Stan McCabe; 8th, Bill Alley; far right, Bill O'Reilly; (sitting) 2nd from left, Don Tallon; 7th, Clarrie Grimmett; far right, Sid Barnes. The tour remains memorable for O'Reilly's 'medal-winning' performance.

OPPOSITE: If your nerves have got ends then the memory of Rick McCosker's incredible courage, batting with a broken jaw in the 1977 Centenary Test, will still set them tingling. Was it the bumpiness of his road to the top, a few potholes that prepared him for such adversity?

FAIRFAX

JACK CHEGWYN COLLECTION/CRICKET NSW

JACK CHEGWYN COLLECTION/CRICKET NSW

ADELAIDE OVAL MUSEUM

SOUTH AUSTRALIA		SOUTH AUSTRALIA	V		WEST AUSTRALIA				
		BOWLERS	WKTS	RUNS	BATSMEN	OUT	B	RUNS	FALL OF WKTS
1ST INNINGS	371	1 MILLER	3	14	VELETTA	C I	2	13	1 FOR 23
2ND INNINGS		2 GEORGE	1	16	McPHEE	B	4	10	2·· 29
WEST AUSTRALIA		3 OWEN			WOOD	C W	1	2	3·· 34
1ST INNINGS		4 SCUDERI	6	6	MOODY	B	4	6	4·· 38
2ND INNINGS		5 SLEEP			ANDREWS	LB	1	0	5·· 38
WICKETS	9	6 HOOKES			ZOEHRER	LB	4	0	6·· 40
CAPES	1	7 HILDITCH			HOGAN	C W	1	2	7·· 40
YARDLEY		8 LEHMANN			MATTHEWS	B	4	0	8·· 40
SUNDRIES	7	9 NOBES			ALDERMAN	C W	4	0	9·· 40
TOTAL	41	BISHOP						OVERS RQD	54
		BERRY	UMPIRES		O'CONNELL	REBBECK			

LIGHT   WEST END   DRAUGHT   WEST END   EXPORT   WEST END   STATE XI   WEST END   EXPORT   WEST END   DRAUGHT   WEST END   LIGHT

WEST END BEERS WEST END

ABOVE: The scoreboard is a classic, and not just because it reflects so perfectly a part of cricket's heritage now swamped by flashing lights and instant replays. Take some time to digest the detail of the events it has recorded. Yes, it was a freakish performance by the South Australian swing bowler Joe Scuderi, but how did he do it, and why did it happen?

OPPOSITE: The answer very probably lies in this image of Scuderi in action in another match against Western Australia — note the ball, seam up and, the length looks full, the line good.

VIV JENKINS

Style, or substance?

ABOVE: The presence of Australia A, who were really Australia B, in the World Series finals in 1995 was administrative high farce. However, it did create a perception that the One-day game was a game that only spirited young men should be allowed to play, and led to an abrupt change in selection philosophy when substitute players were sent to South Africa in 1997. How close is the day when Australia will field truly separate teams and, will there be radical rule changes to accommodate this new breed?

OPPOSITE: By the mid-'90s Australia's 1987 World Cup win was *passe*, submerged in an ever more desperate debate about the One-day game — which players should play it and how should it be played? A key player in the debate was the Australian captain, Mark Taylor, whose style was seen as 'not for the '90s'. Was he really a dud One-day batsman?

VIV JENKINS

VIV JENKINS

David Boon had it all.

to 4.30pm. We boarded, and after half an hour delay we were told the authorities were looking for a lost passenger.

Another half hour later we taxied to the runway only to be told the flight recorder was not working. Off loaded. We arrived in St Lucia at 10.50pm local time, then faced a one hour drive to the hotel. Our gear arrived at 1am and then off to bed.

March 7

Barbados. Kerry O'Keeffe injured by car when running back to hotel this morning. Latest report, his left leg is fractured and in plaster. Lads subdued by Kerry's accident. He is to be in hospital for three days and out of action for at least six weeks.

March 9

Second SuperTest commences in Barbados. Several gates closed as stands full by lunchtime. Final first day crowd estimated at 9000, and Lance Gibbs says the biggest crowd to attend any Test at Kensington Oval on a Friday.

March 13

What started out as a good day finished at 2.30pm when the Test match was abandoned due to a bottle throwing exhibition. It appears the crowd, estimated at 7000, did not consider Fredericks was out lbw to Pascoe when 53 and, a huge rain of bottles came from the stands.

The players were forced to abandon the field. Play was delayed some 50 minutes until the field was cleared but when play could start the crowd chanted "Fredericks, Fredericks, we want Fredericks".

Lloyd and Richards proceeded to the wicket and, again, a new avalanche of bottles came down. This time it was evident that no more cricket was possible. The crowds milled around the players' pavilion shouting "Gosein Gosein", for it was he who gave Fredericks out. They were orderly but could well have rioted if stirred, as Grenada had a revolution this morning.

It would be a pity if this was the pattern we can expect along the trip. I hope not. Seems the players (both sides) instead of accepting the umpire's decision, gracefully, over-react which incites the crowd.

March 15

Last night attended a cocktail party with the cricketers and were entertained with a 20-piece, all female (except the drummer) tin band. Incredible what can be got from old oil drums. They played 'Waltzing Matilda'.

March 17

Some problems experienced with police handling gates. There is a rip-off program between touts and police. It's very hard to stop unless you can be there all day.

A rival magazine bearing our logo is being sold in the stands but it is impossible to control. The military has come to our aid by providing a bus for the Aussies to and from the hotel. The West Indies continue to travel by cab.

March 20
Left hotel 7pm, flight to Guyana left over an hour late. Everybody is tired. Trip from Guyana airport to hotel took about an hour. Seems these people like their airports distant from the cities. Finally to bed at 4am.

March 21
Left hotel at 5pm for Georgetown cricket ground. Wicket very wet, outfield soggy, rain still around. Unlikely any play SuperTest Friday.

The ground appears secure. It is surrounded by a moat and access to gates is via wooden bridges about 10 feet long. The fence is high and wall scaling appears difficult. Some turnstiles are used but I am informed not reliable.

March 22
Raining again this morning. Play has been abandoned Friday and Saturday, will now start Sunday. Pre-sold ticketing procedure is now tricky — this Friday's pre-sold tickets will be good for Sunday, and so on … it will be an experience to be by the gates tomorrow!

March 25
What a day — riots starting at about 2.30 caused abandonment of the day (or match as it seems). The background of the riot actually stemmed from a press statement by a local representative which said play would start at 10am.

Of course this was impossible but neither the public, nor myself for that matter, knew of the newspaper item and the crowd poured in. An announcement at 10.30am advised the patrons of a further inspection at 12.30pm and subsequent to that, another postponement until 2pm. A rather lengthy and silent delay followed and the crowd started to flare.

At 2.25pm an announcement that the captains were conferring, followed immediately by a statement that play would commence at 3.30pm, incited the already volatile crowd and they began to push down the fences, and chairs were thrown onto the ground.

People then began to advance on the members' pavilion, throwing various objects including bottles onto the stand. The West Indian dressing room appeared to be the main target but they soon spread out and attacked the Australian dressing room and the radio box. Many windows were broken as bottles galore rained down.

I was on the top deck of the pavilion at the outbreak and, as the attackers increased, it was necessary to use tables as protectors at the windows, and to carry chairs over our heads for protection from flying objects.

Incredibly no additional police were called until quite late when most of the damage had been done, but when they finally arrived the crowd dispersed into the streets.

Concern was then focused on our return to the hotel. A wise decision to arrange for our transport to leave from the opposite side of the ground was made and, at about 4pm, we left with a police escort.

March 26

A crew of men and boys worked the whole night clearing up the mess created by yesterday's riot. I wasn't aware of gunshots or tear gas but apparently they were used.

One young fellow had a bullet removed from his shoulder, whilst immediate neighbours to the ground suffered from tear gas fired at the mob outside the gate. After both captains, and then managers, were satisfied with security the players were called from the hotel and play started at 10.30am.

The advice to me that the moat around the ground stops people gaining access to the fence is rubbish. Some people place planks against the fence and across the moat, and access from there is easy.

March 28

The feeling is that everyone can hardly wait to quit this place. I hope nothing else happens before we can.

April 4

Dominica. I hear we are not playing at the original ground but on another which is referred to as "a cow paddock". It appears the other one is not prepared.

Trouble at the ground's southern entrance. The entry point is so small that the big rush outside is forcing people to climb the fence.

I alerted the police who immediately put men with dogs outside and foot policemen inside. The problem was quickly halted. Later in the day however the total length of the southern concrete wall was lined with non-payers.

April 5

We arrived in Antigua at 2.05pm. Transport to hotel by school bus. There is a great mess here regarding rooms. I cannot think what may have happened but it took them 'til 6.30pm to find a room for me. The room I have will suit me tonight, but no longer, for I can hardly move in it.

A lot of people in the game thought Kerry Packer's World Series Cricket was like a cool southerly buster at the end of a sweltering Aussie summer's day.

Jack Kramer, who started the pro tennis circuit, said, "I see Kerry Packer not as a pirate, but as a liberator."

And, an editorial in *The Sydney Morning Herald* said, "The players who have signed with Mr Packer cannot be blamed in any way for what they have done. In a world of increasingly commercialised sport they have been badly treated by comparison with other sporting personalities — and they know it. Now they have a chance to better their lot."

A lot of followers of the game agreed. But there were others who thought World Series Cricket was the end of the world, a case for bowed heads and tut-tutting, if not wrist-slashing. The England cricket writer Michael Melford said of the SCG light towers, "It is like seeing the Mona Lisa smoking a pipe." And, someone else offered: "Cricket is meant to be played in God's daylight with a red ball."

And Mr Bob Parish, then a Cricket Board supremo, said, "Private promotion may benefit a few players but it will mean less income to the State associations for the general benefit of the majority of players and the game itself."

Generally, the critics called it a circus and, upon reading Bruce's diary, they might happily decide to offer us the usual shaft of hindsight, "There, I told you so!"

They should be mindful that the year before, a few weeks after Thommo had strutted his stuff in Barbados, Bob Simpson's 'official' Australian team was the target of a riot at Sabina Park, where the crowd hurled empty 44-gallon drums and concrete blocks onto the field, never mind the bottles and chairs.

And, on the tarmac at Antigua as the plane taxied to take-off point — only three hours late because they couldn't find the plane, let alone any 'lost' passenger — one member of Simpson's team said to another, as he gazed glassily out the window at a baggage trolley receding slowly into the distance, "Isn't that our cricket kit?" It was.

In Guyana there was no riot. But nor was there, on most occasions, any electricity in the hotel, running water, and there was not a roll of toilet paper in the town.

Locals were fond of dressing in brown military fatigues and addressing one another as "Comrade", whilst preaching the advantages of communism, one of which, it soon became apparent to the cricket team, was to be able to shave in the hotel swimming pool.

And, on one occasion, Australia's No.5 Gary Cosier leaned out over the top floor balcony of the Pegasus Hotel at midnight and shouted his frustration: "Come on Guyana you can get worse than this!"

One year later, according to Bruce McDonald, and anyone else on the World Series Cricket tour, it did.

It was a roller-coaster ride for Bruce, World Series Cricket. At first, the bitterness of the split touched Bruce, just as it did so many of us who had been 'official cricket' officials, but who had now chosen to be supporters of the new concept.

His devoted service to Sydney Grade cricket in umpiring and club administration was forgotten.

At the 'establishment' Cricketers' Club in Sydney, where he was a popular, hard-working director, acquaintances suddenly ignored him. He was called a "bloody rebel". "I could never come to terms with that," he said.

On the road with WSC there was the odd glitch — and, Bruce, 'Mr Fixit', had to come up with the answers. Batsmen had been complaining in vain for years that the sightscreen at the southern end of the SCG was too low — Bruce had it raised 75 centimetres (two feet and six inches), so batsmen were better able to sight Joel Garner's thunderbolts.

The night games were plagued by a white ball that quickly went grey — Bruce was in charge of the 'repaint factory' in the back of the dressing room where a coat of special, quick drying white leather preparation was applied to the used balls.

"They came up like brand new. At meal breaks I'd go to the umpires with the replacement, or take them out in the trolley at the drinks breaks," he was to confess years later.

And, 20 years on the ball manufacturer has still not been able to come up with a long-lasting white cricket ball. Bruce's repaints might still be the best option.

In the history of World Series Cricket, nothing beats the magic of the night they turned on the lights for the first time at the SCG, November 28, 1978, Australia versus the West Indies. About 50,000 turned up — I wonder how many of them were 'establishment'?

Bruce remembers watching the queues getting longer and longer and getting on the phone to 'Mr P' (Kerry Packer) and telling him, "You've got to see this!"

He remembers hot-footing it around to the Showground next door and arranging six mobile turnstiles to try to cope with the ever-increasing crowd — and then setting them up, and opening them at 'closed' gates, ones normally used for deliveries between the SCG Hill and the Showground.

It was the night the general public was allowed into the Ladies' Stand, usually 'members only' territory.

Bruce: Mr P arrived. There were still thousands outside. He said to me, "Get two bags of change for me ... then I want you to walk down to all those people queued up and call out, 'Six dollars into the Ladies' Stand!'"

I did and they went silent for what seemed like an eternity but it must have been only half a minute ... and then they started to run at me. Mr P and I manned the Members' turnstiles.

Opened them up to the public, a first.

Early November, 1978

WSC Australia are playing the World XI at Mount Smart stadium, in Auckland, New Zealand. It is cold and the pitch is seaming all over the place. Dennis Lillee is close to unplayable. He jags one back and hits the West Indian allrounder, Collis King, high on the inside of his right leg, a blow to make anyone wince, even up in the far off grandstand.

It looks bad. King is down, lying straight out as if ready to be loaded into a coffin. The physio is at work with the magic spray but King remains as if shot. Mr Fixit, concerned, rushes on to the field imagining that the stretcher may be required.

He arrives, and looks down on King, whose trousers are down to his knees. The physio is still applying the magic spray. King slowly raises himself to his elbows and looks down ... "Jesus," he says. "I'm turning white — quick, spray me all over!"

WSC gave us cricket under lights, surely the most dramatic advance in the game since its inception. Some say olden-day players wouldn't have coped with the modern game, but surely that's bunk. And anyway, have modern day players all coped with the game's raised profile?

MO

About WSC-time Gregory Richard John Matthews made his First grade debut with Cumberland. His cricketing talent had been noted — "Has the footwork, anticipation and application of a much more experienced cricketer" was a judgment made when he was 13 years old.

When Greg, at the age of 18, began his First grade career, Cumberland's home ground was no longer the local oval. It was Old Kings, a delightful setting, a circle of white pickets inside another circle, one of gum trees and pines.

The Parramatta River winds back of Old Kings and in those days there was a small swamp nearby, signposted by a jungle of bullrushes, and an adjacent path was a short cut to the Old Kings dressing sheds.

One Saturday, young Greg resplendent in one of the fashions of the day, a toga-style shirt and sandals, his cricket gear in a kit bag slung over shoulder, appeared from out of the bullrushes. His teammates were unable to resist the nickname 'Moses'.

This was abbreviated to 'Mo'. Western Australian Sheffield Shield players might have been closer to the mark after a Sheffield Shield encounter in 1983. They offered up 'Colgate' — for confidence.

The '80s hadn't even begun to hum when Bob Simpson, then a businessman, announced that Greg was his cricket 'character' for the decade. He was so impressed he became Matthews' manager. Bob wrote that Greg was "certainly different ... he boogies around the field or strums an imaginary guitar".

Bob also listed as 'character' Greg's punk hairstyle and the diamond in his ear. Teammates, though, were still assessing his character; 'Boycs' and 'Misere' were other nicknames that popped up briefly.

Greg Matthews became a high profile cricketer post-WSC, when high profiles were about more than just batting and bowling. Lifestyle items, such as fashion and fashionable friends, attracted a modern public following that didn't always care whether Greg made a duck or ate a duck.

To them, it was unconscionable that the source of their entertainment should be given an occasional boot in the backside by a bunch of faceless men operating under the guise of national selectors. Whenever it happened the fan club led the shrill uprising.

It raised an obvious question — just how talented a cricketer was Greg Matthews? Was he really good enough to hold down a regular Test spot? Or was he just a fine Sheffield Shield cricketer who couldn't quite struggle up the next big step to the Test game?

Maybe Greg himself provided us with a clue to his eventual Test fate. He did an interview after missing out on selection for the 1987 World Cup, and said, "I see my future as an allround bowler. Ideally, I would love to bat about No.6 for Australia and be considered part of a spin duo." It was a realistic vision.

He'd scored three quality Test centuries at the time, one batting at No.6, the others at No.7. However, he was only averaging in the mid-30s — was that good enough to displace batsmen like Allan Border, David Boon, Geoff Marsh, David Hookes, Greg Ritchie and Dean Jones in the top six? Any answer to that question would be dependent on selection philosophy at the time, but generally the answer would be "no".

At the time the selectors were choosing Wayne Phillips, the wicketkeeper from South Australia, as a top order batsman — maybe they felt two allrounders in the first six was a luxury. In any case, they were tip-toe times for the selectors, because many of their previous judgments had been compromised by notable player defections to the rebel tours of South Africa.

In some other era Matthews might have been offered a spot up the order. After World War II, Bradman's selection panels often loaded teams with bowling allrounders — Keith Miller, Ron Archer, Ken Mackay, Alan Davidson — who were all capable of batting high.

Rich occasionally batted in the first six in Test cricket, and batted as high as No.4 in South Africa in 1957–58. Mackay was a regular at six, and Greg's grit, and push and poke and plunder style, was similar to the gritty Queenslander's.

If bad luck did dog Matthews then it was his bowling that may have suffered most — his dream of being part of a 'spin duo' never materialised. It's pure guesswork as to whether a regular soulmate might have made a difference, but history does show bowlers, sometimes spinners, can go well in pairs.

Finding a foil for Matthews was no simple matter. It had to be a spinner who turned the ball from the leg. There were a few left-arm orthodox types — Murray Bennett, Tom Hogan, Ray Bright — and a few legspinners — Bob

Holland, Trevor Hohns and Peter Sleep — but for one reason or another, age, retirement, team balance, talent rating or the South African rebel tours, they rarely got together with Matthews.

And, the world cricket 'psyche' was all wrong for a spin duo — the West Indies were proving speed was the way to go. No sooner had Lillee and Thomson and Rodney Hogg moved on than Geoff Lawson, Craig McDermott, Dave Gilbert, Carl Rackemann, Bruce Reid and Merv Hughes were offered the chance to fill the gap in the Australian line-up.

The Australian game plan was mostly three quicks and one spinner, and preferably a spinner to keep it tight because Australia were a wobbly outfit.

The captain Border was under pressure, if not to win then certainly not to lose. And, limited-overs cricket was gaining more and more momentum. Run conservation had become the main tactic in both forms of the game.

They are all factors that might have negatively influenced Matthews' career as a bowler. And, at No.7 in the batting order, he was surely being chosen as a bowler, first.

By the end of his 15th Test Greg had taken 33 wickets. His strike-rate was 81 balls a wicket. Before that 15th Test it had been 100 balls a wicket. That Test was the famous 1986 Madras tie and Greg took 10 wickets, five for 103 and five for 146.

As a former Treasurer Paul Keating was fond of saying about his economy, they were a "great set of numbers". And, figures like Greg's 10 wickets do impress selectors because they show a bowler is doing his job.

Yet Greg never again took 10 wickets in a Test. Never again took 10 wickets in a series and, in fact, never again took a five-wicket haul in a Test. The closest he came was four for 76 against Sri Lanka in Colombo in 1992, his 29th Test, and what was noteworthy about that performance was that he bowled some of the time with Shane Warne, then a rookie, at the other end.

It must have crossed his mind … "at last, a spin soulmate". Greg's Test career reached shutdown after 33 matches. In the end there was little statistical evidence to suggest he was ever a genuine Test class spinner.

Maybe that 10 wicket haul and his impressive Sheffield Shield bowling record confused us all … the different selection panels, and even Greg himself, judging by his 1986 interview.

Maybe we all got it wrong, thinking he was an offspinning allrounder. Maybe at Test level he was really a gutsy batsman who could bowl a bit of steady offspin. He batted in Tests at 41.09 and that's impressive.

Maybe he could have held down No.6, fighting and nudging, sticking around, building the partnerships. In 1996, another interviewer posed this question: "Greg, you haven't scored a first-class century for something like five years. Is that a worry?"

Matthews replied: "My batting has declined since a conversation I had with John Benaud (the Australian selector) in Brisbane in 1987–88. I changed my focus from a player who thought about batting 90 per cent of the time to one who thought about bowling 90 per cent of the time. It was more important to be a bowler who batted."

I came onto the Australian selection panel in the 1988–89 season. On December 2, 1988, NSW were playing Western Australia in a Sheffield Shield match at the Newcastle Sports Ground.

At Greg's request we were walking a circuit of the ground, discussing his cricket talent and his Test prospects.

He had not played in a Test since December 1986, against England in Adelaide. He had been dropped even though he had been a leading batsman (215 runs at 53.75) in the losing team. Another offspinner Peter Taylor had taken his place. In the series Greg's offspinners had earned two wickets for 295 runs. On the walk, my advice to him as a selector was to improve his bowling.

Did he? This was his Sheffield Shield bowling record at the end of that Newcastle match:

Wkts	Ave	5 Wkts/i	10 Wkts/m	S/rate
111	32.46	4	–	83.17

He was next chosen for Australia in the Ashes series against England in 1990–91. This is how his Sheffield Shield form sheet had changed:

Wkts	Ave	5 Wkts/i	10 Wkts/m	S/rate
175	30.32	8	1	79.11

His last Test was in 1992–93 against the West Indies at the SCG, his home ground. By that time his form sheet had improved even more:

Wkts	Ave	5 Wkts/i	10 Wkts/m	S/rate
245	28.48	13	3	74.69

It was ironic that Greg's Test career should have wound up at the SCG, because his successful Sheffield Shield form contains a strong Sydney factor. Of his 359 Shield career wickets, 203 were taken on his home ground at an impressive strike rate of 63 balls a wicket.

And, of his 19 five-wickets-in-an-innings hauls, 13 were in Sydney. All his match hauls of 10 wickets were in Sydney.

But his strike rate at venues away from Sydney was a wicket every 83 balls, which is heading towards the red zone of his overall Test strike rate, 102 balls a wicket.

In that last Test against the West Indies at the SCG he took 2/169 off 59 overs. Some might see that as damning proof, at least statistically, that Greg was unable to transfer his Shield bowling talent to the Test arena.

If you were given the opportunity to clone a cricketer which one would it be? Another Bradman? The great allrounder Keith Miller perhaps? Bill O'Reilly? Or Greg Matthews?

Two Greg Matthews! Just one Greg Matthews is enough for two schools of thought — raise a smile or raise an eyebrow.

There are some cricket people who agree with Greg's former captain Geoff Lawson when he suggests Matthews is on track to become "the best allround player, if not the best player" NSW has ever produced.

Best player? There are others more circumspect about Greg's ability and point out, "Hey, didn't Bradman once play for NSW?" Geoff inspired a headline and there has never been any shortage of headlines about Greg. Why is it so?

Well, when you think about it, it's often for all the wrong reasons. In October 1993, it wasn't because he bowled himself back into Australian selection calculations by ripping out New Zealand just before a Test.

Rather, it was because he refused an invitation — for whatever reason, good or otherwise — to play for NSW against Far North Coast and was dropped by the selectors for the next Sheffield Shield match against Queensland.

Greg was fortunate he received a sympathetic headline. 'Unsettled Matthews Left Out By Blues' could have read 'Matthews Snubs Blues'. A case of 'all his own work'.

There are other examples of Greg, a foot bandaged, and with his own fingerprints on the smoking gun — fined $1000 during a tour to Sharjah with Australia, and in 1992, about the time of the official season launch, the very public crumpling of the Australian Cricket Board sponsor's product.

So, what are cricket followers to make of all this — is he erratic or is he eccentric? In the early '90s some people saw eccentricity in his decision to bowl with his cap on.

Others with long memories thought he was 'taking the mickey' — the great Clarrie Grimmett used to bowl with his cap on. But Greg would be the first to point out that Clarrie was a legspinner with 513 wickets in 79 Sheffield Shield matches to Greg's 359 in 114 matches.

Others congratulate Greg on his commonsense in this matter. After all, a thinning ozone layer versus a then-thinning hairline was not a contest. His teammates have never been guilty of an over-reaction to him. Once when he appeared at a Meet The Blues function at the NSW Cricketers Club wearing a colourful bandana wrapped pirate-style around his head, a teammate shouted, "Hey look boys, it's Willie Nelson!"

And when he made the fourth century of his Test career, 128 against England at the SCG in 1991, so constant were his demands on 12th man Merv Hughes to improve his player comfort level with dry cap, dry gloves, dry shirt, that in the end the big fellow took out Greg's whole kit bag.

For five years I was part of a selection panel that considered every aspect of Greg Matthews' performance in the Sheffield Shield. As it was with any player, the question was always — can he do the job at Test level?

For a long time the Australian selectors were accused of ignoring Greg Matthews' form chart, of showing a lack of tolerance towards Greg Matthews' eccentricity.

The coach Bob Simpson and the captain Border were accused of manhandling him, instead of man-managing him. Not long after Greg's public crumpling of the sponsor's product, the selection panel to whom Border readily offered an opinion, and of which Simpson was a member, managed to invite Greg to play in the First Test against the West Indies at the 'Gabba.

By the Fourth Test it was the West Indian batsmen who had manhandled Greg off the Test scene — four wickets in the series for 228 runs, average per wicket about 57.

September, 1996

The NSW selectors decide Greg can captain himself. He decides to wear No. 36 — his age — on the back of his One-day shirt. In the official media guide he lists his nickname as 'Yeah, Yeah'. Age and Youth in the one package. And, for a few matches, he takes to running onto the field 50 metres in front of the rest of the team.

Consider this: life is a sprint for Greg Matthews. Full on, full time. First is where he has to be. He's always 'with it'. To be without is frustration. He craves to be the centre of attention.

And yes, there are any number of sports people with drive like that. But in the end with Greg there were just too many days when the hoopla got in the way of the howzats.

He'll disappear from the game saying he did it his way, and he'll have no regrets. Others who recognised his talent might wonder if there was a better way.

The test of the best players comes when they are promoted a 'grade' — can they rise to the next level, perform well under pressure? Matthews' batting statistics suggest that he might have been a more than useful Test batsman:

Sheffield Shield Batting				Test Batting			
M	Runs	50/100	Ave	M	Runs	50/100	Ave
114	5532	28/8	37.13	33	1849	12/4	41.09

The Cumbos unearthed another talented allrounder.
He remains one of Sydney cricket's most loveable larrikins,
but he doesn't wear the Cumberland colours. They had to
sack him when he was only 13 years old. Who knows what
might have happened if he'd stayed?

EMU

Ken Hall was a fair dinkum allrounder, bat anywhere,
field in the slips, bowl swing or spin, take your pick. Tough
as they come, too. Had a strange gait, just like Gary
Sobers', but it was another Gary who dead-set cost him
a first-class career.

As the crows fly, and there's a lot of them scavenging on the flood plains in Sydney's outer north-west, it's about half an hour from Windsor to the Penrith district, where Lou took his 20 wickets in a match.

In the local Windsor hospital, on May 5, 1952, Aub and Laura Hall of Wilberforce had a son, Ken.

Like Lou, Ken Hall's earliest talent was spin bowling and, one summer, even though he was barely into his teens, his flighted left-arm orthodox tweakers won over the Cumberland officials and they offered the boy a future in the game. Just as it had been with Lou.

But as quick as his chance appeared, it disappeared. This is what happened: George Horwood was an avid cricket follower who lived at the top of Lou's street in North Parramatta and, when Lou decided he was too old to be managing and advising the Cumberland Under-16 A. W. Green Shield team, George took over.

It was George's practice to try to fine tune his boys by playing a couple of trial matches before the competition started. In the 1965–66 season those matches were played at Richmond, five minutes down the road from Windsor, but so far from Cumberland territory that it was classified 'country'.

And, when Ken Hall, 13 years old and just a slip of a kid, scuttled the Cumberland batting George, not being a mug, selected him for the real thing.

The form turned out to be good; little Ken Hall came up with some big hauls in the Green Shield — five for 27 versus Petersham, six for 51 versus Waverley, five for 65 versus Randwick.

And, George's end-of-season report conveyed his enthusiasm about future summers …"In six matches Ken took 24 wickets at 16.0 … he is available for two more seasons and should prove to be a match-winning player." Reading it 30 years later you could still hear George's lips smacking in anticipation.

Before the next summer the Sydney cricket authorities introduced a rule that only junior players from within a club's area were eligible for Green Shield. Ken Hall never played for Cumberland again, only against them.

Ken was cricket tough, even at 12; he'd play with the other kids in the morning competition, then jump into his uncle Noel's old FJ Holden and head to Sackville, up the Hawkesbury River, desperately hoping that he'd be able to fill in as a fielder for the seniors in the afternoon.

Once, that was the typical Australian cricket education — work experience, an apprenticeship. Rich did it. These days it's all so orchestrated, with every age group, even Under-8s, endless development programs, endless inter-state carnivals, and so on. Trophy-hunting coaches and parents are guilty of pigeon-holing some of our best young cricketers.

A lot of cricketers from the 'old school' doubt the toughness, mental and physical, of many of the young cricketers coming through the modern system. They call them 'soft cocks'. Many are. Talented young cricketers, developed physically and mentally, should be encouraged to play above their natural age group.

Ken Hall hadn't even celebrated his 21st when Prime Minister Harold Holt announced Australia would go "all the way with LBJ". Like Doug Walters, Ken was conscripted and sent to Kapooka, outside Wagga, where he shared a hut with a group of fellow conscripts, fondly remembered as "them all" — from conscientious objectors, who kept jumping out the windows and "pissing off", to another sportsman, Lucky Gattellari, of the boxing Gattellaris, brother of Rocky.

He became Private Hall and because The Army team didn't have anyone to take the new ball he taught himself to bowl late swing.

A couple of years later, Ken Hall came across to Penrith, behind the wheel of his VW 'beetle', mechanically A1 because greasing and changing oil is his business. He came via a landscape of tilled fields dotted with cornstalks and citrus and old, paint-peeled, two-storey weatherboards.

You can take the boy out of the country, but … he was tall, and some would say thin, but by gee, stir him up, give him a challenge and you'd soon find out how wiry and tough he was.

And, only the gravest situation could wipe from his craggy features a bright, hearty smile or silence his infectious laugh. And he loved a beer.

The first thing his First grade cricketing mates noticed was that he walked and ran in a strange bent-legged way, and they didn't miss him when they tagged him 'Emu'.

From the word go he was good for Penrith; he bowled his left-arm swing at a sharpish pace, as sharp as either Bob Massie or Terry Alderman, that's for sure. He could get 'em to go late in the air, mostly in, which came as a bloody nasty shock if you were a smart-arse batsman.

And, there were plenty of those in Grade — they'd let his away-slanters whistle past the off stump, then look back down the pitch and give him the sneer that said, "Up your's mate!" then look down at their shattered stumps when he produced the inswinger. He could move 'em off the pitch, too. More shocks for some.

In the field you'd never stick him anywhere else but in the slips — if the wicketkeeper had a cold Ken Hall could catch it.

This is true: one match when a skier went up off his bowling and the 'keeper shouted, "'keeper!", Emu hipped him out of the way like a rugby centre would a tackler, caught it and said, "Piss off, I catch them with m' teeth!"

When he went into bat he'd crouch low over the bat, and it looked ugly, like a crone leaning on a stick, but his wrists were like rubber hose and his timing as sweet as honey flowing from a jar.

When he got those wrists to work, what a merry dance he'd lead the fielders at cover and point, and square on the onside. You'd bat him anywhere in the order, but when he came to Penrith, aged 23 and maturing, he was best about No.4 or No.5.

By the summer after he'd celebrated his 40th birthday he was long gone from Penrith, where The Player Of The Year Award seemed to be perpetually his, and had gone to Bankstown, the Waugh twins' club. There, he was batting after the 'keeper and, he'd taken up left-arm orthodox spin again.

"Where are you fielding, 'Mu?" I asked him one day. "Still first slip, JB," he says, all straight-faced and serious. Then those craggy features break up and he adds, "And if I could bloody well field there off me own bowling I'd have a bloody lot more wickets!"

In 1995 his great career was drawing to a close and the Bankstown club gave him a testimonial. But what's a testimonial? It used to signal the end of a career, these days it seems to be an invitation to have one last fling. Ken played again the next summer.

In his career, he missed only one day of grade cricket — when his ample nose was busted, split wide open, and bloodied, not after a missed hook but a missed sweep against Murray Bennett, the gentle spin bowler who with Bob Holland reduced the West Indies to rubble at the SCG in 1985.

Emu might never retire. Lou went on until he was a couple of years past his 50th birthday; in the beginning, at Coraki, locals knew Lou as 'young slogger', in the end his Cumberland teammates had taken to calling him by the affectionate title, 'Colt' — as the Bankstown boys do Ken Hall.

It says something about a cricketer's character as well as his talent when he's still playing First grade in his 40s, and enjoying the game. If Ken Hall had been born in another State he'd have gone close to playing for Australia. He had it all, talent, temperament and toughness. But, in NSW his career clashed with that of Gary Gilmour, another left-handed genius.

Penrith, with 'Emu' in the side, were playing Sutherland, the club that was eventually home to another couple of good country cricketers, Steve Rixon and Glenn McGrath.

For no particular reason there was often an edge to these games; in one game I was struck in the box when protectors were small, moulded, lightweight pink plastic and, as I lay writhing on the dampish pitch, the instigator of my grief, a red-faced lad with the unlikely name for a fast bowler of Eugene, stood above me demanding that I "get up you weak-kneed __ !"

On a less stressful occasion, Penrith were enjoying their home batting surface at Howell Oval — which in those days was prepared by Peter Leroy, later of SCG fame, or misfortune, depending on your rating of the grand old ground in the '90s — and Emu was on strike to a fast medium-paced bowler named Graham Barry.

I was at the non-striker's end, backing up, naturally, ever ready for Emu's squirt shot for one into the gap at cover point, or the flick to leg. As Barry went into his delivery whirl his arm struck his side and the ball dropped almost at his feet, a few paces down the pitch.

Emu, eyes brightening and that smile already spreading across his face, advanced on it at a brisk skip, shouting, "Don't touch it, don't touch it!" Even before he reached it he had the bat raised, Babe Ruth baseball style. And, just in case there were some among the converging Sutherland fieldsmen hard of hearing, Emu repeated, "Don't touch it!"

His eyes, gleaming by now, urgently searched the field for a gap into which to smash the stationary ball. This way and that he looked, like a cat playing with its prey. "Where will I hit it?" Then his gaze fixed on the vacant outfield behind me, and a terrible thought crossed my mind ... "Don't hit me!" I screeched, just as Emu's bat began its descent.

He topped it. The ball dribbled forward, possibly about as far as half a blade of grass. I could see Emu wanted to say something because his lips were moving and his mouth was open. The bowler Barry and his fieldsmen livened up considerably at the sight of all this, and Barry moved to pick up the ball, a run out on his mind. He stooped, then leapt back in terror as Emu's bat descended once again!

"Hey, hang on ... you can't do that ... howzat?!" laughed the Sutherland fielders, and out went Emu — hit the ball twice.

The Hall clan was such a cricketing force in the Windsor district that they were invited to take on The Rest in a special match.

There was 'Darkie' (Geoff), a wicketkeeper; Ron, a fast bowler who played NSW Colts; 'Choc' (Colin) a left-handed opener who played Sydney First grade. So did Neal, a loopy leggie, and 'Stumpy' (Alan) a slugger of a batsman. Ken we know about, and there was Ian, Noel, Neville, Broughton and Jerry. They trounced The Rest. And the umpires weren't Halls!

Ken Hall was a no-frills cricketer, always played hard, and to win. So did a knockabout bloke named Brian Riley, but 'Riles' had ginger in him, and a way with words that could promote either a sense of humour or a sense of outrage.

PETES

Petersham was a tough club, in a tough area of Sydney — factoryland, men sweating it out behind blackened brick walls and under galvanised iron roofs. Maybe the fashion of the neighbourhood, blue-collar, influenced the club's tough-talking tradition.

Sledging comes in two flavours, bitter and sweet. Lou, when he was getting on in years, nearing the end of his Grade cricket career, was on the end of some heavy hitting by a young opponent.

The lad sledged Lou. His message, recalled here less colourfully, was, "Try that for size, old man." Lou wasn't into sledging, nor gamesmanship. It was against the spirit of his game. But he didn't mind a challenge, and this kid was a challenge.

Lou moved his field, dropping the man at extra cover deeper, then adopted one of the oldest tricks in the slow bowler's coaching book — he bowled one from 23 yards, thus changing the length, and pitched the ball slightly wider. The kid went for a drive, was deceived by the length, and skewed the ball down the throat of the fielder at deep extra cover.

On his way from the field, the kid had to walk past Lou. As he drew level, Lou turned to him, and said, "You'll find it a lot cooler in the grandstand, son."

How would that have looked on the television these days — Lou standing there, lips working, hitching at the waistband of his strides, as was his habit, watching the batsman depart?

What's the harm in a little bit of verbal cut and thrust between cricketers? Lou's words, as gentle as they were, must have made the kid's blood froth and bubble. These days, of course, our bowling hero would be more inclined to walk aggressively after his opponent, and shout " __ off!" at him.

The subtle 'one-liner', as cutting as a stiletto, has become an abusive 'two-worder'. The shift has taken a great deal of spirit out of the game, which is a great pity.

Petersham's cricketers were so tough they used to 'sledge' themselves. They nicknamed one of their First grade wicketkeepers, 'Fumbles'.

A tough nut to crack was an opening batsman named Max Benjamin, who used to stuff a singlet into his underpants to serve as a thigh pad. On looks alone, Max going in to bat was like Geronimo going on the warpath. Max used to plaster a slash of white zinc cream across his cheeks and the bridge of his ample nose, stretching from one ear to the other.

In a match against Manly he was confronted late on a darkening day, by a combination of tactics and terror. The Manly captain was Jim Burke. 'Burkie' had spent 24 Tests as Australia's opening batsman, being battered black and blue by the very quick quicks, Tyson, Trueman, Adcock, Heine.

This must have impressed Jim, because as a captain he generally applied the Doberman Principle — standing at mid-off, sooling his own quicks onto opening batting opponents with, "Bounce him, bounce him again ..."

Manly's quick was Tommy Hart, and he bounced Max. Soon, Max took one on the head and he reeled away to the side of the pitch as the ball shot away to the fine leg boundary.

Max, rubbing his head and watching it go, then turned to Burkie and shouted defiantly, "This bloke's not quick, I can play him with me head!"

Petersham Oval doubled as a baseball diamond, and a lot of Petersham cricketers played baseball, the game where backchat is an art form. Maybe the 'ghosts' of baseball influenced the club's sledging ethos.

'Petes' had an opening batsman named Kevin Cantwell, who in winter, wore the padded leather bodyguard, the leggings and face mask of a baseball catcher, and sharpened his tongue on the steady stream of batters who came to stance in front of him.

In summer, on the cricket field he would come up with a one-liner quicker than Mae West. His teammates called him 'Crazy'.

Petersham's matches against the great St George club have a traditional 'edge' to them. One bleak season for Petersham, the St George captain Warren Saunders announced in a newspaper report, pre-match, "This is the weakest Petersham side I've ever seen."

Needled, and determined somehow to use this to his team's advantage, Petersham's captain Col Blackman gathered his team around him in the dressing room, and gave them a good, old rev up speech, banging his fist on the rubdown table as he reached the punchline — "... and, whatever you do don't forget that during the week Wacky Saunders came out in the paper and bagged us ... called us the weakest bunch of Petersham cricketers he's ever seen!"

Crazy, from up the back: "And you know what 'Blackie' ...? He's right!"

Crazy just couldn't help himself. To an outsider some of his jibes seemed almost cruel, but he was harmless, and never guilty of bitterness.

Petersham had an opening bowler named Bruce Livingstone, a gentleman, so it will come as no shock to know Bruce was a master of the gentle art of swing bowling.

Bruce was one of a rare breed of Australian cricketers — he retired to umpiring, where he once lodged a claim to fame by giving a hat-trick of leg befores in favour of a legspin bowler named Tom Wood from Cumberland. Tom bowled topspinners only, so Bruce was on safe ground.

Crazy once said Bruce was "an idiot, but a polite idiot". It was said with no malice; it was a generous concession to Bruce's demeanour in two tough disciplines of the game — opening the bowling and umpiring — where many cricketers have always doubted the sanity of the participants.

March, 1977

It's just after the Centenary Test at the MCG, and Petersham are playing St George in a first grade semifinal. Brian Riley, the Petersham captain, and Ian Chappell, the Australian captain, were pitch lengths apart in the world of cricket, but some would insist they spoke the same language.

Riley's nickname was 'Riles', just a simple abbreviation but it could quite easily have been recognition that his tongue was as rough as a rasp. Riley remembers events during the match this way:

Saints were all out for 170. It was a beautiful batting track but right near the end of the day we were four for 60.

I was hanging in there but it was getting shadowy. There were shadows on the pitch and back in the bowler's run up and at the stumps ... and I was thinking about the next day.

Saints had their quickie on, Richard Done [now assistant coach at Australia's Cricket Academy]. He was running in in shadow, delivering in sunshine and halfway down the pitch the ball was in the shadows again.

I got a single off the last ball and said to 'Brooksie' [Centenary Test umpire, Tom Brookes] "How's the light?"

He said, "No go, Brian." Saints brought on their spinner, Murray Bennett, but he's pretty quick through the air. He knocked me over. I was pretty __ ing dirty, I can tell you.

As I went past Brooksie on the way out I asked him did he have two rules, one for Tests and one for Grade?" [A reference to Brookes' decision in the Centenary Test to come off for bad light when shadow enveloped half the pitch late each day at the MCG.]

Black mark for me. Well, I mean ... __ it, four balls after I was out they came off for the light.

Then, in the final we were playing the University of NSW, and I was reported for seven breaches of conduct. I fronted the Association [NSW Cricket] and asked them to itemise them. I couldn't believe it. Things like this:

One of our guys let the ball go through his legs and cost us vital runs. I shouted out, "Hey, what the fuck's going on? Come on, this is a final!"

Then, when I went out to bat all the boozy students up on the hill gave me heaps. And they kept it up. When I got out they really turned it on.

At first I just waved my bat, but on the way off I gave them the thumbs up and the two fingers. What's wrong with that? After all, it was a bloody final!

At the start of the next season the NSW Cricket Association grade committee suspended Riley for misconduct, for one month. Asked what he might put forward in his defence Riley, in his lazy drawl, eyes twinkling behind wire-framed spectacles, and with the constant self-interjection of, "What's all the fuss about any __ ing way?" thought it would be appropriate to offer a few of the above comments.

When a selector is out scouting for talent he doesn't always rely only on his own judgment. He might canvass a second opinion. On another day, at another Petersham versus St George war, the State selector, Ern Laidler, is talking to the Petersham captain Col Blackman.

Laidler, inquisitive, brow wrinkled, head inclined towards the batting action in the middle. "How's Riles going?"

Blackman, suitably serious, emphatic, head nodding: "Batting well, Ern. No problems ... terrific ... temperament's good ... much changed player, Riles." Riley gets out. On the way off there is some verbal self-abuse, he smashes the gate open with his bat, rattles it on the gate post, gets into the dressing room and bounces the bat off the four walls.

Laidler, watches all this, and hears it, too: "You're right, Col ..." And after a moment of contemplation "... he has changed. If anything he's worse."

Riley was a talented cricketer, tall and thin, and a good driver, especially strong over the top. If his team was in a crisis, Riley could still dominate. He was a smart cover field with a clean pick up and a beautiful arm. He'd have been a natural at the One-day game. As you might have guessed, he was also a baseballer.

Some 'names' played with Petersham, among them Johnny Martin and Bob Simpson. Little Johnny was famous for his big sixes and at Petersham Oval once bounced one through a flower garden, across Station Street, and down Park Street. It turned the corner into Parramatta Road, where it rolled to the bottom of Taverner's Hill, heading west.

In one game against Petersham a couple of 'name' fast bowlers, Grahame Corling and Steve Bernard turned out for Northern Districts. Late in the match Petersham, one wicket to fall, were within a few hits of victory. But it was so dark the street lights had come on, and the batsmen Crazy Cantwell and Brian Hughes (now chief executive of Cricket NSW) couldn't see out to the boundary.

Some cricketers say they don't mind losing a cricket match, but we're all human — really we do mind. The NDs skipper, Barry Rothwell, had his mind on the job and brought back Bernard, who was very, very quick.

The ball, a dark blur, reared sharply from the black pitch, Hughes edged it, the 'keeper caught it and the NDs went crazy. Crazy Cantwell went crazier. Harsh words flew.

Even the mild-mannered Hughes reacted totally out of character. "If you ever do that again I'll wrap the bat around your skull!" he shouted to Rothwell.

Rothwell was equal to the occasion: "If you can't see 'em mate, give it away," he replied.

The Petersham captain, Noel Hughes, in his cricket socks, led his Petersham boys onto the field to confront the victors. More harsh words. Both teams then retired to their respective dressing sheds. The Petersham one was the one with the door locked.

Some time later there came a hesitant knocking. Grahame Corling, a beer in one hand and a towel in the other stood there, that sunbeam of a smile spreading across his face.

"Can I come and have a shower in your room?" he said. "I don't want to stay in that one."

Ironically, Corling was credited with prompting the term 'sledging' — he is said to have once sworn in mixed company and was thereafter accused of being as subtle as a sledgehammer. Merv Hughes, another Australian fast bowler, was even less subtle.

MERVS

For half a decade at Test time at the SCG there were two Mervs in the Australian dressing room, Merv Hughes and Merv Seres — the fast bowler and the strapper. Only one of them played serious cricket, but they both had a sense of humour.

Merv Seres was born in 1932 at Newtown in NSW, pure blue-collar country; Merv Hughes was born in 1961 at Euroa, Victoria, merino sheep-big country. Merv S thought he was a fast bowler, but never made it. Merv H thought the same, and did make it.

Cricket lured them from their diverse backgrounds and although it offered one of them more fame and fortune than the other, they were still able to rub shoulders at the highest level of the game. And, it allowed them to become the very best of mates. Cricket can do that — and it makes a better fist of it than any other sport.

When Merv S met Merv H at the dressing room door it was always a contest to see which one could get in first with, "Hey Merv, did you hear the one about …?"

Merv S: "This chap is feeling really crook so he goes to see his doctor, who after checking him over gives him some bad news: 'You've only got three weeks to live … you've got a mystery disease that we only know by the code-name A-34.' The chap is so upset by this he heads off to his local club to drown his sorrows. While he's knocking back triple scotches he finds a couple of 20 cent pieces on the bar, puts them in a poker machine and wins three grand. He has a few more drinks and finds a dollar coin, puts it into another pokie and wins fifty grand. 'You must be the luckiest bloke in the world,' says a chap walking up to him. 'I'm not,' says the dying man. 'I've got A-34.' 'Wow, congratulations,' says the other chap, 'you've won the meat raffle!'

Merv H: "What about the one about the blind bloke? This blind bloke walks into the supermarket, picks up his seeing eye dog and swings it around his head. The check-out chick says, 'Hey, what do you think you're doing?' 'Just having a look around,' he says."

Merv S has a theory about humour and demeanour. Outwardly, the two Mervs were larger than life. All bustle and bubble. Life Be In It types. But, Merv S confesses, they were sort of living a 'lie'. He says, the truth is there are a few stomach butterflies around, and a joke can be handy at those times.

Merv S: "I got into knowing jokes because I used to get a bit nervous. So, I'd tell a joke to break the ice. I've used it all my life. In the dressing room it helps me get on with the chaps. When I'm working on a player, the massage, if he's tense or nervous sometimes a quick joke relaxes him, takes his mind off the game for a second. Merv Hughes … well, I did feel he was a bit nervous, like myself."

However, that wasn't the first impression Merv S gained of Merv H. NSW were playing Victoria at the SCG and Merv H was bowling to the NSW opener John Dyson. He hit him with a lifter, and broke his arm.

Merv S: "I went out to administer first-aid and was aware of Merv Hughes lying on his back at the Randwick end, as though nothing had happened. I thought, 'My God, he's a cool customer!' Everyone else was looking at Dyson and saying, 'My God, is he alright, is he going to die?' and there's Merv Hughes lying down, with his hands behind his head, looking up at the sky.

"And, when the next batsman came in Merv just bowled to him as if nothing had happened. Merv's not an uncaring type. I just think he'd tunnel-visioned himself to bowl NSW out. If he'd have shown compassion he'd have lost it."

A cricket dressing room should have been a culture shock for Merv S. He had arrived after his 50th birthday, via a fondly remembered youth in rugby union, rugby league, and surf lifesaving. All sports yes, but foreign ones to some modern day cricketers, who in the main have never experienced the diversity of sport which was encouraged among the youth of days gone by.

Today it's cricket, cricket and more cricket. Even jobs are spurned in favour of club cricket. It's neither a healthy lifestyle, nor a firm future.

Merv S had tried out for cricket when he was a teenager, going down to Sydney's old Glebe-South Sydney club, where Frank Misson learned the new ball trade so well that he later played under Rich for Australia.

Merv S: "I thought I was a fast bowler. I put my name down then stood at the back of the nets watching their fast bowlers. Comparing talent. After a little while I went back to the secretary and said, "Mate, I'll come back next year!"

So, 'slightly interested in cricket' might have been fair comment on his job application. Still, is it compulsory that a cricket dressing room be filled only with people with linseed oil coursing through their veins? Merv came to the

SCG dressing room with a diploma in remedial massage and rehabilitation. He had a degree in vocational rehabilitation, too, and had been working as the manager of a workshop for the handicapped.

Merv S: "That made me understand life a bit more, working with the handicapped. You don't get upset by little situations."

And, there are a lot of 'little situations' in cricket dressing rooms.

Mike Whitney welcomed him warmly and Merv S appreciated that. "'Whit' … he's one of those blokes you can put all your trust in. He always gave a hundred per cent. He knows cricket, loves the game, seems to impart on people the things that when you're with him make you feel great about the game of cricket."

The NSW opening batsman Steve Small, as fair dinkum a bloke as Whit, used to grab Merv S by the arm and haul him out onto the dressing room verandah where he'd explain to him the fielding positions, the ebb and flow of the game, and the tactics. Soon, Merv S was able to sit down with any member of the team and talk about cricket.

Merv S: "Even though Whit and 'Stumper' (Steve Rixon) are gone I still ring them. One of the great things is I never feel my age when I'm with them. Cricket is the thing I think of most next to my family."

Close up, Merv Hughes looked a lot like one of those 19th century anarchists — swarthy complexion, stubbly beard growth and hooded eyes. Those evil-looking guys who carried in their right hand one of those round shaped black bombs with a wick poking from the top.

Merv threw his own kind of bombs, round and red, and the results were more potent than his many critics were prepared to concede.

When Merv was chosen for the 1989 Ashes tour there was a suggestion doing the rounds that the Australian selection panel had gone into show-business — the prediction was that when Merv approached the bowling crease at Lord's it would be to the accompaniment of 'Send In The Clowns'.

In other words, his personality and not his performance had been the influencing factor in his selection.

Hughes had made his Test debut in the 1985–86 season against India in Adelaide. His lone wicket, Vengsarkar, had cost 123 runs and his form moved the former great England fast bowler, Frank 'Typhoon' Tyson, to explain why Hughes was playing his one and only Test. Frank wasn't alone in that judgment.

Still, by 1989 Ashes selection time Merv had in fact played a few more Tests — 10. And, he had taken 35 wickets. Still not all that flash. His strike-rate was 70 balls a wicket, average nearly 40.

But … 13 of those were in the one game, the Second Test against the West Indies in Perth in 1988–89.

Thirteen wickets in a Test! And the feat was magnified 10 times over because included in his haul was a freakish hat-trick, one which was played out over two innings and a few days.

Euphoria followed — briefly. By the end of the series he had taken only one more wicket. This clear case of bowler's droop inspired his critics, and they were quick to announce that his only chance of generating further hero-worship lay in the clever marketing of the blob of hair growing on his top lip.

The critics forever trivialised Merv's upper lip. More marketable than most it may have been, but from an Australian selector's viewpoint it was also stiffer than most.

Or, put another way, he had some 'guts' — too many, said the critics. It's true 'Big Merv' was 'Too-big Merv' about Third Test time against India in 1991–92, but commonsense tells us not everybody needs to be as slim as a whippet to be any good … Peter Burge, nickname 'Jumbo', a 15-year first-class career, 14,640 runs, average 47.33. Rich: "I tried to get him on a diet at one stage and he couldn't make a run!"

That's part of the charm of cricket — it takes all sizes. Curtly Ambrose and David Boon soon come to mind. The key phrase might be 'cricket fit' when discussing any player's physical shape.

It can be argued that a slim, trim Merv Hughes might not have been able to peform with the explosive success that marked the middle stages of his career; it can also be argued that if he had kept his weight in check his career might have lasted longer.

Armchair selectors despised Merv; fingernails were dug into the seat covers whenever Merv's name was mentioned in the same sentence as success. And real selectors liked Merv for more than just his blood-and-guts mentality — he knew how to play with a batsman's mind. In 1993 he toyed with Graeme Hick's batting *curriculum vitae*, then tore it up with a few short pitchers and the good length leg-cutter.

A summary of Merv's bowling in Tests raises the point that his strike rate — 57.95 balls per wicket — was as good as Ray Lindwall's (59.83).

That is not to say Merv was a better bowler than Lindwall. I'm just saying cricket fans should never forget that Merv Hughes was a useful strike bowler.

Merv had a special talent — he could get his captain 'big' wickets. Ian Chappell, reporting on the 1993 Ashes: "Then, just when it looked like Merv was down for the count he bounced back to remove Maynard and Hussain with two fiery deliveries and boost Australia's hopes of a whitewash."

Merv, hurling bombs. He could turn a game in the space of a couple of balls.

The interesting statistic about Merv's bowling is that he was a potent force in the final innings of a Test match, when a match is won or lost.

This is his comparitive performance, innings by innings:

	Wkts	Ave	5Wkt/i	Best
First inns	70	29.97	–	4/48
Second inns	60	26.33	3	5/64
Third inns	27	28.11	1	5/88
Fourth inns	55	28.73	3	8/87

It's not so easy to pass judgment on another statistic — he had a better strike rate against the West Indies (54 balls per wicket) than he did against England (61).

Was that because he failed to adjust to the slower, less bouncy English pitches? Or did the sight of Greenidge, Haynes, Richards and Co. stir his great competitive spirit more than the sight of whichever cap the Englishmen might have been wearing at the time — the light blue helmet, the dark blue one, the soiled training cap or the traditional cap? It might simply have been a case of Merv bowling too short in England. Or, maybe the West Indian batsmen loved the challenge offered by his short-pitchers.

We have mixed feelings when a cricketer's career ends, simply because some cricketers are our favourites more than others. The influencing factor might be the player's personality as much as his talent. How do you remember Terry Alderman — a flash of white teeth, the outswinger, Gooch leg before?

What about Ian Chappell — his hassle or his hook shot? And, Merv Hughes — bully, buffoon or gut-buster? The ones who think of cricket as some sort of genteel sport think there's no place in the game for players like Merv, who intimidated batsmen with a mix of bumpers, leg-cutters and scowls. But Lindwall was intimidating — he just did it without the scowl, a dividend of modern technology close-ups, as much as of a fast bowler's demeanour.

For all the 53 Tests of his career, the single most compelling characteristic about Merv Hughes' cricket was his courage. No matter how much work he'd done, no matter how much he was hurting he'd never give up. He'd bore in.

His courage was never greater than on the 1993 Ashes tour when Craig McDermott broke down and Allan Border asked Merv to make up for the loss.

Merv bowled nearly 300 overs in six Tests — one thousand seven hundred and seventy eight balls, each effort grinding away, relentlessly rupturing the mechanics of his knees. They would turn to rubble, sooner or later.

We can compare that effort with the 1989 Ashes when Merv bowled 190 overs in six Tests, and his career average per Test, which was 39.

Six months after that 1993 Ashes series Merv played his next Test, followed by his last. The 'next' was at the Wanderer's in Johannesburg, the notorious 'bullring', where, when he was dismissed caught off Brian McMillan's nit-picking bowling, a foul-mouthed fan abused him as he returned to the pavilion.

There was a time when an Australian team in a far-off place might get away with an on-field incident because a lone photographer present mightn't get lucky. And the words of the 10 journalists present were soon forgotten. But now there are 10 television cameras beaming pictures around the world, every minute of every day's play.

Players who contemplate boof-headed behaviour — such as Shane Warne's verbal abuse of Andrew Hudson on that 1994 tour of South Africa and Ian Healy's bat-hurling on the 1997 tour there — fail a simple intelligence test: how will this go over in the lounge rooms back home?

So, into cricket's film archives went the blow-by-blow footage of Merv's unforgiveable confrontation with an abusive fan; Merv banging his bat on a nearby metal advertising hoarding. Nice image — Australian cricket hero attacks unfriendly fan.

Merv's 'last' Test was his next, at Capetown. The great fast bowler didn't take a wicket, or score a run. It was a tough call on a tough competitor (one of only five in Tests, Ray Lindwall, Malcolm Marshall, Abdul Qadir, Wasim Akram, who had taken 200 wickets and scored 1000 runs) who was doing it tough. Merv, a fast bowler who'd have run through a brick wall to take a wicket for his country, had hit the wall.

If Merv H was a rip-and-tear, runaway, angry rhino then it is one of the delightful vagaries of the game that the man who oversaw his selection was as gentle and as unobtrusive as a nudge for one from any silken-wristed opening batsman.

THE COLONEL

Laurie Sawle was chairman of Australian selectors
from 1984 to 1995 — the toughest and the sweetest of
times. He was a calm and compassionate judge whose
influence on the modern trends in the Australian
game should never be forgotten.

Any game that has survived as long as cricket has encourages a continual search for coincidence, however stretched. In 1925, the year when Lou began his teaching career at the little State school on the edge of the farm at North Casino, over on the other side of the continent at East Fremantle, near Perth, Laurie Sawle was born.

He too was raised on a farming property, just across the road from which was a tiny State school; its name was South Coogee, the name of the Sydney suburb where Rich was to spend much of his life after cricket.

And Laurie Sawle became a schoolteacher like Lou … Rich played against him when, as a stoic left-hander, Laurie opened the batting for Western Australia in the 1950s against NSW and scored his only Sheffield Shield century … I selected Test teams with him in the 1990s.

Laurie was a beneficiary of the selection caper very early in life. To stay open, the South Coogee school needed a minimum of 12 pupils. One year it was one short and Laurie, although officially deemed 'underage' at four and a half years, got the nod for 12th 'man' and saved a teacher's job, and possibly a school.

His cricket education was less controversial. His father, Thomas, laid a concrete pitch on the property and bowled mediums to Laurie; his two brothers Stan and Kevin, taller than Laurie, bowled fast enough to give him an early taste of his later life as an opening bat.

Laurie, as befits an educator, played his cricket with the University club where he once experienced the form lapse that makes selectors nervous, and was dropped to the Second grade. The events that followed probably prove, as much as any recorded in cricket history, that the game is uncertain, and that selectors can make baffling judgments.

Laurie's Second grade match was interrupted by rain and on a wet pitch Laurie made a 'pair', any batsman's worst nightmare let alone one who's just been dropped.

But these were dream times for Laurie's University club — two or three of their First grade players, among them John Rutherford, a 1956 Ashes tourist with Rich, were in the Western Australian team. And, because University's next match coincided with a Sheffield Shield match, Laurie went back up to First grade as one of the replacement players.

Somewhat ironic, wouldn't you say, that the future chairman of the Australian selection panel was once promoted on the strength of a pair?

Physically, he is neither tall nor robust. Mentally, he is both. There is a sharpness to Laurie Sawle's features that matches his mind. Often, the skin at the edges of his eyes and mouth is sparrow-footed, creased in the squint of assessment, concentration. The bottom lip bitten, too.

His eyes are gimlet-sharp. His ears are just a tad prominent — antennae. You get the impression that if Laurie Sawle missed any tricks in his 72 years it must have been in a time long, long gone.

If Laurie strolled past you in the street, most probably he'd be sartorially comfortable in a plain sports jacket and trousers, and he'd not turn your head as would say the long-striding, head erect Greg Chappell, another one of cricket's 'kings'. Eh? you say … Laurie Sawle, up there with Greg Chappell in Australian cricket history?

Well, should stats and style be the only guidelines we consider in comparisons of cricketers and their contribution to the game? Laurie's stats as an opening batsman were what the modernists term 'shockers' — 1701 first-class runs, one century, average 28, four times captain, four losses.

Greg's were sensational — 24,535 first-class runs, 74 hundreds, average 52, captain 117 times for 50 wins.

Greg got the MBE for services to cricket. And Laurie? Well, in 1992 he was awarded the Order of Australia for his part in the rise of Australian cricket, a task to which he had devoted the best part of half his life.

Laurie only played first-class cricket for seven summers, until 1960–61; from then, until the mid-'90s, his influence on the first-class game was from beyond the boundary. Watching the game.

Imagine it — half his life spent selecting cricket teams. And for no pay. It was a commitment that brought to mind Lou's remark, "What is it about cricket that produces such love of the game and such loyalty to the game?"

To Laurie Sawle, watching the game of cricket was an attraction no less compelling than the art of scoring runs was to Greg Chappell. And, at the end of the day the satisfaction for each man was just as deep.

It's just that outsiders find it more difficult to acknowledge Laurie's great contribution because it was backstage, not centre-stage.

Laurie said of watching cricket, cricketers and selection: "It doesn't matter whether its four, five or six days, I never get sick of it. To me you can look at so many aspects of the game other than just the scoreboard."

The 'scoreboard' remark goes right to the heart of discussion about cricketers and their contributions to the game, and how they might best be judged.

What does a selector look for in a batsman? Laurie acknowledged the 'general things' — technique and footwork, the obvious ones. But most appealing were the batsmen with unwavering concentration, the ones who could apply themselves over time, the ones who could make big scores.

Lest you think Laurie was advocating the wholesale selection of chartered accountants — run-of-the-mill run accumulators — rest assured he was eagerly on the lookout for batsmen who wouldn't give it up at the first sign of pressure. The ones who liked to get into a fight. The scrappers.

Remember, a big score isn't always just the result of conscientious plodding, the great batsmen make their big scores in a flurry of focus just as fastidious.

And, what about bowlers? Laurie liked the ones who could make the ball do something, swing in the air, or bend or break off the pitch. But no matter what aspect of the game it was, he sought out the player whose performance was a bit different, somewhere above the ordinary.

Commonsense really, but as history shows, not everyone knows how to apply commonsense properly.

To be a selector you need a sense of humour, too, and Laurie appreciated that. When acknowledging his good fortune in being reinstated to University Firsts after his duck 'double', he confessed, "In my first game back up, before I'd scored, I was dropped in the slips. It was a 'sitter' ... I made 122, and followed it with another century the next week!" And he said it with a chuckle.

In the one breath he had acknowledged the luck of the game, and announced his commonsense and his sense of humour. There was a generation gap between Laurie and those he chose but his sense of humour closed it as easily as the famous 'coathanger' links the north and south of Sydney's harbour.

On the 1989 Ashes tour, when he was manager, he played golf at St Andrews with some of Border's team. After failing to play anywhere near his 19 handicap, he observed, "This is a funny course, it doesn't have any fairways."

And, after the team had won at Lord's to go two-up in the series, and Merv Hughes was grabbing $50 bottles of champagne, ripping out the corks, then shaking them and spraying everyone and everything in range, I heard Laurie say to the 'roomie', "For heaven's sake hide the rest, or there won't be any left to drink."

His humour was generally on the dry side. After one Test selection a critic painted it controversial, then inferred that Laurie didn't know what he was doing and that it could only be because he'd never played for Australia.

"Oh, the Australian selectors never gave me a go," responded Laurie, face dead straight. And, then he made the rather telling point that, "If you added up all the players touted by the media you wouldn't need to be a mathematical genius to figure that it doesn't fit into eleven."

People go to Montego Bay, on Jamaica's north-west coast for a few good reasons — to spend money, to frolic in its turquoise waters, to flop on its golden sands, or to party.

Early in Ian Chappell's 1973 tour of the West Indies, the closest we'd come to a party was sitting around the pool helping Doug Walters sing "Sa-a-a-d Movies Always Make Me Cry", or "Itsy Bitsy Teeny Weeny Yellow Polka Dot Bikini". Men will be boys.

The tour schedule said: February 9–12, versus Board President's XI — one of those matches when you expect to play against cricketers the home town selectors think will be their next generation of Test stars.

The pitch for the match was as orange as a punk rocker's hair, rolled clay and cracking, grassless under the baking sun. For Bob Massie, Australia's super swing bowler, it was culture shock.

Barely seven months had passed since he had indulged himself in the combined tasks of sorting and reading congratulatory telegrams and popping champagne corks — he had taken 16 wickets (eight for 84 and eight for 53) on his Lord's Test debut.

That was June, 1972 and the newly acclaimed King of Swing had made merry beneath a shroud of leaden skies and a heavy atmosphere on a pitch that looked helpfully green.

Now, in February, 1973, I was waiting at short forward leg for Massie to bowl, my feet planted, body crouched low, hands cupped at the waist, head straining forward. In those days protective helmets with grilles and shin pads hadn't come into the game, and some of us were silly enough to field at silly leg without even a 'box' on.

I heard the ball, rather than saw it, not as it came past my left ear, swinging in on its way to the batsman, a half-volley on his toes, but as it went past my right ear, rocketing on its way to the boundary.

I sometimes think about that moment, and even today it generates pursed lips, a frown and a slight nervous twitch — a ball's diameter to the left and it would have hit me square between the eyes. I guess I'd have been dead.

The batsman's name was Greenidge, Cuthbert Gordon Greenidge, soon to be of Greenidge and Haynes. C. G. Greenidge was 22 years old, M. (for Michael) Holding was 19, and even then you could see, feel excited by the sweet rhythm of his run-in, if not yet menaced by his still developing pace. C. Lloyd captained that team.

I. V. A. Richards, age 21, played too, our first sighting — brief, as it turned out, because Viv made only 18 and five — of a batsman who was already being rated a champion. His swagger was just a strut then. A dozen days and a Test match later we tangled with Viv again, on his home turf.

It was at the St John's ground in Antigua, where today there's a grandstand named after him. We came to the ground from the Jolly Beach resort, new and luxurious, but a daily return journey of many, many miles, bumping along a rutted tar road in a small yellow bus.

One morning we witnessed the killing of a steer in the town square, a sort of instant meat market. Down the road, the great Dennis Lillee got off the bus and an hour or two later slaughtered the Leeward Islands top order. Young Viv was one of his four cheap wickets, caught Ian Chappell at first slip for five — then Lillee broke down with his back injury and never bowled again on the tour.

But selection judgments, made a world apart, were already in place to generate one of the greatest personal battles cricket — sport — has seen, Lillee versus Richards. Such contests are not unique, but are more prevalent in the individual sports — Ali versus Frazier, Nicklaus versus Palmer, Hoad versus Gonzales.

How many of the modern day head-to-head cricket clashes can stimulate your expectations as did Lillee versus Richards? Maybe Warne versus Tendulkar and Warne versus Lara?

Such contests raise another aspect of cricket selection: how much weight should 'entertainment value' carry in judging any player's worth? Rick McCosker wasn't adventurous enough for some, nor was Ian Redpath. Or Bruce Laird. And, on his own not one was a drawcard. But they had entertainers around them — the Chappells, Walters.

The trick of good selection is also the trick of good batting and good bowling — get the balance right between discretion and valour.

In the mid-'60s, from beyond the boundary of Fletcher Park in Perth, the home ground of the Perth club, Laurie Sawle saw a young Dennis Lillee and, at Bassendean-Bayswater he saw the young Bob Massie.

The sight of Lillee bowling excited him, just as Warren Saunders had been excited by Jeff Thomson — it's the raw pace. "They don't come along often," says Laurie.

Lillee was a tearaway, quick and raw. His enormous determination was obvious, even from the sidelines, before you spoke to him. You could see that he expected to get a wicket all the time. You could see that it never crossed his mind that he might have to give in.

Massie … I wish we had someone like him today, a swing bowler for that new ball period into the wind. We used to categorise new ball bowlers once upon a time, fast, medium and swing.

But these days it seems to be all 'pace' — fast bowlers are all in one bracket … digging it in, not giving the ball air. There seems to be a feeling around that swing bowlers are too slow.

"I don't know whether it's something to do with the coaching, or they're just trying to hit the wicketkeeper's gloves hard," says Laurie, and you can tell he's not happy about it. Nor should anyone be, because it has taken away some of the game's romance, some of its instructive qualities, some of its variety.

'Pace' is a 'generic'. These days 'generic' is a term mostly used by the advertising industry to describe an ad that is repeated over and over to reinforce product message, like people drawing little squiggles for the ABC and going 'doo-dah-doo'. The result can be tedious, if not mind-dulling.

Everyone in Australian cricket knows Laurie Sawle as 'Colonel'; and he did spend time in the army in World War II as a foot-slogger in New Guinea. But that's not how he got the nickname. His organisational skills had so impressed the 'troops' — his fellow boarders at University — they rewarded him with a rank appropriate to his skills.

It's a pity the Australian Cricket Board didn't show the same good judgment when they had the chance to make him chairman in the early 1990s. Instead, they bypassed his passion for the game, his genuine commitment to the future strength of the game, and his absolute integrity.

They overlooked his success in convincing the States that their selfishness in continuing to do their own thing was detrimental to the development process; it was his vision that youth championships properly organised could be usefully fitted around the philosophy of the national selection panel; it was his preference that the Cricket Academy intake undergo a shift in emphasis

— rather than just picking a young team, a better option would be to choose individual players whose skills would strengthen Australian cricket's most immediate needs.

They forgot that he always put the good of the game before anything else. Chairman material, no doubt about that — he had shown he was able to straddle the personalities of the boardroom. "... And the politics," someone might add. Well, not quite.

During his successful management of the 1989 Ashes tour, he had been sounded out by an influential Board member to stand as chairman. He was guaranteed strong support. In modern times that has been enough — the chairman has been 'anointed', regarded by consensus as the best man for the job. It makes sense — who wants a Board divided by 'ayes' and 'nays'?

Then, although Laurie was a 'good thing', South Australia nominated the former umpire, Col Egar. Laurie didn't bother standing even though he'd probably have won the vote.

Which shouldn't surprise anyone. He never called for a vote on his selection panels, just a searching, balanced discussion about the merits of the men for the job, and our decision was made by consensus.

A vote. When you think about it can there be any quicker way to promote divisiveness and then to highlight it?

By the end of the 1996–97 season 15 ex-students of the Cricket Academy had gone on to play for Australia, at either Test or One-day level. Joe Scuderi was not among them, yet on a bleak day at the world's most beautiful cricket ground he showed he was made of the right stuff.

JOE

"Without a water supply the pitch was extremely sporting.
On the morning of the match about all the preparation it
got was the scythe and the roller" — cricket report, 1862.
Cricket pitches today are 'shirtfronts', but that doesn't
mean a team can't get rolled.

At a best forgotten moment in time, some blockheaded politician camouflaged the Sydney Cricket Ground's unique scoreboard with a hideous concrete structure; this environmental outrage was then magnified with an insult to Doug Walters — the words The Doug Walters Stand were bolted on to a block of the concrete.

'Dashing Doug', one of NSW and Australian cricket's favourite sons, deserved a statue. They should have named the toilet block in the bloody concrete jumble after the politician.

After the politicians stripped the SCG of just about all of its magnificence, the ground staff dutifully got into the spirit of things by doing the same with the playing surface and by Test time in the 1996–97 season any cricketer's heaven was hell.

The Adelaide Oval is now Australian cricket's most delightful setting, its centrepiece the traditional scoreboard on the hill and, at the edges, the rolling ranges and the spires of St Peters. The Victor Richardson Gates and Bradman's architecturally grand stand are suitable acknowledgments to great cricketers.

The pitch and surrounds, prepared by the curator Les Burdett are also the best in Australia. Of course, Les has more than a scythe and a roller in his machinery shed, but there would be a cricketer or two prepared to wager Les is talented enough to get by with those alone.

Usually there's a Test match at the Adelaide Oval on the Australia Day long weekend, one of Adelaide's sporting and social high points. However, cricket's administrators sometimes forget when they're on a good thing and, in 1990, on that particular weekend, South Australia began a Sheffield Shield match against the reigning champions, Western Australia.

Like all Sheffield Shield matches it was scheduled to last four days. It lasted three and reinforced the adage about cricket being a strange game.

On a pleasant, summery Adelaide January day what possibly could have possessed the Western Australian captain, Graeme Wood, to offer first bat on a 'Burdett Belter' to David Hookes' South Australians?

And, to Hookes in particular? For 14 summers since 1976 'Hookesy', his eyes ablaze under the peak of that Croweaters' cap he rakishly propped atop his long blond hair, had been delighting the Adelaide faithful with his trademark batting style, carefree and clubbing.

In the 1976–77 season the Adelaide scoreboard rollers had been in overdrive when he scored 163, 9, 185, 105, 135, 156 in consecutive innings.

So, none of we spectators at the Adelaide Oval on January 26, 1990 were really surprised when David issued his RSVP to Wood's kind invitation to bat: another century, 118 off 151 balls.

The scorer, Rita Artis, pencilled in five sixes. Five sixes in one innings is impressive, yet ironically the memorial to Hookesy's cricket career will remain five boundaries — the ones he hit from crowd villain Tony Greig's over in the Melbourne Centenary Test of 1977.

It's a memory that raises the question: whatever happened to a Test career that promised so much? Dogged by impatience probably. He was a six-Test veteran and 22 years old when he rushed off to World Series Cricket.

Eleven innings into his WSC career an Andy Roberts bouncer broke his jaw. Maybe maturity might have been better developed, and less painfully, in the less intense arena of the 'official' game.

Was he too brash? Spinners as diverse as Derek Underwood, Eddie Hemmings, Larry Gomes, Albert Padmore and Geoff Miller often had their way with him. When he was dropped against India in 1985 his career inconsistency was no comfort to the conspiracy theorists.

As a WSC 'graduate' it was reasonable to expect there should have been a substantial improvement in his 'official' Test performance:

In Tests (before World Series Cricket)				
M	Runs	HScore	100s	Ave
6	356	85	0	32.26
In World Series Cricket				
M	Runs	HScore	100s	Ave
64	1717	116	1	24.18
In Tests (after World Series Cricket)				
M	Runs	HScore	100s	Ave
17	950	143	1	35.17

If cricket is fickle, what about the weather? The second day of the match dawned damp. Looking into the distance from the players' rooms the normally blue hue of the Lofty Ranges was masked by the white mists of showery rain. Soon they swept across the oval itself, coming and going like serving staff at a banquet.

Before play began that day the covers were on, then off, then on again. A depressing sight, only one sight less depressing than seeing your favourite batsman trooping off, run out for a duck on his debut, and without facing a ball from some exponent of lollipops.

Hookes, having exercised his heavy Gray-Nicholls the previous day, now saw a chance to exercise his imagination. He declared when rain abruptly halted play — again. About an hour's play in all had been possible after a delayed start.

These days, some captains are so cautious about chasing a result that they'd have thought, 'wet ball', and squibbed it, even with 8 for 371 on the scoreboard.

By mid-afternoon play was finally back on. The pitch was still hard, but had been exposed to the misting rain for brief periods, either during the hour's play in the morning or in the time it took the ground staff to get the covers down after being summoned by the umpires.

The light was certainly not bad, quite even in fact, but it had about it an eeriness that seemed somehow to give the outfield a greener look. Mike Veletta, a 1987 World Cup hero and former Test batsman, and Mark McPhee, a rookie, opened the batting for Western Australia.

It was slow, steady, undramatic, stuff in conditions that were slightly overcast and cold, rather than cool. A boundary was punched, but mostly there were deflections for two, or pushed singles against the bowling attack of Shane George and Colin Miller. George, greyhound-like, young, enthusiastic and at times very quick, came from the scoreboard end; Miller, a swing-seamer, bowled from the Bradman Stand end.

Veletta was the first out, and it came out of the blue really. George had him well caught off a hook shot 'flier' by the running Miller out deepish at fine leg.

Rita Artis noted his time at the crease — 43 minutes. Western Australia were one for 23 and the new batsman was Tom Moody, the Test player. When a captain changes his bowling he expects to make an impact on a match. Naturally, the result can be variable.

When Arthur Mailey was thrown the ball against Victoria in the 1926–27 season it's unlikely his captain expected Mailey's innings analysis would be 64 overs, no maidens, four for 362 or that Victoria would eventually amass a record high team score, 1107. David Hookes threw the ball to Joe Scuderi, a seam bowler of sharpish medium pace.

There haven't been too many 'Joes' on the Australian first-class cricket scene ... a couple who played for Australia were Joe Darling and Joe Travers, but that was at the turn of the century. And, with a name like Scuderi and a birth-place of Ingham, up in north Queensland sugar country, it's reasonable that we might have expected this Joe to have felt more at home shining a cane cutter's machete than a new cricket ball.

But he learned his cricket well enough, and did so well in his cricketing youth that he was nominated for the Cricket Academy. And, he rated a mention at the selection table for the 1989 Ashes tour.

Joe Scuderi was born on Christmas Eve, 1968, an event that can either raise the expectation of two helpings of presents, or heighten the disappoint-ment of being asked by Santa Claus not, "What do you want for Christmas?" but, "What did you get for your birthday?"

On that afternoon in Adelaide, January 27, 1990, all Joe Scuderi's birth-days and Christmases seemed to come at once. Short, stocky and swarthy, as you might expect of a dark-haired, olive complexioned young man of Italian descent, and with a brisk arm action at the end of a bustling run, Joe bowled McPhee with his first ball.

With his 26th ball he ended the Western Australian innings when he had Capes caught by the wicketkeeper. His innings analysis was 4.2 overs, one maiden, six wickets for six. It remains the Sheffield Shield's best 'six-for', challenged only by Colin Miller (6 for 12 off five overs, one maiden) and Simon Davis (6 for 19 off 15.4 overs, four maidens).

Western Australia were all out for 41. The captain Wood made two, which looked good because the last seven batsman raised only three runs between them. The innings was over in 110 minutes.

As a yardstick, Darren Lehmann had scored 41 in the South Australian first innings and that had taken 94 minutes. A procession of Western Aus-tralian batsmen filed off the field wondering, "Gee, what happened there?"

Well, it is possible that the pitch had 'juiced up' a bit. It had been rock hard, with a grass cover as thin as a slice of prosciutto, perfect. But, the rain had given it a light watering, much as a man in his garden might achieve us-ing a very fine hose spray.

And, the covers were on for about three hours, so sweating was a possi-bility. But, it was a cold day ... sweating was surely out of the question. Cer-tainly though, some moisture would have been preserved.

Did the batsmen have a fear that the pitch may behave poorly? From my watching position in the Bradman Stand, directly behind Scuderi, there was no untoward behaviour of the ball, such as irregular bounce or movement. The pitch was not two-paced. And the fact that Veletta survived for 43 minutes, McPhee 64 minutes and Moody 35 minutes supports that.

Did the pitch deteriorate? No. If anything, the bowling got better, because in such conditions fast bowlers, especially young ones, often have an adrenalin rush, get over-aggressive and bowl too short. Remember, Veletta was out hooking.

Were the Western Australians mentally off the pace? It's possible. Long rain delays can impair focus, induce relaxation. They may have been feeling negative about the fact that the captain, who was now expecting them to bat sensibly in less than ideal conditions, was the same captain who the day before had offered South Australia perfect batting conditions.

Some spectators at Adelaide Oval that day said they thought there was a bit of all that in the demolition of the Western Australian batting, but I won't concede that.

I think Joe Scuderi returned the best first-class bowling figures of his life simply by sticking to the most basic fundamentals of bowling — bowling straight, and on a good, full length. And, he had the talent to move the ball, in the air and off the pitch.

And, here's the remarkable proof: the dismissal of Veletta, caught in the outfield wide of fine leg, was the only dismissal completed beyond the width of the pitch.

Every other Western Australian batsman was either bowled, leg before or caught by the wicketkeeper! You can't bowl much straighter or much fuller than that.

Joe had a habit of bowling straight. Of his 154 wickets a third were bowled or leg before. And, as a new ball bowler, he did his job — a third of his victims were the 'top three'. His value as an allrounder was obvious. He averaged 29.26 batting at No.7, and 49.88 batting at No.8.

Joe bowled good outswing but missed the 1989 Ashes tour when Greg Campbell, a rookie swing bowler from Tasmania was chosen. Reading the minds of Test cricket selectors is not to be encouraged, and there are good reasons for that.

ARMCHAIRS

*I used to be an Armchair Selector, a laidback responsibility
to be sure, involving nothing more than tossing a dozen or
more names into an old, fading Greg Chappell cricket hat,
shaking, then drawing out the lucky eleven.*

April 1990

Armchair Selecting is a case of a tinnie or two while earnestly assessing the
national averages or viewing the Test telecasts, then choosing away. Because
Armchair Selecting involves little care, no responsibility and all ego, it is compulsory to program the mind to Gamble Mode.

This means choosing some kid from the backblocks of the Northern Territory to make his Test debut against the Poms; every Armchair Selector
strives to be the first to discover another Bradman or another Walters, the
boys from the bush who made good.

Now it's no more Armchair for me; two summers ago by a quirk of
cricketing fate as strange as that which once decreed the all-mighty Greg
Chappell register fairly close to a flock of ducks in a hat-trick of matches, I
was voted onto the official Australian cricket selection panel.

I say strange only because some found it ironic that about a score of years
before I'd been banned from the game by officials who didn't like a revolu-
tionary boot that I was wearing.

So, I joined the other selectors, Laurie Sawle, Jim Higgs and Bob Simpson.
Sawle, the chairman, has a leanness about him that draws envious looks from
the rest of us as we hurtle towards middle age and its accompanying spread.

Higgs is a ruddy-faced gregarious Victorian, an engineer by profession and
the youngest member of the panel. He played for Australia under Simpson
and Greg Chappell for whom he bowled teasing legspinners, an art that needs
to be dispensed by a person with mischief in his mind and a big wooden
spoon in his back pocket. That's Higgs.

Simpson wears two hats; he is also the Australian team coach. When he
captained Australia in the '60s he was a very smart fielder and, the ultimate
thief when it came to stealing runs when batting, traits he has relentlessly
developed in the current Australian team.

A Real Selector watches a lot of cricket; in 65 days this season, from the end of October to the New Year, I watched 30 days. The venues were widespread: Sydney, Brisbane (three times), Adelaide, Canberra, Launceston and Hobart.

Getting there was ... well, a bit of a wing and a prayer job, given the pilots' dispute — "Welcome yo-all, we do hope yo' enjoy flying with American West" ... or, "G'day, you'll find this Hercules is a bit different to what you've been used to."

A Real Selector loves the game, a lot; I don't find that difficult. The celebrated cricket writer, Neville Cardus, wrote, "The game has infinite variety, played by men free to be themselves. It can shake fire out of us or lull us to a summer time contentedness."

A Real Selector gets no tinnies (on duty), just the odd soda water or an ice cream to keep the mind bright enough to analyse hour after hour of a Sheffield Shield match, the breeding ground of the Test cricketer, or the launching pad for the World Series smashers.

Armchair Selectors get only to see the batting averages or the batsman second-hand via the television; we get to watch a batsman live, to study his footwork, to delight in his powerful, aggressive strokes ... to 'tsk, tsk' silently at his impetuosity.

But there is no little black book for temperamental offenders, just a slight squint to the mind's eye: how will he cope when the going gets really tough on an underprepared pitch or one so green with grass that you'd expect to see Peter Garrett in the groundsman's garb?

Alas, therefore, Cardus's summer time contentedness is enjoyed more by spectators than finicky selectors. To be sure there is comfort attached to the job: there are the armchairs in the executive rooms at the 'Gabba — but the view is just a shade too low and the air conditioning a shade too high.

So, the selector repairs to the discomfort of the too-high-backed green wooden seats in the grandstand right behind the bowler's arm to see how far those Banana Boys can really bend the new ball.

Selectors like opening bowlers who can master the art of making the ball swing in the air or deviate it sharply when it hits the pitch. Pace like fire helps, but it isn't always the bottom line. Finesse might outlast fury.

Even the Border Boys' blitz job on the Poms followed by the triumphs in the tough home campaigns last summer are not enough to make a selector content; there's sure to be 'a cement truck' around the corner, like a scoreline of 'all out for a hundred'! Cricket is a great leveller.

Euphoria for some: 'Peter Who?' crowed the headline writers when Peter Taylor was introduced to the Test team a few summers back.

Despair for another: 'Whit-less Ashes Team' was the headline when Mike Whitney missed the 1989 team to England. Such controversies are often the product of the media in the first place.

The newspaper cricket writers, most of whom have never grasped a six-stitcher let alone tortuously peeled off a jock strap, are the most obvious Armchair Selectors. The day before the Real Selectors do their thing you can pick up any sports section and read: "A probable Test team is ..." and if it doesn't turn out to the writer's liking, well, enter "Peter Who?"

Real Selectors are historically conservative. That does not mean they are afraid to take a gamble on a player, rather that if they do then down the line they must be prepared to back their judgment with reasonable perseverance.

Real Selectors need to be able to differentiate between character and crap, performance and piffle; they need thick, thick skins to soak up the invective, the innuendo when they do take a risk; they need a relative in the medical game to help them cope with fitness (or unfitness) reports littered with terms such as antero-lateral portal, intra-articular ganglion, intercondylar region and inflamed ligamentum mucosum.

And finally ... although PM Bob Hawke has determined that 'Peter Who' was a more appealing front page headline than 'Interest Rates Up Again' and reintroduced the annual Prime Minister's XI matches, it doesn't mean Real Selectors have any regard for marginal electorates.

There might be any number of reasons why selectors choose not to choose a player. Religion is not usually one of them, however ... when I was a young cricketer I had some trouble staying in the All Saints, Parramatta, Under-15 team.

All Saints, denomination Church of England, stands alongside Victoria Road, not far from where Gordon Rorke possibly considered blasphemy a perfectly appropriate response the day Harold Goodwin hit him to the heavens above Cumberland Oval.

Blasphemy was never likely to pass the lips of the fellow who selected/managed/coached the All Saints junior team — he was a true blue Anglican. He told his young cricketing brethren that I needed to be dropped, not so much on the grounds that I was a Presbyterian and, therefore something of a ring-in, but more because I had refused his demand to attend his Sunday School, and thus automatically become an All Saint.

The Lord then moved in a mysterious way — He organised the rest of the boys into a sort of cricketing trade union, which successfully induced the fellow to see the light and retain my services as the team's in-form opening batsman.

Sole selectors cannot be good for cricket. In England Ian Botham was said to have floated the idea that the England selection panel should be eliminated and, in its place, there should be a sole selector/manager, along the lines of the English soccer set-up.

The All Saints experience demonstrates, albeit in its most basic form, that sole selectors can be hellishly unpredictable. And anyway, football is a pattern game, ideally suited to a single mind in charge. Cricket's uncertainty demands more variety of opinion.

That's the trouble with Armchair Selectors — they are sole selectors. My favourite was a gentleman named L. J. Cooray whose outpourings into a word processor used to arrive in my mailbox from time to time during the five years I spent on the national panel.

They were headed Notes For Selectors and included a reminder for me of Sir Donald Bradman's philosophy that in choosing players of near-equal ability, fielding should be the determining factor.

After the First Test of 1992 between Australia and the West Indies 'LJ' became aggressive. The match had finished in a draw, disappointing if you were an Australian. The West Indies were four for nine early in their second innings but eight for 133 at stumps.

The scorebook says they were saved by the captain Richie Richardson's watchful 66, a cool innings. In the face of some disputed umpiring decisions late in the game Allan Border's men lost their cool, and their focus and, worst of all, a wonderful chance to go to a one-nil lead in the series.

LJ was immediately on to the front foot — at the bottom of page one he described me as a "pea-brain". And, what in earlier correspondence had been "suggestions" now became "demands" — he demanded that for the Second Test team we selectors should eliminate the following players from our discussions, and gave reasons:

- Merv Hughes — loses his cool, tries to bowl too fast and is mercilessly thrashed by the West Indies.
- Bruce Reid — injury prone; shouldn't have been chosen for the Brisbane Test because of his poor World Cup record. (I'm still unsure as to what influence the 1992 World Cup form could have possibly had on a Test selection six months later).
- S Waugh — only plays well against teams that have no fast bowlers.
- G Matthews — poor record against the West Indies.
- Dean Jones — ditto.
- T Moody — can't play fast yorkers.

That's the scorched earth approach to selection — LJ might not have realised it, but he had made a large crater in the outfit that had almost got the money in the First Test. This was what he had left:

Boon, Taylor, _____ , M Waugh, Martyn, Border, Healy, _____ , _____ , _____ , McDermott, _____ .

And, this was his solution: "Having selected McDermott you would be well advised to choose the best medium pace bowlers in Australia who swing and move the ball, bowl accurately and use their brains."

But LJ failed to name one of them. Laurie Sawle always thought Armchair Selectors had a decided advantage over Real Selectors — "Their combinations are never tested," he said.

For the most part, Armchair Selectors are harmless and good entertainment. Their theories generally promote healthy discussion about the game, player styles and tactics.

Not so harmless are those among the modern media hunting headlines with their tape recorders and zoom lens, the ones looking for any one-minute grab that will take 10 years off the life of that day's hero. In the '90s it's all called new technology, 25 years ago it was just a 'knife job'.

In January 1972, the sporting editor of *The Sydney Morning Herald* made an extraordinary attack on Ian Chappell and his captaincy during the fourth unofficial Test match between Australia and The Rest Of The World XI.

> On his performance yesterday Ian Chappell should not be in charge of a ludo team, let alone an Australian side bound for a Test series in England. To describe his captaincy yesterday as woeful is to be kind in the extreme.
>
> His management of bowlers, field placements and changing situations was pathetic. Moreover, Chappell's persistence with leg spinner Terry Jenner was an ill-concealed attempt to bowl his South Australian team-mate into the Australian side to tour England at the expense of Kerry O'Keeffe and perhaps others.
>
> I hold no brief for O'Keeffe as a Test bowler but he was not given a 'fair go' by Chappell yesterday. Jenner, on the other hand, was given every opportunity to impress the watching selectors and to get figures 'on the board'.
>
> Chappell gave him the ball after both the luncheon and tea breaks and on a number of occasions just after a wicket had fallen. Batsmen are most suspect at these times. Their concentration has been broken or there is a newcomer to bowl at.

Despite this 'help', Jenner bowled what used to be called a 'load of old rubbish' and thoroughly deserved his unflattering figures of one for 69 off 18 overs.

That the World XI, with a long tail, managed to recover from six for 68 to a total of 277 is to Chappell's lasting discredit. Consider what he did to that big-hearted powerhouse Dennis Lillee.

With only eight overs to go before the new ball could be taken, Chappell gave him the old ball and then, the supreme insult to a fast bowler, only one slip, a gully and the next man no closer than 20 yards to the bat.

As one great fast bowler of recent years said to me: 'If a skipper did that to me I would give him back the ball and tell him exactly where to put it.'

Suffice it to say that Jenner, operating his 'lollypops' from the other end was given an almost identical field to that of Lillee.

Even when Lillee was given the new ball Chappell set only two slips (one of whom was removed to the covers three balls later) and a gully.

Not much of an encouragement for Australia's best fast bowling prospect since Alan Davidson retired.

The comments prompted two notable responses: Ian Chappell said nothing (publicly, anyway) but came out and scored 119 the next day and, about a fortnight later, the editor of the *Herald* received a letter.

As chairman of the Australian Board of Control I find it incumbent upon me to write and protest against the article by your sporting editor on January 10.

As a TV spectator of the game, I believe these criticisms were unwarranted or grossly exaggerated. But they were dwarfed by his blatant imputation that Chappell unfairly gave his team-mate Jenner advantages to the detriment of O'Keeffe.

Such an insinuation of lack of integrity against the man who is currently Australia's cricket captain is a serious charge. Chappell already has a great record as a worthy Australian representative. What qualifications has your sporting editor to judge a cricket situation?

So far as I am aware he has never played in a first-class cricket match. Chappell has been a Test player for many years and already has vast international experience in many countries.

That his judgment of what to do and when to do it on a cricket field should be questioned, not only in quality but to the extent of integrity, by a man in your sporting editor's position forces me to rise in Chappell's defence because obviously he, himself, is not in a position to refute the allegation.

At a time when a very large section of our publicity media is rediscovering the qualities of cricket as a national asset and giving it a 'fair go', it is disappointing that someone, whose position to influence people's opinions far outweighs his knowledge of the subject, should descend to such criticism.

Chappell is too big a person to be interested in petty State jealousies. (Signed) D. G. Bradman,
(Sir Donald Bradman),
Kensington Park, SA.

Sir Donald going public in such a way was rare. Other letters to the editor followed, noting the "violent rupture of his silence barrier" and his "long-standing disinclination to talk to the press".

Clearly Sir Donald was very angry. Yet, his response was a fair while coming — why? One can only assume it took him that long to investigate thoroughly the background to such a detailed attack on Chappell.

Sir Donald sent three messages in that letter. The least important was to a sporting editor whom he had discovered possessed a limited knowledge of the tactical skills of the game at that level, and whose main interests were golf and trotting.

The most important was to any doubters among the cricketing public — look, this sporting editor has dodgy cricket credentials, but you can believe me when I say our cricket, under a new captain, is starting to pull back from its recent depressing run of Test losses against South Africa and England.

His final message? It covered the matter of 'petty State jealousies'. It was almost a throwaway line in his response but I'd wager at least one NSW cricket person felt the blood rush of a guilty blush.

When you've been in the media for all of your life, as I have, and you read a comment piece like that, with detailed references to bowling changes, field placings and so on, all from the pen of a man who has never played first-class cricket, you ask yourself one question: "Who loaded the gun?"

Then a few more: "Who was the sporting editor's 'great Australian fast bowler of recent years' who had a theory about where Chappell should stick an old cricket ball? Why was he so shy ...? Why didn't he want the remarks attributed to him? How many more of the sporting editor's criticisms of Chappell came from that source ...?" Sir Donald had that fast bowler, for one, squarely in his sights.

And, if the sporting editor held no brief for Kerry O'Keeffe, who might have? Well, Bill O'Reilly was writing for *The Sydney Morning Herald* at the time ... and, if he had been in the press box that day, and had been reinforcing what all we cricketers knew of Bill's forthright thoughts on 'lollipop' legspinners, well ... it's possible Bill was in full flight that day.

But, even if Bill did think O'Keeffe was a better bowler than Jenner surely it was hardly a starting point for the sporting editor's outrageous conspiracy theory.

Anyway, how did Jenner and O'Keeffe compare over their careers? Between 1970–71 and 1975–76 Jenner played nine Tests against England and the West Indies.

Wkts	Ave	Best	S/rate
24	31.21	5/90	78.37

O'Keeffe played 24 Tests between 1970–71 and 1977, against England, New Zealand, Pakistan and the West Indies.

Wkts	Ave	Best	S/rate
53	38.08	5/101	101.58

In Sheffield Shield they performed like this:

Matches	Wkts	5/10	Best	Ave	S/rate
Jenner					
87	234	8/1	7/127	34.71	72.69
O'Keeffe					
58	187	11/1	6/49	27.18	63.97

Neither Jenner nor O'Keeffe passed the 1972 Ashes selection test. Mallett and Gleeson got the nod. Two decades later two other members of the brotherhood of spin made it to England — Tim May and Shane Warne. Never tag them as twins, for two more diverse characters you'd be pushed to meet.

MAYSIE

Which bowler would you rather watch in action, a good offspinner or a good legspinner? The legspinner, of course, for they are the stuff of Australian cricket legends — Grimmett, O'Reilly, Benaud, Warne. Name a legendary Australian offspinner.

Arthur Mailey said:

It requires little or no talent physically or mentally to bowl an off break. It is the natural spinner schoolboys allow to fall out of their hands without knowing it. I soon realised there was no future for me in big cricket with this kind of ball and turned to the less disciplined but more amusing 'wrong'un'.

While I am loth to give anybody credit because he is able to bowl off breaks I do give a measure of credit to those who are able to add hostility because of their knowledge of flight, spin and break variation.

Arthur, had he still been with us around the mid-'80s, might have given Tim May some credit, however slight, for his attempts to master the art.

From 1985 until Shane Warne, Australia's cricket fans had to endure The Battle Of The Offspinners, as first Greg Matthews, then Peter Taylor, then Tim May endeavoured to make the spin spot in the Test team his own, with only brief challenges from the legspinners, Peter Sleep and Trevor Hohns.

January 14, 1993

Tim May would probably not remember the date with much fondness, and I can't blame him for that. It was the night the Australian selectors more or less 'sent him packing' and, in so doing, I regret to say we left him open to some abusive barracking from the fans at the SCG.

The Australians were playing Pakistan in a day/night World Series match and May had been relegated to 12th man, having lost the offspinning spot to local hero Greg Matthews.

But Tim was subbing and having a shocker. Tim's nickname within the team was 'The Master Of Disaster', and he was living right up to it by way of misfields and missed chances, his 'yellows' were well streaked with grass strains and dirt splodges from his endeavours in the SCG infield.

Suddenly he was pulled from the field, reminiscent of a football code interchange when a player is hauled off after spilling a pass that could have won the game. It looked like Tim had been punished, and the crowd saw it that way and paid out on him mercilessly.

What really happened was this: the Australian selection panel was at the game to discuss two points — the squad for the World Series finals which were about to begin, and the possible line-ups for the Fourth and Fifth Test double-header against the West Indies, which followed the limited-overs finals.

We decided May was not a possibility for the One-day finals, but he was a strong possibility for the Fourth Test in Adelaide — his home pitch, and spinners had been profiting there more than in previous summers.

That presented us with a major problem. If we dropped May out of the One-day finals, which were the only international lead-up matches to the Fourth Test, then he would get no cricket — unless we were able to pull off a small scale, military-like operation.

The next day, January 15, May's home State South Australia were to begin a Sheffield Shield match against Tasmania in Hobart. Could we get May into that game, even though he hadn't been named in the South Australian team, even though he was in Sydney, and even though it was 8pm on January 14, match eve?

So, we sent a message out onto the SCG to Allan Border — "Send May off." Border thought it was something to do with May's misfielding misfortunes and hedged, probably thinking that it was rougher than usual treatment of a player for such misdemeanours.

So we had to send out a clarifying message. May was jeered from the field, and wasn't all that cheered either by the news that we selectors wanted him to consider our offer to suddenly reorganise his cricket career.

It was a tough call, but a sensible one. How irresponsible would it have been of the selectors to have left May in the One-day finals squad, knowing he would almost certainly be just an onlooker?

So, having convinced May of the desirability of the switch we then had to tell the South Australian officials that May was available. What if they didn't want to pick him? It was about 9pm when Laurie Sawle traced Peter Philpott, the South Australian coach, to a Hobart eatery ... and the answer was, "Yes, we'd love to have him."

The next phone call was to get May booked in on the first plane out of Sydney the next morning at 6.30, arriving in Hobart about match starting time. But there was another problem. Because the season had reached its World Series stage, May was only travelling with his 'yellows', not his 'whites'.

May called his wife Katherine in Adelaide and arranged for her to get his whites onto a flight out of Adelaide the next morning, a flight which fortuitously linked up with May's coming from Sydney.

And, so began the rebirth of Tim May's career as Australian cricket's No.1 offspinner. It had been a long and laboured progress. About four years in fact.

Tim's tardiness in realising his great potential went back to 1988 when he took 50 wickets for the summer and got the nod to take on the West Indies in the Second Test in Perth. He celebrated by stubbing the little finger of his bowling hand in a fielding mishap, causing dislocation.

There was talk of permanent ligament damage, even surgery, but as things turned out that was reserved for Tim's dicey right knee, which despite the knife and therapy of allowing it to lie motionless on a soft cushion for long periods, threatened to remain chronic.

The result was that the bowler with the talent to become No.1 offspinner was suddenly No.1 cripple and No.3 spinner. Yet during his stint in spin bowling's equivalent of an RSPCA shelter, neither Peter Taylor nor Greg Matthews was able to make it happen at Test level.

May's comeback Test was the famous Fourth Test against the West Indies in Adelaide in 1993. Typically, The Master Of Disaster had another scare for team physiotherapist Errol Alcott, never mind his captain, Border.

In trying to field a ball he trod on his thumb! He was treated for a gash and joint damage, but came back to bowl his best-ever spell and take an amazing five wickets for nine runs.

In the middle of it he said to Border, "This is scary AB, they're just coming out so good." Border thought about that for a moment and then replied, "Yeah, well just keep treading on your hand."

May's clumsiness attracted critics like lamp posts attract ladies of the night, and his five for nine was soon consigned to the basket marked 'flukes'. May showed them in the Test at Lord's in 1993 that it was no fluke — and, he didn't fall on his hand proving it.

One of the most satisfying moments in that Lord's victory by Australia came when May got Alec Stewart leg before on the last day. At that stage, Stewart and Foster were showing enough guts and commonsense to suggest England might just get out with a draw.

Stewart was playing May and Border with his pad and doing it so effectively there was a just a hint of frustration in Border's frown. Then May went around the wicket, pitched one in line that Stewart parried with his pad, expecting it to turn down the famous Lord's slope. But the ball went with May's arm, barely moving off line.

Stewart had been completely deceived. It would have hit middle stump about halfway up. It was the wicket that won the Test for Australia. It was fitting that Lord's was the scene of another big step in May's comeback from cricket misery.

It was there on the 1989 Ashes tour, when he was feeling fairly down, that his wife Katherine reminded him he had a sense of humour. She suggested to Tim they might put their youngest in the Lord's creche during the Test.

This puzzled Tim. He'd never heard of a creche at any cricket ground, let alone Lord's. Katherine said, with a smile, "Well, the commentators keep talking about the nursery end."

Ashley Mallett is acknowledged to have been the best of Australia's most recent offspinners. The numbers stack up.

Matches	Wkts	5/10	Best	Ave	S/rate
Mallett					
39	132	6/1	8/59	29.85	75.68
Matthews					
33	61	2/1	5/103	48.23	102.80
May					
24	75	3/–	5/9	34.75	87.69
Taylor					
13	27	1/–	6/78	39.56	82.48

Australia's Ashes victory in 1993 was not without controversy; a desperate England played their Australian Connection, English-born cricketers who had been raised in Australia, trained at Australia's Cricket Academy, and played in the Sheffield Shield.

GOOSE

When England chose Western Australia's occasional fast bowler Martin McCague (born in Ireland) to play in the 1993 Ashes series we Australian selectors were condemned for allowing McCague to slip through our fingers. Did we?

July, 1993

Do you believe that stuff about a pet and its master being look-alikes? During the Martin McCague case I had a phone call from a chap named Barry who bellowed for my resignation as an Australian selector.

On, and on, and on he went, like one of those religious zealots who sometimes come and stand outside your screen door on Sunday mornings.

I bet myself that Barry was sure to be the proud owner of one of those little yapping dogs that bite strangers on the ankle. Barry charged me with neglect of duty because I admitted I hadn't seen McCague bowl during his short and intermittent career with Western Australia.

And he was unimpressed when told that two of the other selectors had. It was not good enough that I should rely on the judgments of the other selectors, I should have been able to view McCague's bowling personally, said Barry.

It was then that I started to think maybe Barry didn't own a little yappy dog, more likely it was a goose.

Because Barry, on his knees before the great god Technology, announced that the obvious way to ensure that every selector sees every player of potential Test status is to call for the video.

That is, players should be videoed in action in a Sheffield Shield match, even a Grade cricket match, and the cassettes whipped post haste over to me for assessment, or to any other selector similarly in the dark. I can hear the shouting from the video cassette manufacturing industry now: "Barry for selection chairman!"

What sort of videos does Barry have in mind? Will they be technical-only, targetting the one spell of bowling, or a half-hour at the batting crease? A snippet of fielding perhaps?

Or will they be feature length and address some of the things selectors really want to know about, like the pitch and weather conditions, a player's temperament and how he might handle the subtle changes in pressure that will confront him at the highest level in the game?

I can just imagine fellow selector Jim Higgs, the engineer by profession, telling a major client, "Look you'll have to cancel our consultation on that $600,000 road project, I'm watching Martin McCague videos all this week."

We all saw McCague on video via Channel Nine's Ashes coverage of the final day of the Third Test. We saw a lad physically strong and facially stern, with a run-in that looks like it's got some development in it yet.

We saw he has an open-chested action with a widely splayed front foot, and that he bowls at a sharpish pace. We didn't see him get a wicket (although we knew that in the first innings he took four, including Mark Taylor, David Boon and Steve Waugh).

What sort of assessment could a selector make on a video of that final day's play? Zilch! He could make a few guesses, such as, "The pitch looked flat" and "The sun was shining", but he could never tell from a video how flat or how hot.

They might not seem to be important factors, but they become so in any assessment of McCague's final day performance.

Did he look a little ragged in that final session when Gooch called on him to get the breakthrough that could have won the Test? Any selector at Trent Bridge, late on that final day, could reasonably have thought McCague's pace was down and his line and length less consistent.

Why? Tiredness? A case of a hot day, an unhelpful pitch, the pressure of his first Test, playing over five days for the first time ...

Does Barry advocate we have player interviews on these videos: "Excuse me Martin, I was wondering if you could tell the selectors why you didn't get a wicket in your last spell?"

The McCague case — from Down Under to Old Dart — is a great story-line for a cricket fairy tale, but it doesn't, as Barry maintained, show up any weaknesses in the way the Australian selection panel goes about its job.

Only the pig-headed refuse to concede that selection is just a matter of opinion, and the England panel — Ted Dexter and Co. — in their wisdom, decided that McCague was ready to make his Test debut.

The Australian panel had a different view. Dexter's men made their judgment on his form in a few dozen matches in County cricket. We made ours on McCague's fewer than a dozen appearances in two seasons for Western Australia.

Our selection procedure was simple; when we met, whether it was face-to-face or by telephone hook-up, each of us would give a report on players we had watched, detailing form, potential, statistics, match conditions.

That was expanded during discussions and might have taken in technique — say footwork in a batsman, and even his career statistics, as some sort of guide to his consistency. It always took in temperament, and always the situation in the match when the player either made good or went off the boil.

Naturally we tried to pick match-winners — the players which our intuition and experience suggested to us would be able to turn a game our team's way, particularly when the odds were against us.

If one of those potential match-winners was a new face, one that not every selector on the panel had seen, and by general agreement of the panel he could be the goods, then chairman Laurie Sawle would change the roster to ensure every selector did see the player under match conditions.

That happened last summer (1992–93) with Michael Slater, a late starter for NSW. It was a simple formula, and going on Slater's success on the 1993 Ashes tour and beyond, it was effective.

When Martin McCague quit Australia, age 23, he had played 11 Sheffield Shield matches. On his debut, age 21, against Victoria at the suburban St Kilda ground he took five for 105.

In all he took 32 wickets, 14 of them on his home pitch, Perth. His average was 33.94, his strike rate a wicket every 64 balls.

Australian selection rating: Has some promise.

When England picked him up, age 24, he took four for 121 on debut; he played two more Tests, and took two more wickets, average 65.00, strike rate 98.83; he hasn't been chosen since the 1994–95 Ashes tour.

Possible England selection rating: Failed to realise promise.

It's not unusual for Australian selectors to choose a young, possibly immature batsman, but immature fast bowlers rarely pop up; Craig McDermott, age 19, was the most recent exception to the rule, a rare athletic talent.

McCague might have been a better bowler if he'd had a longer, tougher education in the game. That is, more Sheffield Shield experience and a lot fewer English County experiences.

Over time, there have been thousands of cricketers who have either switched clubs or districts to satisfy their urge to do better. Occasionally it works, but mostly it's the 'soft' option. What about those players who can't make it, and can't switch, either?

GEESE

Miss Ashes selection and it's a case of make your own arrangements about cricket in England. There is something about playing in England, on a village green in the pale, golden evening of a long day, that can often transcend playing the game anywhere else.

Lou: "The experts say an Australian player will improve greatly by playing a season with an English County team … so, why aren't more English County cricketers champions?"

It's a fair talking point nowadays, but when Lou said it it was a fairly tough call. Lou smarted for a long time over Jim Laker's 19 wickets at Old Trafford in 1956. He couldn't abide anything that smacked of a rort and he reckoned the Old Trafford pitch was 'doctored' with marl, a crumbly soil used as a fertiliser. He marked England hard thereafter.

But Australia's humiliation at Old Trafford was the very reason why many young Australian cricketers chose, in earlier days, to spend a winter in England, mostly in the Lancashire League, trying to fathom the vagaries of uncovered pitches in weather that was often damp.

Australian selectors choosing the Ashes squad in those days, if confronted by a tight decision might have asked, "Which player will best handle England's fickle pitches?" There was a widespread perception that if a cricketer had played in England it enhanced his Ashes prospects.

Possibly it was a bit of a furphy — the good players will surely adjust to strange conditions, and fairly quickly, won't they? Nevertheless, in cricket it is difficult to overlook the 'Roman Theory' — learn from the locals.

I had a season with the London club side, Stanmore, in 1968. Our opening bowler was 't'old Yorkshire pro' named Frank Hodgkiss. One day we were walking onto the field when all of a sudden Frank exclaimed to the captain, Brian Hall, "I've got it Brian, I've got it! Look!"

Brian looked and saw that Frank, still walking nonchalantly, was expertly picking the seam of the ball — with one hand, and it was the hand with which he was holding the ball! Most seam-pickers need both hands.

Frank had manicured his thumb nail until it was the perfect image of a screwdriver head. He could pick a seam so clean it would cut the palm of your hand if you were unlucky enough to have it come awkwardly to you in the field. I wonder how Frank would have fared under the intrusive lens of seam-cam?

The Stanmore pitch looked like the old Luna Park carpet slide, raised at each end and a dish in the middle. There'd been a spit of rain the day I made my English debut. I faced a baldy, bandy legged, medium paced seamer with a lowish, round arm action. Veteran.

A six-week boat trip before I'd been facing Victoria's sharpest seam bowlers, John Grant and Alan Connolly, in the Sheffield Shield on the MCG. This first ball on Stanmore Common was shortish, at off stump. My reflex said: Back foot drive. I played three, the third of which was a little early for the speed of the ball … caught and bowled by the old bloke. ·

I walked off, across the boundary line, into the pavilion and heard a couple of my new teammates telling Brian Hall, "That Sheffield Shield must be an ordinary competition."

These days, on covered pitches as blunt as a bulldog's 'button', the English 'experience' is no longer the stern test of a visitor's skill that it used to be. Australia's young cricketers go to England mainly for a quid, a few play major league cricket, a lot play minor league, a lot more play club cricket.

What real benefit can there be in that? The matches are one-day affairs, either decided on a limited-overs basis, or by the quaint system of a 'winning' or 'losing' draw. Batsmen come back boasting extraordinary run aggregates, fast bowlers come back hacks.

Jason Arnberger, a young graduate from the AIS Cricket Academy, a forceful opening batsman on the fringe of Sheffield Shield selection in the mid-'90s, spent his winters in Scotland. What's the point of a young cricketer in that position, a few good scores short of making the strong NSW team, doing that?

How could playing every six months in a cricket competition of a markedly lower standard possibly have improved his game, or his fitness? What could he learn? It could be argued that, if anything, the Scotland experience has held back Arnberger's career prospects.

When you're standing in the change sheds, feeling your age, noting with alarm how your muscle tone has stretched whilst around you there are men half your age toning their muscles by stretching, you get the idea it's just about all over.

And, when you walk out into the sunlight to be greeted by the match organiser, the popular scribe Peter Roebuck in his trademark broad brimmed hat, and he invites you not to the practice nets but to the rooms for tea and scones, then you know it is all over.

But fear not, for there is a cricket heaven — Tom Morris's at East Lydeard near Taunton in Somerset. I arrived in late July, 1996.

Tom's a dairy farmer. Breathes cricket. Churns out high, looping leg-spinners — what else? Tom's got a twinkle in his eyes that matches the mischief of his everpresent grin. Any legspinner's credentials.

Fact was, Tom tossed them so high Sir Arthur Conan Doyle's wonderful make-believe story about Spedegue came to my mind. Spedegue was the unknown bowler who practised in the New Forest until he had perfected a ball sent skywards that would drop right onto the top of the stumps.

Spedegue's Dropper was as famous as Warne's Zooter. Sir Arthur's story had Spedegue's ingenuity winning him selection in a crucial, deciding Fifth Test against Australia.

Sadly for Tom, selectors could find no place for his talent in the local scheme of things, so Tom started his own team, and called it The Flying Geese.

In one corner of his Somerset farm Tom fashioned the team's home ground, its perfect pitch surrounded by a gently rolling, green outfield. Under a cluster of trees to one side there is a small, shingled pavilion with a clock, and neat scoreboard. A labour of love.

Away in fields in the near distance, through a scattering of trees, Tom's cows chew cuds and, on a large nearby pond the geese gather. Late in the day they take flight with a thunder-clapping of wings that startles fine leg and reminds him there's a game on, against 'The Geese'.

On one side of the ground, at the boundary line, a sparkling creek runs, its waters shin-deep. It is protected from the big hitters by a wicker fence, but none too well for often the ball scoots under it, and into the water.

This is the signal for Tom to add one more touch of character to the game that thrives on it more than most. In early days of The Geese he laid on fishing nets, and a young fellow in 'wellies' to retrieve the ball. But nowadays he takes from his pocket a whistle with a special high pitch, and blows it.

Four dogs come a-running — Prickles the border terrier, and three labradors named Rajah, Pluto and Jupiter, all of them trained to retrieve pheasants. The labradors bound to the creek and plunge in — retrieving the ball! And the game can go on.

It was just as Roebuck had predicted over the tea and scones: "'JB', you may never have seen anything like this before in your cricketing life, and may never again."

Letter from Tom, February 1997

Dear John,

Cricket has always been my first love of all the ball games. Ever since I could read I've always been interested in games of cricket. I used to know all the County championship scores from day to day as well as Sheffield Shield, Currie Cup, Ranji Trophy, the Plunkett Cup, you name it I knew it.

Somerset has always been the team I supported; Bill Alley was my hero and I still think he was better than Ian Botham.

Flashes of cricket moments still appear in my mind from those school days. One of the clearest is of your brother bowling Peter May behind his legs when it appeared Ted Dexter had won the game for us at Old Trafford in 1961.

I was never a good player although I played in my school First XI for several years. I think it was just my enthusiasm for the game which kept the cricket masters putting my name down on the team sheet.

However, after I left Agricultural College in 1969 I did not play a game until 1984 while I tried to sort out the farm left to me by my parents. Then one Sunday I was asked to play in a game with some farmer friends at Roadwater, a lovely little ground.

I don't remember the result or how I played, but I do remember thinking that I had been missing something very special. We had all enjoyed ourselves hugely. On the way home I said to Tara [Tom's wife] that 'it must not be another 15 years before I play my next game'.

However, to get a game of cricket on a prepared pitch with your friends is almost impossible as all the clubs have regular fixtures on Saturday and Sunday; irregular games between friends were out of the question.

So I decided then to make my own pitch … a home for homeless cricketers.

Having taken some advice from a few experts, who had beer mugs in their hands, I set about doing what I could. Originally there was a stream running through the middle of the square and the rest of the field was a bog. By raising the level of the field we were able to drain it. We levelled the ground a bit and in 1985 we reseeded it.

We built the pavilion in the spring of 1986 and determined to play our first game on June 10, a Sunday. I sent out formal invitations and everyone said 'yes'. I hadn't got a clue how to prepare a wicket but the day dawned cloudless and warm, Tara laid on a superb tea in the house, and we all had a great day's cricket.

The TV cameras turned up to see this strange farmer with his new cricket field and we all went down to the pub and celebrated.

In 1988 we set up The Flying Geese. We prepared a fixture list and we also converted the Old Dairy into tea rooms and changing rooms. I sent out 80 letters inviting people who I thought might be interested in joining a club ... one where the cricket would be played fairly, and hard, but most importantly would also finish with a good social with the opposition, as I feel too much sport is now played for the game only and not to meet and drink with the other side.

Seventy-eight said 'yes', and so The Geese were formed. I have always done all the ground work. I have found the secret of a good hard, long lasting wicket is plenty of water about 15 days before you are going to play on it. After I re-seed the square I always put about 50 ewe lambs on the field — they always wear their whites and seem to enjoy their stay!

During the early 90s we played about 70 games a year, about 35 Geese games and the rest solicitors and the like. We've slowly reduced the number of games played because I couldn't physically run the farm and prepare and host that number of games.

We have found over the last ten years that the ground has completely run our summer months. Friends no longer ask us out for barbecues, or tennis parties because we can never go.

Although I've enjoyed it more than anything I've ever done, met lots of people, got drunk more times than I should have done, scored lots of dazzling runs, taken outstanding catches and ripped out more middle orders than I care to remember, I have decided that if Tara and I are to see anything of our children then we have to stop playing cricket here — except for one or two family games where we entertain our friends.

The decision has been made and I know that I shall miss it.

Yours Tom.

So, a dairy farm, where there's plenty of room to swing your right arm ... Tom's place was my greenest pasture. However, a cricketer's times in Harare in Zimbabwe can be rougher and tougher. Shane Warne survived, then thrived.

DAKTARI

Australia sent a 'B' team to Zimbabwe in 1991. The captain was Mark Taylor, who went on to captain the 'A' team successfully. All players were chosen with a view to the future and, in most cases, the faith of the selectors was not misplaced.

Managing Australian cricket teams can be a tricky business because there are a myriad of personalities at work, and play. A sense of humour and a blind eye can be valuable allies for any manager.

If one manager, Bill Jacobs, is fair dinkum about an experience he had then a deaf ear might be handy, too. Bill cared for Ian Chappell's team in the Caribbean in 1973.

The day after arriving in Montego Bay, Bill was invited to meet the local mayor, Trevor Cooke and, after exchanging greetings the mayor announced, "I will introduce you to your liaison officer — your team will be shown the better sights of Montego Bay."

Bill: "Where is he?"

Mayor: "It's not a 'he', it's a 'she' … Cecille, Cecille, come over here. This is Mr Bill Jacobs, the manager of the Australian cricket team."

Bill: "How do you do Cecille, it's nice to meet you."

She said, "Get rooted!" Bill said, "I beg your pardon?" She said, "Get rooted!"

Bill: "I'm not sure what you're saying."

Cecille: "Get rooted."

Bill: "Very well, then, I'll see you later."

Cecille said, "Get rooted," and walked away.

Bill says he later found out that Doug Walters and Greg Chappell had told Cecille that in Australia 'get rooted' was a common expression which could mean 'good morning', 'good evening', 'lovely to meet you', and 'goodbye'.

Less unlikely shenanigans happened on the 1961 Ashes tour when Syd Webb was manager of the Australian team. Syd had a mannerism, possibly a by-product of his legal background, of thrusting his hands into his suitcoat pockets when speaking at an official gathering.

The players had noted that. At Hever Castle, when it came time to leave, they sneaked a few pieces of Lord Astor's finest silverware into Syd's coat pockets and at the drawbridge, the 'front door', when goodbyes were finalised, they waited expectantly.

Syd stepped onto the drawbridge and up went the arms, elbows bent, fingers of both hands extended downwards, thumbs protruding, looking like a gunslinger preparing to draw ... into the pockets, then suddenly out again, clasping a spoon and fork and wondering why.

So, in 1991 I set out with Taylor and the B platoon, destination Zimbabwe. Among my managerial possessions I had the Australian flag, a baseball glove, 12 dozen cricket balls, 15 boxes of malaria tablets, one physiotherapist (Errol Alcott), one twin (Steve Waugh) and another 12 players (Taylor — captain, Michael Bevan, Jamie Cox, Stuart Law, Denis Hickey, Tom Moody, Peter McIntyre, Tim Nielsen, Shane Warne, Rodney Tucker, Paul Reiffel, Wayne Holdsworth). It did not always go well.

Prior to departure airline staff announced that the names of two of my key players, the fast bowler Hickey and the wicketkeeper Nielsen, were nowhere to be found on the passenger flight list.

I was still an Australian selector at the time and one player, with a keen sense of observation, suggested it must have been because "they were both from South Australia ... ho, ho, ho". South Australian representation in Australian teams had been terrible, and still is although the rise and rise of Blewett and Gillespie is a sign of revival.

Seat allocation placed me next to a fast bowler, Holdsworth. He had on his lap one of those music playing machines shaped like a continental loaf of bread, and about as long, made of black, hard plastic, and with a handle, which, if you walked around with it for long enough you'd be listing like the Titanic, and deaf. The flight lasted 17 hours, give or take a cassette tape or two.

The liaison officer in Zimbabwe was Russell B. Tiffin, the national sales manager for an oil firm, but there was a physical hardness about Russell, and a mental edge that told us it was a good bet that he'd spent a fair bit of his most recent past in the armed forces. The SAS perhaps.

This led some of the boys to think Russell was a bit hyperactive, some even tagged him as aggressive, but the bottom line was Russell was just nutty about cricket (later, he was to join the international panel of umpires), a fanatic to whom the prospect of being able to rub shoulders with Steve Waugh and Mark Taylor meant the world.

Upon our arrival, Russell instigated a debriefing session for us at the

Harare Sports Club and, although it was an unofficial welcome, we went along in our official team uniform — the plain tie, plain cream shirt, plain green blazer and fawn trousers number, not so much a fashion statement as a self-conscious burp.

Russell insisted on buying the drinks — "You'll have a Soapy!" and "You'll try a Sneaky!" were demands rather than invitations. The local thirst quenchers were pure alcohol mixed with what turned out to be hopelessly inadequate quantities of soda and lemon juice.

When I woke up in my hotel room the morning after, I was as surprised by my state as Bill O'Reilly must have been by the medals at Mareeba, or Syd Webb by the cutlery — I was still fully dressed, still in the team uniform, shoes, blazer and all.

The itinerary made no mention of Victoria Falls. It seemed ridiculous to me that we should have come all that way yet not see one of the wonders of the world. So, I raised 10,000 Zimbabwe dollars (not as difficult as you might think!) and Russell B. Tiffin did the rest ... he organised an air charter.

At six in the morning we found ourselves at a small airfield outside Harare, playing guessing games as to which plane was 'it' — the Tropic Air 20-seater that was going to get us to Victoria Falls, and back. None of us picked the World War II Dakota.

Our hostess was Janet, an attractive blonde lass, recently married, and whose new husband was there to fondly farewell her. Her face told the story: I'd rather be spending this glorious morning with him than with a plane load of cricketers. The pilot introduced himself as Robin Hood. True.

Wonderful old plane the Dakota; I think we were all impressed when we reached the Falls, and then absolutely dumbfounded when Robin managed to do a reasonably tight figure of eight in her!

On the return journey, much of it in darkness, the old girl started to yaw; young Janet announced that Robin wished us to know that it was 'nothing', that the auto pilot had retired hurt; I was just behind the open door to the cockpit and I could see Robin's foot feverishly working away at the rudder. Great for the Achilles.

As I watched all this fancy footwork, and looked out through the window into the inky blackness, a chilling thought occurred to me — on board was the cream of a future generation of Australian cricket and I wasn't sure if I'd arranged the flight insurance! And it was Friday the 13th.

The players gave me none out of 10 and awarded me the team gong — they called it the Daktari Suit, an atrocious little number made up of khaki shorts and shirt with a black tiger-stripe, and a khaki slouch hat; long, white socks and desert boots were compulsory accessories. I had to wear it for a day, and at any time I was in public.

This test of my sense of humour by the players came near the end of the 21-day tour, by which time the suit had been worn by just about every other team member, and was considerably the worse for wear, mainly in the area of the fly zipper, which had been reinforced by a safety pin.

And, it came on a day we were to play golf at noon at The Royal Harare Club, meeting in the foyer of our hotel at 11.30am for an 11.45am departure.

I left my room so I would reach the ground floor at 11.44am and move directly to the team bus, thus spending no time in the crowded foyer. I left the lift at the ground floor and started briskly for the hotel entrance, and heard, "Telefoon ad de desk for a Midder Beano of Ostrarlee ... Midder Beano, pleeze."

Unbelievable! It was Laurie Sawle, the chairman of selectors, calling from Australia for a tour review. I guess we spoke for 15 minutes, during which time the players never missed a chance to point out "that big-noter in the Jungle Jim gear talking on the blower".

There were several motives behind the selection of Australia's B-team: one was to have a look at Mark Taylor as a future captain, another to assess player character, but mainly we were looking at legspinners. There were two in the team, Shane Warne and Peter McIntyre, both inexperienced, total rookies in fact. The tour would be an ideal test-tube.

A close third was the fervent hope that Steve Waugh could drag himself out of a form slump — he had been dropped for his twin Mark against England at the start of 1991 (eventually, he would miss 13 of the next 15 Tests).

A 'second' tour like the B-team's to Zimbabwe can offer a batsman the chance to score what are often referred to as 'easy runs', and they can do a lot to reignite a good player's confidence or build the character of a fringe player.

Taylor's team easily won the two four-day 'Tests' by nine wickets and 10 wickets, but never looked as unbeatable in the three One-dayers, the first of which they lost by six wickets and the last of which they won by eight runs, only because Holdsworth, riding the boundary, took a catch so freakish that even the occupants of Castle Corner stopped drinking to applaud.

Zimbabwe were five for 208 chasing 248 when Tucker bowled a waist-high full toss going down legside to Ian Butchart, a delivery known as the 'happy birthday'. Butchart helped it on its way in a big way and it was going up and away for six until the sprinting Holdsworth down at fine leg flung himself headlong into the air and plucked it with his right hand.

At the time, the closeness of the limited-overs results meant little but 10 months on it seemed they must have meant a lot, because the International Cricket Council granted Zimbabwe Test status, or full international status. Yes, that's right … a team that had just been smashed by Australia's B-team was upgraded to A-level.

It raised the question — what possible use could be served by giving such status to a cricketing nation as substandard as Zimbabwe? Another question was just as pertinent — why did it happen when it did?

We all support the ICC's brief — to spread the cricket message to every corner of the earth, to have regard to the future development of the game. But what were Zimbabwe's credentials for a successful cricketing future?

The decision seemed to reflect the age in which it was made, when everything happens so fast tomorrow seems like yesterday. The most likely reason for their admission was convenience — to make up the numbers for the 1992 World Cup. The limited-overs agenda seemed to have superseded the Test agenda, and who knows for whatever agenda down the line.

The 'no' voters would have argued this:
- Zimbabwe's star player strength was too old — David Houghton, Ian Butchart, Andy Pycroft, Malcom Jarvis, Ali Omarshah, Andy Waller were in their 30s, John Traicos his 40s.
- The player base was hopelessly narrow, and the intra-country competition completely uninspiring.
- Zimbabwe's performance against Taylor's team in the longer games in Harare and Bulawayo was substandard — they played 'Japanese', save face, and for the draw. They scored at a fraction over two runs an over.

The 'yes' lobby would have argued differently:
- The population of 11 million, 50 per cent of whom are under 15, is the future.
- Admission will result in a higher profile for the game, new sponsorship money and an opportunity to attract overseas players to help develop the local competition, and to coach.
- Once South Africa, Zimbabwe's next-door neighbours, were granted re-admission, if Zimbabwe were not a full status country, then it was certain the game would wither, then die in Zimbabwe — talented players of the new generation would head south of the border, in much the same way Graeme Hick migrated to England.

Whatever they argued, they won the day against commonsense. Even if the numbers of those youngsters who take up cricket multiply mightily every year, the job of coaching them up to 'speed' is a daunting one.

I suppose anything's possible ... in the year 2040 one of the game's oldest administrators might even be heard to say, "It was a very, very good thing that we did for Zimbabwe before the turn of the century."

Zimbabwe threaten to be about as successful as New Zealand have been. The real risk is that the quality of the game, particularly the Test game, will be further compromised by the presence of Zimbabwe.

This was expansion, purely for expansion's sake. Or, to steal a piece of 'rag trade philosophy' — never mind the quality, feel the width.

It got sillier. In the 1996 World Cup three more teams, Holland, Kenya and United Arab Emirates — whose composition wasn't unlike that of a so-cial pick-up outfit — joined the the competition.

And a cynic might add, the decision was probably a nice little earner for the Pay TV microdish installers. One extra team would have been good for cricket, but clearly it was bad finance. Money rules, OK?

Full Test status was too generously granted to Zimbabwe. Before even thinking of offering it the ICC needs to consider two things:

- greatly improving the development structure, so second-tier countries like Holland and Kenya play many more matches against the B-teams of established Test countries;
- maintaining sensible 'space' between the two forms of the game.

The One-day arena is clearly one in which lesser teams can fluke a win, and therefore at least appear to be more competitive than they could possibly be in the longer form of the game.

Why doesn't the ICC create two aspects to full status — couldn't One-day status be the first step towards Test status?

Those who would promote a blanket open-to-all policy do the game the greatest disservice. To allow the underdeveloped nations to try to play full Tests against long-established Test nations is dangerously naive.

When the vote on Zimbabwe was taken someone forgot to ask the magic question, "What if ... the West Indies have to host Zimbabwe in a three Test series in the Caribbean, or Australia have to host Holland at the MCG?"

Test cricket will disintegrate.

It comes as a surprise to learn that it was Australia who seconded Zimbabwe's entry into the international arena. That's because Australia, after inviting them Down Under for the 1994–95 World Series, then insulted Zimbabwe by treating them as a second-rate outfit.

The Australian Cricket Board's decision to ask Zimbabwe — and England and Australia too — to match it with an Australian B-team, the results of which contests weren't even officially recognised, was ordinary.

The sort of snooty, selfish, muddled thinking that cricket officials try on now and again. It was the verbal version of the infamous two-fingered salute. It was big-headed — we voted for you but you're just a bunch of duds and we can beat you with our second best team.

And, what did the decision say about Australia's commitment to helping develop the fledgling cricket nation? You wonder what the manoeuvre might have meant down the line when the ICC came to vote on particular issues. Australia might have been lucky to get Zimbabwe's nod.

And, you wonder too if the Australian Board gave even a passing thought to the potential damage it might have done to Taylor's main team. The Aussie versus Aussie concept created unwarranted tensions among the Australian cricketing public, and unwanted tension among the players.

And, just so the public didn't get the impression they were being conned, the marketing people kept calling the B-team the A-team.

The selectors' job was a total nightmare because the Cricket Board said it was okay for them to switch Australian players between the two teams! "Eeni, meeni, mini, mo ..." Crass, a cricketing farce.

Nothing was more farcical than when the deciding final series arrived and Australia had to play Australia B and the B-team's best bowler during the tournament, Paul Reiffel, was promoted to the A-team — but made 12th man! The concept created fierce debate. If you didn't like the idea of a couple of Aussie tribes going head to head you were accused of being too precious.

Well, imagine if, back in the early '80s when Australia was being pointlessly crushed by the Caribbean kings of cricket, the West Indies Cricket Board had deigned to put their B-team into the field for a One-day series? Australia beaten by West Indies B ... never mind the Australian Cricket Board's outrage, imagine how dirty the Australian fans would have been!

The impact Taylor's 1991 B-team tour had on Zimbabwean cricket can't be gauged — zilch, most probably. We did no coaching. Why? Surely the two Cricket Boards could have arranged an itinerary that involved some instructional time at schools? Money perhaps, no vision or just lack of real commitment?

Half a dozen years on and Zimbabwe have won one Test which nails them firmly to the floor of the Test nations, (see table opposite).

The win was in Harare in 1995 and they beat Salim Malik's Pakistan by an innings and 64 runs, an upset result about which the odds on offer would have been about 40 to one. Still, when you think about it, isn't cricket a bookmaker's dream? Uncertainty and all that.

Team	Tests	W	L	D	T
Aust	567	237	160	168	2
Eng	735	249	207	279	–
SAf	209	53	86	70	–
WInd	331	128	80	122	1
NZl	252	36	104	112	–
Ind	309	57	102	149	1
Pak	235	66	54	115	–
SL	70	9	33	28	–
Zim	22	1	10	11	–

They have some established good players like the Flowers, Andy and Grant; and Alistair Campbell has graduated to the captaincy. New faces Paul Strang, the legspinning allrounder, and the quick Heath Streak, have given the game a lift. But it remains a concern that Andy Waller and Ali Omarshah, both aged 37, turned out in limited-overs internationals in 1996. In the end, the ongoing strength of Zimbabwean cricket can only be measured by the numbers of young blacks playing, and coming through.

Taylor's tour though did have a lasting impact on the Australian game. Mark Taylor became Australia's 39th captain in 1993. Tom Moody recovered from this 'hiccup' to play in the 1992 World Cup …

Put to bet first by Zimbabwe, who won the toss, Australia B withstood the loss of kingpin Tom Moody, who fell when he chose to hazard a late dash for the odd run after Andy Waller had covered a hit by the visitors' captain Mark Taylor. Moody found himself run out for a paltry six runs as a result of his unintelligent gamble.

Bulawayo Chronicle, September 16, 1991.

Stuart Law played one Test, but mostly One-day, and made it to the 1996 World Cup. Shane Warne and Peter McIntyre both bowled legspin for Australia, Warne like a superman, McIntyre like a tradesman.

Steve Waugh made it back and eventually became the world's No.1 rated batsman; Paul Reiffel was an Ashes success in 1993, a tour on which Wayne Holdsworth's fast bowling was as disappointing as it was in Zimbabwe.

Tim Nielsen, Rod Tucker and Denis Hickey never went on to play for Australia, either in Tests or World Series. Nor, by 1996–97, had Jamie Cox, a talented opening batsman from Tasmania.

Some players who have trouble making it with mainland States often take the soft option and switch to Tasmania; Cox's aspirations for an Australian spot, an acknowledged tough assignment, might have been advantaged by the reverse, a switch to the mainland in his maturing years, when he was about 23. Tougher competition at Grade level, say in Sydney, would have sharpened his footwork, a weakness.

Which leaves one more player, Michael Bevan. Well, who would have believed it? He joined the team in Zimbabwe from the English Leagues. His role? Batsman. Pure. At Mutare, where Taylor's team played the Zimbabwe B-team, Bevan played a shot never to be forgotten.

It was only batting practice, but the shot was all modern technology — the laser beam hit over cover. We've all seen it a few times since.

Because there were no practice pitches at Mutare, two centre pitches were prepared, one for the match, and one for practice with a removable net squared around it. It was the last ball of pre-game practice and Bevan hit it on the up.

The front foot came positively out, the bat raised, the body weight coming forward, knee bent, the bat sweeping down, the right elbow high, the bat sweeping through in a perfect arc. Contact.

And away it went, the ball, with lovely clean timing, up and over where cover would have been fielding, straight towards the elevated scorebox, under which the groundsman stashed his roller and gear.

Luckily, the man wasn't *in situ*. The storage area had an 'open' front, the other three sides protected by a heavy hessian coverall. Bevan's hit struck the back one with a mighty thud, tore part of it away from its sturdy fasteners, and continued on for a few more metres.

By 1993–94, in the Ashes Tests against England, he'd lost his No.5 spot in the batting order to Greg Blewett; by 1997 he was batting No.7 and his part-time left-arm over-the-wrist spin had made him one of Australia's most potent bowling strike forces. The accidental allrounder.

That's cricket — just when a selector thinks everything is going to plan someone does something totally unpredictable to make him out to be a total idiot. Shane Warne's career nobbled a few judges, too.

WARNE

Because the most notable inclusions in Australia's B-team to Zimbabwe were the two rookie legspinners, Peter McIntyre and Shane Warne, that got right up the noses of some notable cricket people. In hindsight they probably wish they'd had more foresight.

Lou was always a good judge of a cricketer. I think he had an instinct to go with a good eye. In our countless discussions about the game, around the dining room table, he'd always enjoy advancing a theory or two about a young cricketer he'd seen, whether the action was in the local park or in the centre of the television screen.

When I told Lou we'd picked Trevor Hohns as the legspinner on the 1989 Ashes tour, Lou remarked that when he had seen 'Cracker' earlier in his career with Queensland he had rated his batting potential, not his bowling. 'Cracker's' first-class record leaves that judgment up in the air — batted at 27, bowled at 37.

On the 1989 Ashes tour Hohns took 26 wickets, 11 in the Tests and we on the selection panel were happy that we had been able to include a relatively effective legspinner in a bowling line-up in which we hoped the main quicks, Lawson, Alderman and Hughes, would take the bulk of the wickets.

Happy, not so much because we were preserving a rich Australian cricket tradition by including a wrist spinner, but because it gave the skipper, Allan Border, a bit of variation — the attack was much better balanced.

On returning to Australia, Hohns quit the game to see more of his family and his new business; gloom was cast over the panel and, its best mate, doom, arrived the moment the first Test of the summer finished in a draw.

Australia's four-man pace attack had bombed the Kiwis mercilessly for four days at the WACA, but couldn't budge Greatbatch on the fifth. Without Hohns, our spin attack, our balance, was Border and Jones, two part-timers.

And, when the next Test of that summer — at the 'Gabba, against the inexperienced Sri Lankans — also ended in stalemate, there was some determined lip-biting around the selection table.

Choosing four pace bowlers at the WACA and 'Gabba was a reasonable theory given the nature of those two pitches at the time, but it turned out to be a dud tactic. Change was needed.

For the next Test against Sri Lanka in Hobart we ignored three off-spinners, May, Matthews and Taylor, to choose a legspinner who had played only 12 Tests over 10 seasons, whose Test bowling average was 51.17 and whose strike rate was a wicket every 105 balls. Peter Sleep — and, he was 32 years old. This cricketing version of mouth-to-mouth sent out a message: the selectors think a legspin bowler is a necessary part of the Australian bowling attack.

So, Sleep makes 47 not out, and takes three for 26 and two for 73. And, Australia win the Test by 173 runs. Sleep plays in the next Test against Pakistan and gets 23 and a duck, and takes one for six and one for 64. And Australia win the Test by 92 runs.

But, it is Sleep's last Test for Australia. He loses his spot to the offspinner Peter Taylor. In the next Test, Taylor makes 33 and one, and takes none for 57 and two for 94. The Test is drawn.

Now, that might seem like a gross over-simplification of what happened in those matches, but if you were a headstrong supporter of wrist spin over finger spin then the point is worth making.

Peter Sleep was the spin bowler who, earlier in his career, was approached by a selector who asked, "How'd you like to bat against yourself, son?" There is a certain 'edge' attached to the message to ensure the person to whom it is directed 'gets the message' — and it's true, Sleep was never the most accurate legspinner to ever cock a wrist, nor was he the most street-smart cricketer ever to pull on the baggy green.

Coming off Ashes glory 1989, Border & Co., although still rebuilding their confidence, had been expected to hammer New Zealand and Sri Lanka and then match it with Imran Khan's stronger Pakistan outfit. But they couldn't beat the Kiwis, they'd struggled to beat Sri Lanka one-nil, and now they led Pakistan one-nil with two Tests to play. Might they go backwards if they got a belting at the hands of Pakistan in the remaining Tests?

How hard should we selectors push the risk factor? Sleep, with a Test bowling average that batsmen dream about, had to be a risk. We opted to retreat and play the offspinner — Taylor was a form bowler in the World Series. Safety first.

By omitting Sleep, despite his reasonable contribution in two Tests, the panel was announcing it didn't think he was the spin bowler who, down the line, was going to help Australia to beat the West Indies and get back to the top of world cricket. Who was?

There was a legspin vacuum. The next summer against England we decided there was no other course than to go back to Hohns ... "Make a comeback, Trevor, we think that against the West Indies (after the Tests against England) you can be the winning difference." He said "no", business and family remained the stumbling block.

So, we went with Matthews' offspin against England. His seven Test wickets cost him 60 apiece. In the 1991 touring team to the West Indies we chose Matthews and Taylor, the first time I could remember an Australian team heading off to the Caribbean without a legspinner, and I'd been following their fortunes since 1955, when Rich went.

Only two legspinners' names had come up at the selection table. One was Shane Warne from Victoria, a lad who had spent some time at the Cricket Academy, but he was barely out of his teens, a blond with as much baby fat as bravado.

The other was Tim Zoehrer — a second wicketkeeper who dabbled in legspin. Desperate times ...

Warne — and a few other names that would crop up down the line like Martyn, Lehmann, Bevan, Fleming and Julian — had been to the West Indies in 1990, on Australia's Youth Tour.

The Cricket Manager on the tour was Steve Bernard, a fiery NSW fast bowler in the '70s; he was only a raw-boned young tearaway when his powerful swayback, whiplash action had caught the eye of Jack Chegwyn, during one of Cheggy's country tours to Orange, in the central west of the State.

Later in his cricketing life Bernard became the chairman of the NSW selection panel, then replaced me on the Australian panel. This is how Bernard judged Warne's tour in his official report:

> Shane demonstrated good control and also has a good variety of deliveries. He has a good spinner's head, and is prepared to keep a full length and maintain an attacking stance against a batsman who tries to take to him.
>
> Shane was the highest wicket-taker on tour, and I believe he can be successful as an allrounder if he is prepared to work on his batting. The ability is there to make a competent No.8/9 batsman.
>
> Shane was an excellent tourist and was paid the honour by the West Indies team of being given their tie in recognition of his personality and the fact he mixed well with the opposition when many others would not be bothered.

Warne's stats were: six wickets in the 'Tests', at 30 apiece; tour matches, 17 wickets at 16 apiece. That tour was in September, 1990. In November that year, Victoria chose Warne for a Sheffield Shield match against Western Australia at St Kilda.

His match figures were one for 102. On the strength of them, he was dropped. Only the bravest, or most foolhardy band of national selectors would have sent him back to the West Indies, a few months later, this time to bowl to Viv Richards or, worse still, have his fingers busted by Ambrose, Walsh, Patterson and Marshall.

History shows that even though Matthews and Taylor were Test-tough, they did not enjoy the 1991 Caribbean experience — between them, in three of the five Tests they took five wickets at about 70 apiece.

But, with Bernard's report on the table and aware of Jim Higgs' knowledge of Warne's potential, we knew there would be no worries about sending him off to Zimbabwe with a first-class reference as thin as 'one Sheffield Shield appearance'; names like Pycroft, Arnold, Flower and Campbell were less intimidating than Greenidge, Haynes, Richards and Richardson.

It was indicative of our urgency that we chose another legspinner, McIntyre to go with Warne. Then the flak began.

Warne and McIntyre didn't just share a talent for legspin. They were both from Victoria, but the Victorian selectors' first choice as spinner was a left-arm orthodox named Paul Jackson and we didn't pick Jackson in the team to Zimbabwe.

This was the state of play for the three Victorian spinners in the Sheffield Shield at the time of the Zimbabwe selection process:

M	Wkts	5/10	Best	Ave	S/rate
Jackson					
30	73	1/–	6/55	37.30	96.62
McIntyre					
13	21	–/–	3/55	60.95	133.86
Warne					
1	1	–/–	1/41	102.00	222.00

On the strength of that it is possible to revisit Laurie Sawle's assertion that the scoreboard doesn't always tell the whole story. At the end of the 1996–97 season this is how their Sheffield Shield careers had changed:

M	Wkts	5/10	Best	Ave	S/rate
Jackson					
73	180	2/–	6/55	37.58	94.83
McIntyre					
51	159	5/2	6/64	45.09	91.08
Warne					
22	81	5/–	6/42	33.23	77.33

"Vision is bullshit." I think it was the former NSW Premier, John Fahey, who said that when trying to score a point off PJ Keating, the Prime Minister who used to polish the crystal ball when he wasn't polishing his bovver boots. Fahey's opinion of 'forward planning' is not on record, but we can only hope that in 1996, when he became the nation's Minister of Finance he had changed his mind.

The Victorian Sheffield Shield coach at the start of the '90s was Les Stillman. If he didn't think the Warne-McIntyre Zimbabwe experiment was bullshit, then he certainly didn't think it was much of an idea.

In 1991–92, in a pre-season interview he argued that the pair had been elevated to national prominence too soon, that there would be pressure on him to choose the pair in the Victorian team when they might not deserve to be chosen ...

"I mean, whom should we drop from the pace attack? Merv Hughes, who's a Test player? Damien Fleming, who's up there with Terry Alderman? Paul Reiffel ... Tony Dodemaide ... James Sutherland?" railed Les, dropping a few names.

He continued, "Last season we picked bowlers according to the number of wickets we thought they would get, not because of their bowling style, and we will continue that policy this year."

We can ignore the first point because that was just Les letting off some steam and being a bit silly (Fleming up there with Alderman), or, we can ask the obvious question, not so much, "Who's James Sutherland?" as "Where is James Sutherland?"

But on the second point — was Les really suggesting that there was a chance the Victorian selectors, according to him no respecters of style, might choose five offspinners on the grounds they thought they would get the wickets? Whatever happened to balance in a bowling attack?

The headline on the interview said, "The Conspiracy Theory — Spin in Victoria". The Stillman interview had all the ingredients of an attempt by

Victoria to establish a mischievous proposition that the national selection panel was getting too big for its boots, that it was dictating selection policy to State selectors, therefore putting the winning of Shield games as second priority. Now, that *is* bullshit.

The player balance of the team to Zimbabwe merely showed we were engaged in a bit of forward planning which we hoped might benefit Australian cricket, especially in the immediate future because the West Indies were due on our doorstep again.

And, as for the conspiracy theory ... to what end? To stop Victoria winning the Shield? It was all sheer fantasy.

Stillman raised another point during the interview:

Spinners need time, particularly in district cricket, to develop their bowling. You get someone like Shane Warne, who is a very promising legspinner, but he's only 21 and very inexperienced.

He would have been lucky to have taken 30 wickets in district cricket and yet he's wearing the Australian cap in Zimbabwe.

I think it is excellent that he has been recognised because he has the potential, but I would like to see him get much more experience in district cricket so that when he comes to play Shield cricket he is ready to make the jump up in standards.

There is commonsense in that view, and I'd say it probably applies in most cases. But another view questions the quality of development he might be exposed to in district cricket.

And, "quality" is the key word here — a dull district cricket captain who sets dud fields? Or maybe a captain who is a pace junkie? Or, even one who gives the spinner an over before the lunch and tea breaks — just to make sure his development is really steady.

The Australian selectors didn't know it at the time but Warne is a freak. The fact that he was able to rub shoulders with, exchange tactics with, and socialise with senior Australian players like Mark Taylor, Steve Waugh and Tom Moody matured him rapidly on the Zimbabwe tour.

And anyway, if he hadn't been in Zimbabwe he'd have been trialling in the St Kilda nets for district cricket, weather permitting. In three weeks in Zimbabwe he bowled 153 overs and took 15 wickets — an unkind commentator would note that's only 15 less than Les thought Warne had taken in his whole district cricket career.

A few seasons further on and Jackson had moved north to Queensland and helped them win their first Sheffield Shield, and McIntyre had gone to South Australia, and helped them win their first Sheffield Shield in 14 years, and he'd played in an Ashes Test. Warne had matured into the best leg-spinner in the world. The best ever some said.

New Year Test, SCG 1994

It was just after tea on day three and 'HC' — Hansie Cronje — was about to face 'JC' — Shane Warne. It was the 26th over of South Africa's second innings, they were a wicket down, and the total was 47, still 76 runs short of making Australia bat again.

Cronje had scored 18. Although this wasn't Warne's first over of the innings we could feel an adrenalin surge, and quickening pulses among cricket's true believers, the fans of the ebb and flow game. Eventually 100,000 of them turned up to see possibly Test cricket's sweetest victory of all; certainly it was South Africa's, by just five runs.

At that moment, as Warne eyed Cronje, we thought the Proteas were about to wilt. The expectation was: get Cronje and South Africa's house would soon be in disorder, a house of cards. Until that moment, Warne had been bowling with a stiffish breeze from the Randwick end; now he was to come into it.

The switch also allowed him to aim at the spreading dust patches made by the stomping feet of fast bowlers in their follow-throughs, targets about the same size and shape as the hoops Warne uses in his practice drills.

Ball one: a stock legspinner, tossed up into the breeze, good loop, dropping and drifting towards the legs. Cronje, two quick steps to the pitch of the ball, kills the spin and plays it to the onside. Good timing, but a comfortable rather than a confident shot.

Ball two: will Warne try for the orthodox — another looping leggie, pitched wider, looking for a stumping? It's another legspinner, but it's short, not quite a long hop, but short enough to attack. Cronje has to answer the question that has necked his teammate Cullinan three times so far — is it the flipper? He plays safe. He blocks it, comfortably. Only then may it have crossed his mind: "I should have pulled that for four."

Ball three: the same length as the ball before, short, but not the legspinner. It's the flipper and Warne's hope is that Cronje will have been fooled by the previous ball, think it's another long-hop leggie and this time, go for the pull shot, exposing his stumps and pads to the sharp, low skid of his wicket-taking ball. Cronje blocks it comfortably. If he didn't pick it, he very probably expected it.

Ball four: if Cronje can pick the flipper then Warne has to come up with something to unbalance South Africa's stand-in skipper for the hurt Wessels. That's not easy because Hansie looks as if he might not mind wearing a hair shirt in a heat wave, and chewing old leather to boot. Tough as gristle. The ball Warne chooses for this special effect is a ripping topspinner. Or was it a wrong'un? Even from high up on the sidelines and aided by a televsion replay it was hard to tell.

Whatever, it pitched just short of a length and leapt at Cronje, seeming to take a batting glove as well as the thigh, then scuttled away just wide of the grasping hands of the diving Boon at short leg. Warne's deliveries are 'stilettoes' and don't demand an ambulance for batsmen as did Jeff Thomson's Exocet missiles, but Test cricket is as much a mind game as anything else and that Warne delivery had as much to recommend it as any Thommo rib-cruncher.

Cronje showed nothing, but he may just have wondered: Where did that come from? Warne was back on top.

Ball five: Cronje might not be confused but one thing is certain — he's wondering a bit harder about this next ball. What will it be? Flipper, floater, wrong'un, top spinner ...?

It's just a legspinner. Well not quite 'just' — it lands a ball circumference outside leg and on a perfect length. Cronje, tall, gets well forward trying to cover it with his long reach, but it flits sideways, past the outside edge of a dead bat, but not into the off stump as it did with Mike Gatting 10 Tests before.

Ball six: If Cronje's rattled he's not letting on, but Warne and the Australians know he's lucky still to be there. Warne's last shot is another legspinner with less rip, hoping for less turn and therefore an edge to Healy, or Taylor at slip. Cronje's forward defence is tight enough this time.

It was an unforgettable span of play, a couple of minutes of cricket combat that reminded us all of just what Test cricket is all about. And it took a legspinner to do it.

Any talk of Warne and legspin history in Australia always covers Bill O'Reilly, Clarrie Grimmett and Rich, all different styles, all different personalities, all match-winners.

The simplest way to compare them is to take the end-point of the careers of O'Reilly and Grimmett and, because Warne has yet to play as many Tests as Rich, to match Warne's current status with Rich's career at that time (See the table on page opposite).

Purely from a selection point of view the most eye-catching statistic is Grimmett's talent for taking five wickets in an innings, and 10 in the match. A destroyer, and a captain wouldn't have been able to toss him the ball soon enough!

Tests	Wkts	5Wi/10Wm	Ave	S/rate
O'Reilly				
27	144	11/3	22.60	69.61
Warne				
27	124	6/1	23.63	67.86
Grimmett				
37	216	21/7	24.22	67.19
Warne				
37	170	9/2	24.10	65.58
Rich				
58	231	15/1	26.46	74.65
Warne-current				
58	264	11/3	23.95	63.04
Rich-record				
63	248	16/1	27.03	77.05
Warne-record				
55	249	11/3	24.04	63.37

In view of Warne's early Victorian experience, you may see some humour in the following: in the six seasons the young Grimmett (from age 25) was in Victoria, the selectors only picked him five times. He moved to South Australia.

Warne was a major player in a revival of legspin worldwide, a kiss of life for a game being bludgeoned to death by slow over rates and pace. The new wave of legspin didn't just influence Test match results — it performed a facelift on limited-overs cricket.

TINKER

Limited-overs cricket is one-dimensional cricket. Its saving grace is that it can be played at night and watching cricket under a full moon is magic that lasts. A mix of spectator agitation and player boredom can be the catalyst for inevitable change.

What is it about One-day cricket? Does it attract a second tier of spectator interest? Is it a licence to make money? Is it television ratings-driven? Does it widen the player base? Or, does it just give the players some welcome relief after the intensity of a five-day Test match?

It's possible there was a time in One-day cricket history when the latter applied, when the same players, with one or two changes, were chosen for both the Test team and the One-day team.

Of course, it's less the case in the late '90s. More and more countries are separating the selection process, and more and more players, on the fringe of the Test game, are specialising in the One-day format because they see that as their meal ticket, rather than the stepping stone to the Test team.

About the only concession Australia used to make to the different tactics in the two forms of the game was always to select Simon O'Donnell in the One-day team. Now they're sending One-day specialists to overseas contests (South Africa, 1997) and sending home victorious Test players.

This puts more pressure on the selectors during their judgmental sessions, but not so much that we need two panels, for that surely would be a recipe for chaos. Or would it? I suppose so long as there was a constant to the two panels — the same chairman — then there is no good reason why the format wouldn't work. But, I don't see why one astute group of selectors couldn't handle both jobs.

After Australia had been beaten, a sort of a capitulation, by India in the one-off Test in Delhi in October, 1996 — it should be noted that David Boon had retired the previous January — Allan Border gave an interview to an Indian magazine, *Sportsworld*.

He was asked to respond to two points:

- Was it reasonable for Australia to excuse the Test loss by damning the turning Indian pitch?
- Did Australia miss having someone like Boon in the batting line-up?

This is what he said in answer to the first question: "It is a question of playing your innings according to the circumstances and the pitch of the day. That is what Test match batting is all about. You can't be a one-dimensional player. You have to be able to play the ball between waist and chin on a fast bouncy wicket and, you've also got to learn to play the long, dour innings on a difficult turning track."

On the second, he said: "I'll tell you, Australia's disappointing loss in Delhi won't be the last occasion when an ugly five-hour Test century or a typical David Boon innings would be seen as a blessing. For the first time in a decade he wasn't there to waddle to the crease, chew thoughtfully on his gum and ponder what the moment called for."

If you are inclined to agree with the proposition that One-day cricket is one dimensional, then AB's message that you can't be a one-dimensional Test player, raises for administrators, cricketers and their coaches, and selectors the old chestnut — is One-day cricket having a negative influence on traditional cricket? Consider the recent plight of Michael Bevan, a champion One-day batsman but troubled on the Ashes tour by short-pitched bowling, an aggressive tactic outlawed in the One-day game.

In the expressway that is the '90s there mightn't be time to listen to AB's wise counsel, yet there is so much to consider:

- How closely should administrators monitor the volume of One-day cricket? What is saturation point for players; when will they suffer physical and mental rundown? Will there still be a place in the One-day game for the 'character players' as well as the sloggers?
- If it's glamour, glitz and bright lights that most influence the young cricketers of tomorrow, does that mean the 'Rockys' like Boon will be out by 2000? Is grit to be superseded by grunt-only?
- That question raises selection philosophy and why there could be a case for two panels — just in case the adrenalin rush to choose youth becomes so overwhelming, should we not preserve a Test panel with some patient, reflective minds on it?
- What about pay rates for players — should Test and One-day players get equal pay? What if a smart lawyer works out that Michael DiVenuto is entitled to more dollars than the Test No.3? If there are different pay rates might not that have some influence on a player as to which game he might pursue?

- Can some administrators really be serious when they talk about limited-overs Test matches? If so, what are the chances of someone applying for a heritage order on Test cricket as we know it?

Do you think that this worldwide trend towards more expansive selection philosophy might really be a confession that the One-day game had become too stereotyped? If that was the case — a negative trend, crowds starting to stay away or, soggy television ratings — then mightn't we need to change not just the faces of the players but the rules of the One-day game, too?

Television ratings might partly explain the Cricket Board's 'Australia B insult' to Australia, England and Zimbabwe in the 1994–95 World Series. Who'd want to watch Zimbabwe play England? was a thorny question.

The answer was, hardly anyone. Crowds at Zimbabwe matches averaged a lowly 7,613. Compare that with the overall average crowd attendance of 25,941 a game, which rated solidly against any other season.

The Cricket Board can cope with seasonal financial downturns, and indeed has always had to — The Ashes one summer, New Zealand the next. But if such disenchantment with Zimbabwe was to impact negatively on the TV ratings then the broadcaster faced losing considerable advertising revenue.

What happened was this: without any Australian influence the ratings figure was as low as 15; with Australia B it reached 25, and when Australia played it climbed into the low 30s.

Television ratings are always more likely to turn doughy before attendances at grounds. Pre-series reserved ticket sales and 'live atmosphere', and all that's good and bad that goes with it, are crowd constants.

Lounge-room luxury is a flick-of-the-switch thing — what's more exciting tonight, Grant Flower sussing out Phil Tufnell's finger spin or Inspector Morse tracking down The Toecutter? When the punters switch off, that's the danger sign.

If that happens, what are the Board's options? Some modern marketing initiatives have been naive — prizes for spectators who catch six-hits, some kid watching the toss, players in shorts, school fete standard dancing girls, and batsmen entering the arena to signature tunes like 'Wild Thing'. Naturally, there were no takers for 'The Great Pretender'.

It got worse — songs like 'Hit the Road Jack' and 'See ya later, Alligator' blared out after departing batsmen, most of them Australia's opponents. Nothing like a bit of bad taste to spur on a yobbo, or ten thousand.

Cricket's 'suits' need to be careful they never lose sight of the old, but still true marketing theory — you can dress up a can of dog food, but the product is still dog food.

It's the cricket that counts. Get that right and the rest will look after itself. Is the cricket right?

Any rule changes must be simple. The bottom line in any good One-day game is simply what is called 'the equation' — 38 runs from 32 balls and, can the batsmen do it?

The equation is there all during the match, but no one gives a hoot when it's 214 runs off 258 balls. It's only near the end of the game that the equation creates peak interest.

So, if the administrators are tempted to tamper with the rules nothing should complicate the climax — everyone from players to spectators to viewers must be able to appreciate the runs/balls equation.

The game falls into three basic sections — first 15 overs, overs 16 to 40 and, the last 10 overs. If any aspect of the game needs surgery it is the middle phase, the pedestrian overs, when the field goes back and the batsmen start knocking the ball into the gaps for ones and the odd two. Formula cricket. For spectators it's time to go and get a hot dog. What about bored viewers?

That's the time when batsmen should be offered more scoring opportunities through some rule changes. Don't worry about the bowlers — W. G. Grace got it right that time long ago when he adjusted his broken wicket and told the bowler, "They came to watch me bat, not you bowl!"

Consider these possibilities:

Fewer fielders outside the circle after 15 overs is fine, but there needs to be a proviso — of those left inside the circle, more should be in designated 'catching' positions.

That should offer batsmen more gaps, and larger ones and hopefully encourage more inventive shot-making than the chip out to midwicket, or the push to long on.

However, the number of 'catching' positions should not be so great as to create conditions too similar to those in the longer form of the game, or the disparity between the two games will be diluted, and that would be fatal.

Why not introduce bonus runs for boundaries hit between overs from 16 to 40?

The silliest suggestion so far on bonus runs has been to turn fours into fives and sixes into sevens. It makes for a bigger score, but hardly more brilliant cricket, or more compulsive watching. It's like moving the boundaries in.

Lou: "Nothing can be changed by the wholesale changing of the laws of the game if the changes will not result in a positive improvement in the game.

Take the case of the introduction of a law to shorten the boundaries. All it accomplished was to make it easier for the same boring batsmen to get runs more easily."

A more useful result might be obtained by rewarding teams for batches of boundaries, or six hits — say, for every five boundaries a team hits they get a bonus of 10 runs. If they hit 10 boundaries they get 25 bonus runs, and so on.

The marketing whizkids will love it — great graphics on the ground big screen! But, if they hit nine boundaries, they only get the 10-run bonus. In other words, the intention of the bonus boundaries rule would be to encourage batsmen to go for it a bit harder. And, for bowlers and captains to try a bit harder to prevent it happening.

Bonus boundaries might have the effect of bringing forward what Dean Jones liked to call 'the happy hour', the final overs of an innings when the batsmen were a little less cautious about playing the big shots.

And, overs 35 to 40, when batsmen know a few more boundaries can mean more bonus runs, would surely be more exciting. A bonus run rule is surely a natural follow-on to the bench player innovation.

Bench players. Already captains are using 'pinch-hitters' from within the original line-up. But bench players, those coming on from outside the eleven, should never be allowed to reach the nonsensical and confusing proportions they have in the rugby league code.

Two substitutes, a pinch-hitter and a strike bowler, are fine, but with a proviso — yes, they should be nominated before the match, much the same as the 12th man is now, but, they should only be used up until the 40th over. They shouldn't be allowed to have a direct influence on the final equation, which should remain untainted and the true test of each team's capacity under pressure.

Many will say 'yeah' to such changes. Those who say 'nay' will argue that the game's not 'broke', so why try to fix it? But, why not try to improve the cricket spectacle, and try to encourage more people to the game?

There is one rule change that administrators should make without hesitation:

The no-ball rule. In One-day cricket, administrators should scrap the controversial front-foot law, and revert to the old back-foot one. The earlier call would allow the batsman a good, old fashioned free hit. It might even be a worthwhile experiment with a long term view towards changing the situation in Test cricket.

I met him on a train, a total stranger. It was 1984. And, as eager as he was to get off at his station, Penrith, he was just as eager to show me a computer printout. It was a fascinating document, the likes of which I hadn't seen before. It detailed every one of Dennis Lillee's 355 victims in Test cricket. Some milestones were:

No.1, Adelaide, January 1971 — John Edrich, ct Stackpole;
No.100, 'Gabba, November 1975 — Viv Richards, ct Gilmour;
No.200, MCG, February 1980 — John Lever, bowled;
No.300, 'Gabba, November 1981 — Wasim Raja, ct Laird;
No.355, SCG, January 1984 — Sarfraz Nawaz, ct Phillips.

This stranger's name was Ross Dundas and, I soon discovered, he had something of a fetish for cricket statistics. Why? Elementary, really. He was born in 1953, an Ashes tour year, and grew up on a dairy farm at Mullumbimby, a short drive up the highway from Lou's place at North Casino.

As a kid he listened to Alan McGilvray on the radio and filled in the scoresheets at the back of the ABC Cricket Book. And, when he came down to the big smoke to pursue a career as a computer operator, he finally settled at Penrith, where Lou had bowled up that piece of cricket history. Today Ross Dundas runs the electronic scoreboard at the SCG. When I was selecting, his information could be invaluable. Ross can't quite tell you how many times Dennis Lillee's right forefinger squeezed sweat from his eyebrows during his career, but he can tell you everything else ... victim No.87, Lord's, July 1975 — Graham Gooch, ct Marsh for six.

Of course, a selector relies on his eyes and his experience in the game, even his instinct when it comes to making judgments, but if there's indecision then statistics might assist in the judgment by showing a form trend.

The selector who tells you he doesn't bother with statistical references is having a lend of himself. The good selector just doesn't let the stats get in the way of his better judgment.

Courtesy of Ross Dundas's computer, here are some points about the One-day game. Because One-day cricket is a pattern game, like football and basketball it fits snugly into the computer age — 'click button A for action'. One-day cricket has the slick image yet a lot of Test matches are more unpredictable.

One-day cricketers tend to establish a pattern, then play to it. It only needs a few successes to create a 'fad' — Simon O'Donnell's slogging and his slower balls; Dean Jones and his running between the wickets; Jayasuriya's and Kaluwitharana's blockbuster openings; Allan Donald coming back in the middle of the innings, not the end.

Take Geoff Marsh, one of the real success stories of Australia's great winning run from the 1987 World Cup until he retired. Tip-and-run Geoff.

But what about the player whose unlikely One-day style was on just as many lips as any of those names, Mark Taylor?

By the end of the tour to South Africa in 1997 Taylor was out of form and out of the Australian One-day team, at the time a proper selection judgment, even though he was the captain. The important point to make there is that he was an unsuccessful captain. The team was losing.

His dropping prompted the verdict, "The One-day game is simply not his game," but it was not a recent judgment. It had been in place since the 1993–94 season, when a campaign began urging the selectors to choose Matthew Hayden and Taylor in World Series on a rotation basis.

The suggestion came from Queensland, and a cynic might have been inclined to wonder whether it was intended to influence the eventual captaincy changeover from Border ... after all, if Taylor the vice-captain couldn't make the One-day team how could he be captain of Australia? On the other hand, Queensland's Ian Healy, the wicketkeeper, was assured a spot in both forms of the game ...

It put Taylor under a great deal of unnecessary pressure to change his style. His non-slogging batting style was perceived as being wrong for what is touted as the fast form of the game. So, you might wonder how two players of stodgy style, Geoff Marsh and Mark Taylor, can be so differently judged in the One-day arena.

What would you say if told that 'the duffer' Taylor's World Series career compares quite favourably with the hero Marsh's? Taylor's batting strike rate (runs per 100 balls) is 59.14, Marsh's is 54.35.

Other notable batsmen we can compare statistically with Taylor have been Desmond Haynes 59.42, Richie Richardson 56.45 and Javed Miandad 57.89. Yes, 'Hammer' Haynes on virtually the same strike rate as 'Tubby' Taylor!

Marsh won six WS Man of the Match awards and Taylor three, plus two Player of the Finals awards (one shared). Taylor has figured in 10 century partnerships, Marsh in 13. Taylor shares the Most Catches in a Match, four. Taylor once rated as Australia's most successful captain in World Series — only by 0.51 per cent, but nevertheless, the best.

Of course, it doesn't really matter to Taylor's critics how well his record stands up statistically; they merely labour the point that his style is not the style for the roaring nineties. If Hayden's style was acceptable, the substance might not have been — strike rate 45.09.

Bob Simpson's coaching style, the tip-and-runners, Marsh and Boon, and his pace change bowlers like O'Donnell and Steve Waugh, altered the face of the One-day game for half a dozen summers.

Then along came Sri Lanka's sloggers just before the 1996 World Cup, and suddenly the Australian tactics looked old-fashioned, and batsmen with reputations like Marsh, Boon and Taylor looked out of place. Enter the young gunslingers like DiVenuto and Ryan Campbell.

Style. It's like a Pierre Cardin wardrobe — seasonal. In a game as predictable as limited-overs cricket, we can be sure of one thing — one day, the tip-and-run tacticians will come back into fashion. Unless, of course, some marketing guru insists that in future all boundaries be no further than a sand-wedge from the centre.

One of the myths about One-day cricket was the one about wrist-spinners being undesirable. It's just that when the One-day revolution began, when World Series Cricket introduced the white ball and night play, the business of wrist-spinning was in temporary receivership, except in England where it was totally bankrupt.

Back then, the champions at both forms of the game were Clive Lloyd's West Indians and their attack was a battalion of fast bowlers with a bit of back-up from Larry Gomes and Viv Richards. They were a couple of part-time, flat off spinners whose accuracy wouldn't have been out of place in front of a dart board in an English pub.

Because the West Indies had so much success with their formula every other team in the world decided it was just that — the winning formula. A few fast or medium pace bowlers, and finger spinners were suddenly the fashion.

The great sadness about it was that just about every junior coach decided to get with the trend. Upon seeing a youngster tossing up a loopy leggie at training the coach promptly advised him there was no mention of such expensive nonsense in his game plan.

Now, in the '90s, we've gone the other way. If you can find a cricket coach anywhere in the world who doesn't have a wrist-spinner in his team then you might feel inclined to take some time out to tell him he's unfashionable.

But, for the sake of the game, and its future, you would be more sensible to discuss the benefits of diversity of styles in a bowling attack. Variation, and balance will usually win the day.

Because it is such a one-dimensional game, One-day cricket can provide watchers with some of the great talent comparisions by statistics. These comparisons apply to all One-day Internationals, not just Australia's World Series.

The battle of the allrounders. Steve Waugh doesn't bowl much these days, and the rest, Ian Botham, Imran Khan, Kapil Dev and Richard Hadlee have retired. Will we ever see such dynamic talent again, all in the one era? Dev's batting strike rate (92 runs per 100 balls) over such a long period is extraordinary.

Player	Matches	Wkts/S-r	Runs/S-r
Hadlee	115	158/39	1751/76
Imran	175	182/41	3709/72
Botham	116	145/43	2113/80
Dev	225	253/44	3781/92
Waugh	218	172/45	5032/74

And, doesn't that all raise a point — where are all the allrounders in modern cricket? Players like Keith Miller, Rich and Alan Davidson, who were all dynamic bowlers ... and equally dynamic with the bat.

Why is it that bowlers like Jason Gillespie and Shane Warne, who clearly understand the technical points of batting, don't bat like batsmen, properly. These days bowlers seem to be either pinch-hitters, or 'rabbits'.

Australia has a Cricket Academy that should be more strenuously addressing the development of allround potential. And, every Sheffield Shield team has a coach, as does Australia. Generally, this indifference to batting by bowlers can be put down to mindset rather than a lack of talent.

Nor is the development of allrounders being helped by an insistence by captains that the first six places in the batting order must go to 'pure' batsmen. There was a time when the strength of Australian cricket was its allrounders. We must hope we'll see the day again.

Pakistan's Abdul Qadir was a cricketing pioneer — a legspinner asked to take on the One-day big hitters when offspinners were fashionable. How does he rate against his successors, Shane Warne, Mushtaq Ahmed and Anil Kumble?

Player	Matches	Wkts/S-r	Best
Warne	73	128/32	5/33
Kumble	113	159/38	6/12
Mushtaq	124	141/45	5/36
Qadir	126	141/45	7/37

Dennis Lillee, Michael Holding and Joel Garner trampled across world cricket, in any of its forms, for a decade. How do they rate against the modern fast bowlers Craig McDermott, Curtly Ambrose, Wasim Akram and Waqar Younis, and Allan Donald?

Player	Matches	Wkts/S-r	Best
Younis	156	264/30	6/36
Donald	87	147/32	6/23
Lillee	63	103/35	5/34
Garner	98	146/36	5/31
Akram	232	333/36	5/15
McDermott	138	203/37	5/44
Holding	102	142/38	5/26
Ambrose	141	193/39	5/17

Also, check Wasim Akram's performance against the list of allrounders. His batting is as explosive as his bowling — 2180 runs at a strike rate of 89 — which arguably makes him the world's most valuable One-day cricketer.

You won't be surprised that Viv Richards is One-day cricket's hell-for-leather batsman. No one comes close to his strike rate — but there are some surprises among the challengers from other countries.

Player	Matches	Runs/S-r	50/100s
Richards	187	6721/91	45/11
Aravinda	204	6407/82	43/8
Tendulkar	143	5079/82	31/11
Anwar	118	4135/82	17/11
M Waugh	132	4411/78	27/10
Gower	114	3170/77	12/7
Crowe	143	4704/72	34/4
Cronje	115	3473/68	22/2

It might be worth noting that the three batsmen closest to Richards have played most of their cricket on the flat pitches of the subcontinent.

World Series stats are a dream for trivia buffs:
- Allan Border sometimes called on Craig McDermott to do some pinch-hitting. Craig's batting strike rate was 80.85, but he scored more ducks (11) than anyone else. High risk, perhaps?
- Dean Jones was dismissed three times in the nineties, 98, 93, 92, and stranded in the nineties twice, on 99 and 93 — what might have been.

The list of that sort of stuff is endless, but the stats can also show up a trend. According to the table below it is a trend that should be of some concern to the Australian Cricket Board.
- On a season-by-season basis the majority of Biggest Victories and Narrowest Victories occurred before 1990. The top ten Highest Individual Innings were played, bar one, pre-1990. Only three of the Record Wicket Partnerships were compiled after 1990. Two-thirds of the Most Expensive Bowling Performances were before 1990.
- The huge season was probably1982–83 when Australia, England and New Zealand hit 503 fours and 53 sixes. The brightest season was 1984–85, when Australia, the West Indies and Sri Lanka, scored at 81 runs per 100 balls.
- The most recent season, 1996–97, between Australia, West Indies and Pakistan, was the second dullest on record judged on strike-rate—a thick edge over 62 runs scored per 100 balls.

Season	Fours/sixes	S/rate	Visiting Teams
1993–94	280/15	61.88	NZ, S Af
1996–97	340/25	62.47	Pak, WI
1991–92*	269/21	62.78	Ind, WI
1992–93	273/15	64.33	Pak, WI
1995–96*	340/16	64.51	Pak, SL
1994–95	327/10	65.12	Eng, Zim, Aus B
1986–87	278/21	65.38	Eng, WI
1987–88*	349/20	70.57	NZ, SL
1989–90	320/42	72.49	Pak, SL

* Denotes World Cup year

Yet, on the basis of fours and sixes hit the 1996–97 season rated much higher. If batsmen hit more boundaries you'd expect a high run rate, so why were there so many 'dot balls'? The answer may lie in the team totals; in 14

World Series matches the team batting first set a target of more than 200 only four times. Surely that's the best available proof for any One-day captains who doubt the theory about the best way to restrict the run rate is to take wickets.

I suppose the tough question is why did it happen? Are bowlers getting better or are batsmen getting more careless? Were pitches spicier? Or, are captains more clever, even more attacking?

Note the extraordinary number of sixes in 1989–90. Most of the dull cricket has been played post-1990. What happened? Perhaps the players were suffering cricket fatigue?

About that time there was a massive increase in One-day matches worldwide. It has continued. In 1996 there were nearly five times as many One-day matches as Test matches.

When the Australian Cricket Board announced in 1997 that the selectors would be choosing separate Test and One-day teams, its strange timing (just after the Ashes victory) created an inference that the much-criticised Test captain (Mark Taylor) would not be in charge of the One-day team. It was just one more test of the captain's character.

TAYLOR

Mark Taylor is one of the most successful Australian captains, but not even his bold leadership style and winning record could save him from a mostly mindless media campaign to get rid of him when he began to suffer a run of indifferent batting form.

It says something about the modern Australian media that a solid citizen like Mark Taylor has never been a pin-up captain. I guess he's just not a 'nineties-guy'. No gel in the hair and he's round, when physically he should be Matthew Hayden-esque.

Not so much as a millimetre of bronzed skin on the little bit he shows. No eye-catching earring. No on-field histrionics. Hell, he's less effusive than Allan Border, whom we all acknowledged was a rock.

Taylor doesn't leave the front of his shirt unbuttoned like Rich, but buttons down his sleeves. He doesn't get aggro like Chappelli. He doesn't walk tall, nor as elegantly as Greg Chappell. Face a mask, he sort of rolls.

He's got a slightly cock-eye, one member of the modern sporting media has said he "talks slightly faster than Donald Duck on speed", and he so annoys some people with his jaw yawing gum chewing habit that they actually make time to write letters to newspapers to complain about it.

And, worst of all, he failed occasionally to order his opponents to follow-on, when all the captains out there in armchair land knew he should have asked them to.

My God, where is this man's laser lightshow of personality? Why isn't he simply oozing charisma? Shouldn't someone have told Mark Taylor early in the piece that substance is out and schlick is in?

Bradman was going on 90 in late 1997, so the modern cricket society would probably think his opinion about cricket captains was as old-fashioned as Taylor's persona.

But Bradman reminds us all of what we should always expect of a cricket captain: "A good captain will be a fighter; confident but not arrogant, firm but not obstinate, able to take criticism without letting it unduly disturb him, for he is sure to get it — and unjustly, too."

Anyone with a moderate mind and a sharp eye for the game, who watched Taylor closely during his years on top down under, might have been inclined to think he was Bradman's kind of captain.

Remember when newspapers offered 'expert' sporting opinion? The bloke whose name had appeared on the scoreboard on Saturday, was the same bloke whose name graced the columns of the morning paper on the following Monday.

"Jawbreaker Jones Writes For Us — Exclusive", the street posters would screech, inviting you to indulge in 10 cents worth of wisdom from one of the game's greats. In the case of some great cricketers, notably Rich, Bill O'Reilly, Ian Chappell and Arthur Mailey, it was all their own work.

But Jawbreaker didn't write his at all — he was actually under a ray lamp somewhere, trying to change his bruises from black to blue and his column was the work of a 'ghost'. That is, Jawbreaker's thoughts were committed to print by a professional journalist.

Was that really such a bad thing? When done properly — one committed journalist working consistently with one 'expert' — ghosting can provide a valuable insight into a sport, its tactics and those who fashion them. Good ghosting can provide a balance to another critic's viewpoint.

Sometimes, circumstances devalue it. The respected Sydney rugby league writer, the late E. E. Christensen, was once asked to ghost three players in one day — a front row forward, a fullback and a halfback — all from different teams, all born in a different country and speaking with different accents, all with massive discrepancies in IQ, and who had played in three different matches on different sides of the city.

Because ghosting raised ethical concerns among journalists, from the minor — not a real journalist, not a paid up member of the union — to the major — won't bag his own team, won't bag his opposition, the phrase 'conflict of interest' received heavy airing, as did the word 'bias'.

Two things happened: one, the qualification 'as told to' started to appear at the bottom of ghosted articles, thus crediting the ghost but creating a slightly negative perception about the sporting editor's 'exclusive' line. It was a development to be applauded.

The other was a determination to clean up the image of sports writing, to get rid of the jockstrap image. So, 'creative' writing talent became all important, more important than any intimate knowledge of the sport about which the journalist was offering 'expert' commentary.

It is arguable whether this creative trend, the new fashion, has provided sports reporting, particularly cricket, with a desirable outcome.

Consider this preview of the 1997 Ashes contest in *The Australian*: "The arrival of the Australians has again encouraged the usual nonsense about Ashes tours being the ultimate when they are becoming increasingly irrelevant." In another tour preview the Ashes series was likened to an end-of-season football jaunt.

The judgment is based on the writer's own sterile perception of the game, on the recent track record of England, and nothing else. Does he ask the players if they think the contest is irrelevant? Where is the supporting evidence? Is there a player prepared to offer, "I'm not going on that junk Ashes tour!" And the fans? If the Ashes tour is irrelevant why were pre-Test series sales at sellout levels?

And the writer ignores one of cricket's lasting characteristics, its ebb and flow. Players will have a run of outs, today's hero is tomorrow's has-been, and generally teams will perform according to whichever trend is in play. The writer also forgets that The Ashes is well documented history, forever reminding us of many of the game's greatest tussles. We live in hope for as many encores as the fingernails will stand.

England beating Australia — only occasionally, mind you! — is good for the game. I'm entitled to be old-fashioned when it comes to judgments about cricket commentary because I have a deep love of the game. It's in the blood. Late in his life, when he was approaching his personal 'nervous 90s', Lou wrote: "The spirit of cricket entered my heart while I was at high school ... there is still a deep love of cricket in my heart."

I subscribe to the theory that unless you have spent some quality time in the middle then you might not care enough about the game, its players and the pressures, and pleasures, under which they operate.

And, if you don't really care about the game, if cricket is just another sporting contest, then you should think twice about offering yourself to the public as an expert, as many in the new cricket media do.

Some of them have become so precious about their right to take the long handle to the players in the game that they themselves have never played, never enjoyed, never got to know intimately, that they refer to some ex-player commentators as 'the cricket mafia'.

That's certainly not to insist that ex-players are always right in their judgments, merely to say that in the main they are more likely to consider the fabric of the game before they try to create a headline.

The new cricket media are encouraged to ignore the nuances of the game because it is their editor's most earnest hope that a smart headline will 'neck' some poor individual.

They are not particularly interested in the ebb and flow of a day's play, no longer interested in enjoying with a team its success, instead they seek out failure, or manufacture and peddle controversy.

March 27, 1997

A feature story, headlined "What Gazza Shares With Shazza", appears in *The Sydney Morning Herald*. Its author compares Shane Warne, never in his cricketing career known to have gone by the nickname of 'Shazza', with 'Gazza', a thug named Paul Gascoigne who plays soccer for England. It is the classic case of an article being written to fit a clever headline.

The article is accompanied by an illustration known as a 'photomontage', in which Warne and Gascoigne appear to be training at the same ground, and happily chatting to one another. They're not. It is a classic example of the tricks that can be played by computer imaging.

The article brought this respone from Rich, in a letter to the editor:

If it can be shown factually that Shane Warne has assaulted fans, punched photographers, is a wife basher, has received a suspended jail sentence and exhibits behaviour ranging between being daft as a brush and mentally ill, or any one of those things, then the article by John Huxley has some merit.

Otherwise, it is one of the worst and most disgraceful stories I have read in 41 years as a journalist.

Maybe it's not just the new sporting media which is inclined to this sort of character assassination, maybe it's the nature of all today's media, the dividend from Watergate where a couple of super-snoop journos brought down a corrupt American president.

Now every journo wishes he could be as famous as a Bernstein or a Woodward and bring down a VIP. Who cares how trivial his sin? Tolerance is out. Shane Warne smokes a cigarette and it's on the front page — a quiet news day, perhaps?

But for me, as someone who cares for cricket, much sadder than all that was the destabilisation of the Australian team leadership during the 1996–97 season, a media beat-up which reached frenzy status in the middle of the very successful 1997 tour of South Africa and then riddled the first weeks of the Ashes tour, and even its victorious end.

Monday, March 17, 1997

There's a headline in *The Australian* newspaper. It is at the top right-hand corner of page one. A cricket story on page one of the serious national broadsheet daily … it must be important. The headline says: 'Why It's Time to Dismiss Mark Taylor'.

Gee, we're sacking the Australian captain — and, in the middle of a tour! In fact, in the middle of a Test series.

The author is the well respected Mike Coward. The article goes on for about 1,000 words, spilling from page one to page four. It begins … "Some things in this life we are not good at talking about. Death, terminal illness and sexuality are subjects which quickly come to mind."

A rather unique opening line to a comment piece on the lovely old game of cricket, you'd surely agree. For a split second you get the idea that it might be another ho-hum story about cricket being a dying game, or well stuffed, at least.

A tad over the top, of course, but that's Mike Coward's style. He's a wordsmith, and highly regarded for it. Mike's point is that people in cricket's high places are off the pace because they are reluctant to sack the Australian captain.

Mike says the reason the captain has to go is simple — he can't score a run to save himself. Maintaining all the drama of his opening, Mike eventually announces mid-article: "We can't avert our gaze any longer. We can't continue to look the other way. It is now 15 months and 17 innings since Taylor has scored a Test match 50 and it is becoming increasingly difficult to see from just where his next score will come." (A few days later Taylor made 38 — alas, 12 short of 50.)

Others in the cricket media were peddling Taylor's form lapse as a 'festering crisis' in Australian cricket … never mind the fact that we'd belted the West Indies and South Africa, and under Taylor had become the world champion Test nation. But some even went out of their way to qualify that achievement … 'a captain is only as good as his team'.

At least one former player backed Mike at the time. Neil Harvey, also a former selector, said Taylor should go. But Neil would, wouldn't he? Whenever the media wanted to sack Allan Border they usually phoned up Neil — a man as forthright with his opinions as he was with the bat. Next day's street poster would be along the lines of, 'Border Must Go, Says Harvey'.

Neil went by the nickname 'Ninna' but there's a bit of circumstantial evidence around that in matters of selection he could have copped 'Choppa' — he was a selector when Bill Lawry got the chop as captain of Australia and he was a NSW selector when I was sacked as captain over The Boots.

But of course, sackings go with the selector's territory. Two points can be made about Neil: (a) he helped to choose both of us, Lawry and me, and (b) on the tour to South Africa in 1957–58 Neil, who was a tour selector and vice-captain, is reported to have refused to consider team captain Ian Craig's offer to stand aside.

Judges less inclined than Neil to don the black cap took a wait-and-see stance on Taylor, nominating the circumstances that prevailed at the time.

In considering whether or not to join the queue demanding Taylor go out and find a sword and fall on it they asked a couple of questions, the questions a reasonable selector would ask himself in the circumstances: (a) the Australian team was performing strongly; (b) Taylor's opening partners were doing nothing much with the bat, either; and (c) the vice-captain, or captain-elect was Ian Healy. They were all important provisos in any balanced discussion about dismissing Taylor.

MILLER WOULD GIVE BENAUD CAPTAINCY

While Ian Craig's team has been successful in South Africa Craig himself has failed.

That's why I believe the Board of Control should seek another captain for the team which this year will try to win back the Ashes from England.

And I think the man they should appoint is Richie Benaud.

The situation in South Africa now is similar to that which existed in England in 1956, when Ian Johnson's form did not justify his place in the Test sides.

In the first four South African Tests, Craig has averaged 14.3 runs in a team which has assembled big scores.

His continued failure

average against the weaker South Africans.

His scores in Pakistan and India were 0, 18, 40, 36 and 6.

It was not the kind of form that ensures Australian selection in the future —yet Craig was not chosen, but was made captain over the heads of more experienced and considerably better players.

His job in South has been the suc ers—an that in

—and Richie over came a chan I am su mind h tain. part ort

What is it about a tour to South Africa that seems to bode ill for Australian cricket captains? Near the end of Australia's highly successful 1958 tour, Ian Craig's indifferent batting form prompted some critics to advocate he be replaced. But it was tame stuff compared with the witch hunt Mark Taylor endured.

The questions to be considered were these:

<u>Why was there a preoccupation with the score of 50?</u> Are fifties the only way to judge an opener? His job is to take the shine off the ball. The media could have looked a little deeper into Taylor's performance — over the same period of time since his last 50, he had occupied the crease for longer than an hour in 50 per cent of his innings. What were the circumstances when he did that?

<u>How should we rate Mark Taylor as a cricketer</u> — is he purely a batsman or is he an allrounder, with two aspects to his game, opener/captain? Three even

— champion first slip fielder. Clearly, he's an allrounder. It is fair to judge him as any bowler/batsman allrounder would be judged if he was having a dead spot with say, the ball.

If we have to drop an opening batsman should we retain Matthew Hayden? What's more important to the team, Hayden's indifferent batting form (he was out of his depth and averaging about 25) or Taylor's successful captaincy?

And, is it smart to sack a captain whose team is winning Test matches like we haven't won them since Ian Chappell was in charge — just in case the opponents get an adrenalin surge and the team suddenly stops winning under another untried captain?

Now that could create a crisis, possibly even a festering one. It might even envelop the coach and the selectors.

Very early in the season of 1996–97 the first story about the team leadership appeared in *The Australian*, suggesting that the Australian vice-captain Ian Healy could lose the 'keeping job against the West Indies to a rookie, Adam Gilchrist.

Extraordinary, when you think about it. Why on earth would someone in the Australian media suggest that Australia, on the eve of the toughest Test series of all, might drop the world's best, toughest wicketkeeper and replace him with a novice?

It was one of those headlines that raised the age-old question, "Who loaded the gun, and why?"

The answer very probably lay in the second leg of the story — Healy was the Australian vice-captain and Shane Warne, recently appointed to the Victorian captaincy, was the player being tipped as most likely to get Healy's vice-captaincy.

We should ask the question: were The Bushrangers, as The Vics like to call themselves in the '90s for whatever reason, pushing their own man because Healy had a less than impressive debut as stand-in captain for Taylor on the off-season short tour to Sri Lanka?

The switch never happened, Healy stayed, and rightly so. Then, later in the season, when Australia did poorly in the World Series limited-overs contest, stories appeared saying there was a chance Healy would take over from Taylor during the series.

This was yet another re-run of the 'Taylor's not a One-day player' line, because he didn't leave scorch marks on the outfield like Sri Lanka's Jayasuriya. Funny thing was that the summer before Taylor had been Australia's leading run-getter in the World Series, 423 at a strike rate of nearly 70.

Questioned by the media about the media's own proposition that he might take over as captain, Healy said that whilst he wasn't interested in the Test captaincy he'd be very relaxed about taking over the World Series job if he was asked to.

That never happened, either. Then, as the headline writers found more and more statistics to turn Taylor's form glitch into a slump during the Tests in South Africa, the media offered up another scenario — Steve Waugh would be a good captain for the forthcoming 1997 Ashes tour.

Healy said he didn't mind that idea, either, that Waugh would be a great Test captain. Surely a wiser course for Healy, the team vice-captain, would have been to pour bucketfuls of very cold water on all the media conjecture — "I've got nothing to say about that stuff" — instead of a litre of paraffin.

It made some think that Healy coveted the captaincy. During the South African tour, when he did take over from Taylor in the One-day matches — and, with great success — he renounced his earlier claim of disinterest in the Test job, suggesting maybe the media hadn't properly understood his earlier comments about his captaincy preferences.

Maybe all these positions on the captaincy question just proved Healy was a naturally outgoing, outpouring type, prepared to make a stand — how else could we explain the machinations of a mind that gave the world, via live television, the infamous bat-hurling in the Test at Centurion against South Africa?

At that moment the media's pre-season prophecy was accidentally fulfilled, although it only became official when the Ashes touring team was announced — no more Healy vice-captain, guillotined by his own hand.

But it wasn't the media's chosen one, Warne, who got the job. Instead the selectors, or the Cricket Board, gave the vice-captaincy to Steve Waugh, a move they had once before been reluctant to make.

The media then made the following deduction: "Waugh one step away from captaincy — out-of-form Taylor has been placed on notice," was the headline in *The Australian*. Talk about the relentless pursuit of their own driven prophecy.

It is very true that Taylor's indifferent batting form offered the media as many free kicks as they wanted to take, but the game and all that is great about it would have been better served by a media less preoccupied with necking the captain and more inclined to reasoned discussion about his predicament, and whether it really was a problem for the team.

Consider this headline, which appeared in *The Australian* after Australia lost the Third Test against South Africa, a 'dead' Test. It announced — 'Taylor Crisis Hits Team Cohesion'.

That's mighty serious stuff. And, what was offered as the evidence of this disturbing trend? Nothing, actually, just "mutterings within the team about workload imbalance". Which player said this? Who knows, because no one was named, or no one was game enough to put up his hand. No comment from anyone.

Instead, there was this snide piece of conjecture by the author, Malcolm Conn: "It is hypothetical whether Ian Healy's unacceptable behaviour [the bat-hurl] which earned him a two match suspension would have taken place had Taylor been more in control of his own game and, by implication, more respected in the team."

Now there's a leap in perspective for you — it's possible Taylor's run drought inspired Healy's bat-hurl. Any fair-minded person reading that, and aware of all that had gone on before, might have been inclined to wonder if there was a witchhunt underway.

If there had been any sort of a captaincy crisis early in Taylor's form lapse, and there wasn't, then as time went on and the Ashes tour got underway, the media certainly did its best to ensure that it would become one, and a festering one at that.

Every day was a get-Taylor headline day: "Taylor guaranteed two Tests for openers to decide his fate"; "Tubby fails as Waughs seal win"; "Tubby in the middle in search of some form"; "I've definitely snared my vote, says Taylor"; "Taylor leads way to shower"; "Day of reckoning underlines Taylor's struggle"; "Taylor teased then trapped"; "Noose tightens after Taylor's fourth-ball duck"; "Taylor unearths just 30". And so it went on, and down, like the stockmarket share index in the 1987 crash.

Then, just when we all thought things couldn't get any worse, they did — Bob Simpson and Ian Chappell, historically at odds in matters cricket, agreed ... Taylor shouldn't be in the First Test at Edgbaston.

Of course, it wasn't so much the Simpson-Chappell consensus that was disturbing, rather it was their conversion to the media's self-fulfilling prophecy that Taylor had to go. I'd have thought that as former holders of the office of captain, wholehearted support for Taylor might have been a more reasonable stance.

Greg Chappell joined in; he chose the first day of the Australian winter to deliver his judgment on how personal failure can bend a cricketer's mind: "Mark Taylor is in no fit state to be captain of the Australian cricket team ... he is caught in a mental whirlpool ... affecting his footwork ... captaincy has deteriorated over the last six months."

Then, the lowest moment of all, two days before the First Test, this newspaper front page.

"Taylor has told only a close circle of friends about his decision (to stand down)," it said.

It was, of course, a complete fabrication. And, even after The Ashes had been retained and Taylor had managed a century and a series aggregate that was quite satisfactory given pitch conditions, the urge to hang him was relentlessly pursued: 'Tubby Gives First Hint of Retirement'; 'Taylor Gives Nod to Waugh as Next Australian Captain'; 'Taylor to Play Shield if He Loses Test Job'.

Arguably, these were the bitchiest nine months in Australian cricket history.

What happened to Mark Taylor's form? How can a batsman who had made a couple of hundred short of 6,000 Test runs suddenly hit the wall, not the ball? Do the eyes suddenly go? Does the fitness fail? Or, does the mind get confused, as Greg Chappell maintained?

The magic of the broomstick putter has eased the pain for golfers strangled by the 'yips', but slump cricketers have no such godsend, no bewitched bat to cope with a rapidly advancing ball that seems to get smaller as the scores dive lower.

To properly asses Taylor's career twitch a reasonable starting point might be to look closely at his whole international career, which falls into four distinct parts — success, trough, super success, slump.

Success: his opening partnership with Geoff Marsh. Marsh the elder, Taylor the rookie finding his feet. The marriage worked — 29 Tests, Taylor made eight hundreds and 17 fifties, and they had four century partnerships.

Trough: life after Marsh. Eleven Tests, sharing the new ball trauma with Wayne Phillips once, Tom Moody three times and Boon seven times — no centuries, two fifties and one century stand.

It's fair to say that in all three relationships Taylor was expected to adopt the senior role, even with Boon because he had been reinstated to opening after batting at No.3. The great expectation was 'Taylor the boss', but it was never fulfilled.

<u>Super success</u>: with Michael Slater. They were the perfect pair, any cricket selector's dream — right-hand, left-hand, smasher, stayer, equals balance.

Until Slater was mysteriously axed from the team, their pairing over 33 Tests was one of the game's real successes. Taylor hit six centuries, 14 fifties and he shared 10 century partnerships.

Just as the experience factor with Marsh had lessened the pressure on Taylor's early career, so too did Slater's exuberance. Taylor was able to play his contented, second-fiddle role — his natural game, dab it here, push it there.

<u>Slump</u>: opening with Slater's replacements — that is two, not one! — both rookies, Matthew Elliott and Matthew Hayden, and both left-handers. It wasn't just a perception that Taylor was expected to lead the way, it was a prediction. His form slump can be traced to Slater's axing.

During this fourth phase of his career another factor came into play — an operation on a troublesome back. Have you ever had a bad back, ever experienced that muscle spasm that makes you think you'd be perfect for the lead role in The Crooked Man?

A bad back creates a mental nervousness about almost any strenuous physical performance. A little twinge raises the big question — is the back about to go again? The form of any cricketer — whether he's an opening batsman or an opening bowler — Dennis Lillee or Bruce Reid had famous backs — is likely to stay a little average until he's sure he's fully fit.

Was that Taylor's curse, probably coming back too soon after the operation and touring India, or was it 'divorce' from Michael Slater?

The bad back would certainly have influenced his batting style, because his weight transference would be compromised, and his bat would be coming through at an angle rather than straight.

In other words, playing across the line. That can cause any number of problems from played on, to bowled, to caught in the cordon to leg before. There was no shortage of those forms of dismissal when Taylor was struggling.

All of those factors may have contributed to Taylor's decline. But we should never, ever forget the tidal wave of negative media pressure, the incessant headlines revelling in his unsuccessful attempts to come to grips with his problem.

In the end, it seemed that it all got to Taylor. He made a quite extraordinary confession: "The only problem I have now is purely a mental one." 'Only' ... as any cricketer will tell you, 'mental' is always the highest hurdle on the way to success.

It was May 31, the day before Greg Chappell had performed his psychoanalysis on Taylor, a few days before the First Test of the 1997 Ashes series, and not the ideal time to be confessing to mental stress with a baying media in your face demanding, "For God's sake man, piss off!"

I wish Taylor had tried one thing: when he returned from South Africa I thought he should have arranged a centre wicket practice with his Sydney club, Northern Districts, and spent four or five hours in the middle, nonstop, against who-cares-what-standard of Grade bowlers, just to get back his rhythm and his confidence. Revisit the fundamentals.

That said, Taylor could reasonably revisit his previous form lapse and maintain such an extreme measure had been unnecessary to rediscover his touch on that occasion.

Taylor's first trough was deepest when the West Indies were touring Australia in 1992–93. He had gone 16 Test innings without scoring a fifty and, although he was the team vice-captain, the selectors made him 12th man. Not quite dropped.

The 12th man's job conveys some hope, but carrying out the drinks today when only yesterday you'd been everyone's favourite to be the next captain of Australia, might have created a certain air of despondency in Mark Taylor's mind.

Certainly, it inspired a steely determination, because next time out, one Test later against New Zealand at Christchurch, he made 82 and never looked back — until his second slide.

I was a selector, and therefore a willing party to his dropping in 1992–93. It had to be done. Taylor was making no runs, and therefore making no contribution to what was a stuttering team effort.

I am open to a claim of hypocrisy for supporting him during his later form slump, but by then he was the captain, and contributing solidly to his team's success, there was no question about that.

Should any Cricket Board in its right mind sack a winning captain? Not if it can possibly help it, surely. Imagine an NAB shareholders' meeting and someone in the media jumps up and proposes that the company's successful chief executive should be sacked: "Hey, why don't you get rid of the bloke whose theories and man management are making you all that money."

Cricket in the '90s is big business, and more than ever relies on lucrative

YOU'VE JUST LED AUSTRALIA TO ANOTHER TEST SERIES TRIUMPH PUTTING US AT THE APEX OF WORLD CRICKET. DON'T YOU THINK YOU SHOULD STAND DOWN?

Ironically, it was *The Australian's* cartoonist Peter Nicholson, rather than the cricket writers, who got the Taylor affair into the right perspective.

sponsorships and a strong cash flow. Can you imagine a sensible Cricket Board putting all that at risk by sacking a winning captain? Imagine trying to explain to the sponsor that he might no longer be backing a winner … but you'd like him to increase his handout, anyway. It simply defies commonsense.

The Taylor case prompted claims that Australia had discarded the traditional practice of picking the best team and then choosing the captain. I had no problem arguing that Taylor's allround status — best first slip, best captain, gutsy opener — entitled him to be in the 'best team', but what struck me about the status of those peddling the traditional line was that over the years they had been the ones most likely to shun the traditionalist view on other aspects of the game.

Anyway, how rock solid is the claim that "the best eleven cricketers will be selected and a captain chosen from them"? And, why shouldn't the best captain be regarded as one of the best eleven cricketers?

In its most simplistic form the 'best eleven' philosophy could create a scenario where a country might have three different captains in three successive Test series, depending on personal success, tactical success and the whim of the selectors. That sort of stuff happens in Pakistan.

It's true the Australian selectors choose a team, then nominate a captain. The chosen captain is the one player they believe can inspire the team to smash the opponent. The captain will, at least, be a solid performer and, if he does brilliantly himself then so much the better.

But once the captain is nominated then in subsequent selections he is the first man chosen. Of course, he could be sacked for any number of non-cricket reasons — criminal, wrong boots, etc. — but realistically, the captain should only come under pressure if his team starts to play poor cricket and to lose, and to lose badly and consistently.

That's why Bill Lawry got the chop, not because he was out of form, and if it wasn't the reason why Kim Hughes resigned then it should have been. It's why Ian Botham, a champion player but losing captain, was sacked as England skipper mid-series in 1981 and Mike Brearley was brought back. Brearley won the Ashes and was generally a winning captain — 31 Tests, 18 wins — despite his poor batting average as an opener, about 20.

The only area where there was any justifiable concern about Taylor's captaincy record was in the One-day arena, where Australia hit a soft patch in 1997.

Some cricketers thrive on captaincy, some lose their personal touch. You might be surprised at how some of the more famous Australian captains have fared, especially those whose personal performance slumped while their teams thrived. And, vice-versa.

Compare the batting form of Bob Simpson and Mark Taylor and then their captaincy win percentages. Note again the intriguing similarity in the careers of Taylor and Woodfull:

Captain	Ave as non-capt	Ave as capt	Win % as capt
Simpson	33.68	54.07	30.76
I Chappell	37.27	50.00	50.00
G Chappell	51.80	55.38	43.75
Bradman	98.69	101.52	62.50
Hassett	45.85	47.03	58.33
Benaud*	26.87	27.14	42.85
Border	50.01	50.95	34.40
Lawry	47.34	46.83	34.61
Hughes	38.97	35.22	14.28
Taylor	46.98	33.47	54.54
Woodfull	53.13	42.94	56.00

* Bowling stat

Good selectors always have an eye out for good strike bowlers, fewest balls per wicket or the consistency with which they are able to take five wickets in an innings.

And, they often think the most useful batsmen can be the ones who figure in a lot of century partnerships. Those big partnerships can break bowlers' hearts.

In Sheffield Shield, Taylor shared 29 century stands, half of them before he was first chosen for Australia in 1988–89. Most of them (11) were with the very aggressive Steve Small. In Tests he shared 29 too, most of them with the very aggressive Michael Slater (10); there were eight with David Boon, four with Geoff Marsh, three with Border and one each with Steve and Mark Waugh, Justin Langer and Rick Ponting.

The Ponting partnership should be noted. It was worth 126 runs. It was against the West Indies at the 'Gabba, the first innings of the First Test of the 1996–97 summer.

It was a partnership that arguably set up Australia's eventual victory by 123 runs yet, one Test later Ponting was dropped. And that happened a Test or two after the retirement of Boon who, as you have seen, was another good batting mate of Taylor's and a team stabilising influence.

Arguably the selection process was confusing and risky and, worst of all, destabilising. It says much for Taylor as a captain that he was mostly able to inspire his men to maintain a winning edge, and to do it when under increasingly intolerable personal pressure.

History should judge Mark Taylor's captaincy as generously as it might judge a successful Prime Minister, although Taylor might prefer not to be in the same boat as a politician, even if it was Bob Hawke, who aspired to be a cricketer. Politics and cricket — do they mix?

POLITICS

Is there any place in cricket for politics, generally a grubby little game? Petty politics compromise commonsense. There was a good chance there were some politics around when the time came for the Cricket Board to agree on a vice-captain to Mark Taylor.

Some people think that politics plays a part in the selection of the national team, that some self-centred political agenda being run by a rogue selector, or two, can influence who's in, or out.

In the final judgment, surely no cricket selector, particularly an Australian one, is going to be so selfish, so stupid as to choose a player not on ability, but on the basis of State boundaries, lest it weaken the team's winning chance and, by implication, damage his own reputation.

At the end of 1992 the Australian cricket team was subjected to shameful abuse, not in Colombo, or Guyana, or at the Wanderers, but at the WACA ground, in Perth — a home game. Australia was squashed in a World Series match against the West Indies.

The catalyst, it was announced, for an outbreak of fruit-hurling and foul language, was the non-selection of a Western Australian player in the Australian line-up.

The Western Australian Minister For Sport, Mr Graham Edwards, was reported as saying, "I thought there were Western Australians who were good enough to be in the team, but then again we are often seen at the wrong end of the selection decisions taken in the eastern States."

Ever noticed how something strange seems to happen to politicians when they get the Sports Ministry? Perhaps they can't handle the petrol fumes at their first GP meet. The fact is they become instant experts on all ball games — football, baseball, basketball, volleyball, handball, netball. Even "shadow" Sports Ministers get into the act — they talk about "balls-ups".

Mr Edwards seemed to be inferring that we 'eastern' selectors, Simpson and Benaud (NSW) and Higgs (Victoria), rambo-ed our way into the selection telephone hook-up and said, "Bugger winning, let's do a hatchet job on Laurie Sawle (WA) and get our mates in."

Mr Edwards should have put his hidden agenda theories aside long enough to consider the following about the most obviously absent Western Australians:

- Bruce Reid was a player with an injury problem in his bowling shoulder; if Mr Edwards had been a member of the selection panel and wanted to be sure such an injury would not recur in an upcoming five-day Test, where would he have given the shoulder a test run — in a four day Sheffield Shield match (where the selectors played Reid in preference to the World Series), or for a maximum 10 overs in a limited-overs match?

- How would Mr Edwards have fitted Damien Martyn into this first-up World Series team? In 1992, not even Edwards would have opened the batting with Martyn, a middle-order player. But that was the only spot Martyn could possibly have filled.

    After all, Dean Jones had a pretty fair One-day record, the Waugh twins were outstanding allrounders and Border was the captain. No room for Martyn in the middle.

Some people from out of the west are a little paranoid, inclined to believe in Kipling's "east is east and west is west and never the twain shall meet". The depth of their feeling, and the breadth of their ignorance, can be gauged by this letter from a Western Australian to the *Australian Cricket Magazine*: "To play the match at the WACA with no local representative was an insult to WA cricket and, to the people of WA in general. As far as I am concerned the crowd was not out of line and the players got what they deserved."

The comment defies commonsense. The clear suggestion is that the Cricket Board should crank up its public relations/promotional machine and order the selectors to choose players according to the venue. Enter the token cricketer.

There's another glitch in that thinking — what about when the team is playing away from Perth, say at the MCG, is it okay to drop the Western Australians and pick Vics? And so it would go on. Can you imagine anything sillier?

Politics shouldn't be confused with an occasional selection practice — 'horses for courses'. For instance, sometimes, a Western Australian fast bowler might bob up in the Test team at the WACA, where the breeze, 'The Fremantle Doctor', and the pitch's unique high bounce can unsettle bowlers from other States.

In my time politics never got a look-in at the selection of any Australian team; the clearest evidence I can offer of that is the selection for the Fifth Test against India at Perth's WACA in 1992 — Geoff Marsh, the team vice-captain, and a popular Western Australian, was a controversial omission.

Politics might have occasionally permeated the Prime Minister's XI process, but you'd have to ask Bob Hawke about that!

State administrations, and their selection panels do dabble in politics, and more often than not it is a registration of interest in the Australian captaincy. Be assured, the commander-in-chief's job, and that of his deputy, has been a powerful motivator for administrators, but rarely players.

Consider this timetable:

- Between 1948 and 1956 Australia's captains had been Lindsay Hassett and Ian Johnson, Victorians. From 1957 until 1967 Australia's captains had been Ian Craig, Rich, Neil Harvey, Bob Simpson and Brian Booth, every one of them from NSW.
- At the start of the 1967–68 season, Simpson announced it would be his last as Australian captain. His most likely replacement was Victoria's Bill Lawry, the vice-captain. Given the age most players retired at in those days, and because Lawry was about the same age as Simpson, the appointment seemed likely to be a relatively short one.
- In December, 1967 NSW made Doug Walters captain. He was only 22 years old, but his personal performances had been inspirational — in the 1964–65 season his 253 against South Australia and five for 92 against Western Australia had swung for NSW a Sheffield Shield triumph.
- There was a great similarity between the careers of the former NSW and Australian captain Craig, and Walters: both were country-born, Craig at Yass, Walters at Dungog; Craig scored 213 not out for NSW against South Africa when he was just 17. At 21 he was captain of NSW and became Australia's youngest captain, 22 years 239 days.

  Walters played Sheffield Shield at 17, and he made a century in his Test debut, aged 19.
- In April, 1968 Lawry captained the Ashes tour. His vice-captain was Barry Jarman, the 32-year-old wicketkeeper from South Australia. Four young players in the team were Walters, Ian Chappell, Paul Sheahan and John Inverarity.
- At the start of the 1968–69 season the NSW selectors re-confirmed Walters as NSW captain.
- Lawry and Jarman remained in charge of Australia during that season's West Indian Test series until the Fifth Test, when Brian Taber replaced Jarman as wicketkeeper and Ian Chappell was made vice-captain to Lawry.

- That Fifth Test team was chosen early in February; in January, Walters had 'lost' the NSW captaincy, replaced by Brian Taber.

Clearly, the NSW administrators saw Walters as 'another Ian Craig', another potential Australian captain, but when those same men became aware that Doug wasn't going to get Jarman's vice-captaincy job they sacked him and gave the NSW captaincy to another player whom they hoped might.

Am I a cynic, or a conspiracy theorist? Is it too tough on the NSW administrators to suggest that Doug Walters ended up being just a political pawn? Or, is it a good thing that administrators push up for the Australian captaincy? I guess it all depends on how they go about it.

When Doug lost the captaincy it was announced that he had 'voluntarily stood down'. In the 1968–69 NSWCA Yearbook Doug's resignation was officially recorded this way: "Walters announced he would prefer to stand down … that he could not devote sufficient time to the team and his own cricket, business and domestic activities."

Doug remembers it all quite differently, the original appointment, via a conversation with a high-up NSW administrator: "They were making me captain to give me some experience with a view, perhaps, to my taking on the vice-captaincy of the Ashes team to England in 1968."

And, on his voluntary resignation … "I was asked to stand down and to make a statement that the captaincy was affecting my cricket and I would like to be relieved of my duties. I felt — I think probably for the first time in my life — a surge of anger."

Few players covet the captaincy and Ian Chappell bears that out. He said, "Until I was appointed vice-captain to Bill Lawry for the last Test of the 1968–69 series against the West Indies the prospect of one day becoming captain of Australia hadn't even occurred to me."

It would be un-natural for a vice-captain not to think about promotion, but it's the administrators who get really excited about captaincy prospects. The king-makers. What does it really mean to a State's cricket to have the Australian captain, or vice-captain in the ranks? Taking a line through Ian Chappell's philosophy leaves us with the inescapable impression that all it does is put the penthouse on the administrator's ego.

Captaining a first-class cricket team is a tough job, one that calls for maturity, as much as playing talent. Administrators seeking to stake a claim for the Australian captaincy sometimes seem to forget that.

Remember Damien Martyn, the blazing young batsman who grabbed a middle-order spot against the West Indies in 1992–93? He was 21 when he made his Test debut and, at 23, became Western Australia's youngest captain.

Halfway through the following season he stepped aside — the reason, to concentrate on his batting.

Some might be concerned by Victoria's appointment of Shane Warne to the Sheffield Shield captaincy in 1996–97, but Warne's youthful looks are a blind. He was in fact 27. The only question to be answered as far as the Australian captaincy was concerned covered his maturity, and man management skills, because tactically he was smart.

The Cricket Board is fond of telling us that the selectors choose the team and the Board decides the captain. That's not quite right — the selectors nominate a captain and vice-captain, then the Board concurs, or not.

During the Mark Taylor crisis during the 1997 tour of South Africa, the Board overturned the selectors' wish that Taylor come home after the Tests and miss the One-day series. And, so it should have. A move as radical as that needs some telegraphing.

But, would the Board have been as supportive of Allan Border if he had come under the selectors' hammer late in his career?

When the Australian team returned from South Africa in 1994 just about everyone expected Allan to retire from international cricket, simply because Allan himself had created just such an expectation long before.

He had publicly recognised there could be no more timely moment to go — captain of the first Australian team to tour South Africa in 25 years, a little bit of cricket history to go with the rest he'd created with his bat.

And, before the tour there had been a Testimonial match and a Testimonial dinner for him. The Cricket Board had even announced that after cricket there would be a job for him. It wasn't a reward like a politician gets a gold pass, but a proper recognition of his great talent, and his complete commitment to the game.

It was, simply, a classic case of the self-fulfilling prophecy. But, 'AB' came back from South Africa averaging nearly 40 in the Tests, and with a rampaging strike rate of 90 runs per hundred balls in the One-dayers — all of a sudden, the word started to go round that AB might like to stay on for a while.

Well-meaning mates, and well-wishers started urging the selectors to say, "Play on, AB!" And AB did nothing to discourage it.

Egoism is a much despised state, and critics often confuse it with single-mindedness, pride, self-confidence, or even arrogance in a cricketer. If AB had an ego then he had certainly never needed anyone to stroke it, such was his success. And, only a poor judge would have considered anything AB ever did on the cricket field as egocentric.

But he was single-minded. And pride? AB had that, and in large lumps. We'd all seen it, admired it ... he'd been the guts and glory of the Australian team for a decade, or more.

Opposing bowling attacks found AB stubborn. And so he could be in real life. He liked to dictate his own terms. In the matter of retirement he felt he should be allowed to go in his own good time. The media's expectant "When are you going?" was answered with an increasingly emphatic "When I'm ready."

AB's mind was possibly working down these lines: "There's another Ashes series coming up (1994–95), and, following that, another chance to beat the West Indies ... we'd gone so close in 1992–93 ... now, that would *really* be a good way to go out, winning back the Frank Worrell Trophy ... only another two series ..."

Maybe AB started to think the fans were right. Yet, surely that defies logic. After all, AB had a reputation of being one of the toughest markers in the game when it came to assessing another player's temperament or talent.

If AB really did think he could play another two series wasn't he ignoring a few cracks developing in his own game? AB had a problem, mind you certainly nothing as major as the one that later confronted Mark Taylor.

AB was still scoring runs, but his great talent consistently to take the game up to the bowlers at Test level seemed to have gone missing. He'd get on top but didn't seem to be able to dominate.

Short balls around off that he'd once have dealt a mighty blow square of the wicket, he'd now let go. Loose balls were going unpunished. The champion's 'edge' was fading from his game. But, England were still rebuilding and the Windies were in wind-down ...

These were dangerous times for one of our greatest cricketers. He was old to be still playing, at least by Australian standards — 39 going on 40. What were the odds — that he would continue to play in that comparatively stymied style, or that he would experience some sort of spirited revival?

If he played on, AB risked getting the sack, and nobody in Australian cricket needed that, least of all a stand-out like Allan Border. The Board and the selectors were offering AB a chance to go gracefully. That's more than they did for Bill Lawry when they sacked him from the final Test against England in 1970–71.

Unfortunately, it all became such a mess that when AB finally announced his retirement from the international game, it appeared as if he'd been given 'the push'. AB certainly wasn't blameless in fuelling that perception.

Nor did the Cricket Board help, either. It made a strange move, one that had 'hint to AB' written all over it.

The Board called in four senior Australian cricketers to interview them about the state of the Australian game, and its future directions. The players were Mark Taylor — Border's vice-captain — Ian Healy, David Boon and Steve Waugh.

No Allan Border. The public could ask why. After all, he was still the captain at that stage. The 'talkfest' gave the impression that the Board didn't think Border had anything useful to contribute, but that wasn't really the case. His views had been well documented at a dinner he had with Board boss, Graham Halbish, not long before.

But the public weren't to know that. Whatever, the interviews sent out a clear message — AB's out. Border resigned and when the Board met about a week later to consider the make-up of the team's new leadership it's highly probable politics was the name of the game.

The Board heard an assessment from the selectors, Steve Bernard, Trevor Hohns and Jim Higgs, via the chairman Laurie Sawle, on the candidates for team leadership.

The gist of it was that on balance the vice-captain Mark Taylor was the best man for Border's job, but Steve Waugh's tactical talents were highly thought of. In fact, he was perceived as the player along with Taylor with the best cricket brain in the team.

But anyone thinking that Steve Waugh might be captaincy material had to balance his tactical talent against three concerns — (1) what had, in fairly recent times, been a somewhat brittle hold on a regular team spot; (2) how the onerous job of captaincy, with all its pressures on and off the field, might affect his improving form; (3) his temperament, intense, AB-like.

AB and the Board had had a couple of minor bingles during his time as captain, scrapes that prompted the less relaxed among administrators to run nervous fingers around a collar that suddenly seemed a bit tight.

A week later the Board voted Taylor-for-captain, and it was a shoe-in. There was a supporting voice for Healy, apparently expressing the view that Taylor's style would be too similar to Border's. How wrong can you be! The vice-captaincy was not as clear cut.

The Board consistently denied that it had been a 'job interview' when it had called Taylor, Boon, Waugh and Healy to Jolimont House and, it is entitled to be believed. But, consider this:

On the later date, when its members heard from Laurie Sawle, the day they chose Taylor as Border's replacement, they had to confirm the new vice-captain. The selectors' nomination was Healy.

This is what happened then: as you might expect, the NSW directors were more impressed by what they heard about Steve Waugh's smart cricket brain than they were by any negative influences and, they nominated him.

Queensland backed the selectors, and wanted Healy. That was fair enough, too. They'd made him Sheffield Shield captain in 1992, four months before the start of the season, accompanied by a glowing reference from the Queensland selection chairman Max Walters — "An easy decision," he said. "It always is when the guy is a standout candidate to captain Australia."

You might ask yourself then, why did it take Queensland so long to recognise such a super leadership talent? Well, to their credit, they certainly hadn't fallen for the 'youth trap' — Healy was 28.

So, the Board faced a head-to-head contest between Waugh and Healy — a vote. How would it go? NSW, Victoria and South Australia each had three votes, Western Australia and Queensland two, Tasmania one.

Then, from out of the blue, South Australia nominated David Boon. Why would South Australia nominate Boon? If it had been Tasmania, Boon's home State, fair enough. And, doesn't that raise another point — why didn't Tasmania nominate him?

Certainly, there was no doubting Boon's character, his commitment, nor his career record. But his captaincy record was less than enterprising — 29 matches for three wins, 16 losses and 10 draws. Still, captaining a Tasmania struggling to emerge is a tough job.

Vice-captains are generally chosen because they are either next in line, good tacticians, or strong team motivators. Boon was 33 years old so he could hardly be seen as heir apparent to Taylor. So, on what grounds did South Australia make their nomination?

Suddenly, the vice-captaincy was a three-way contest, 14 votes from six States to be split among three candidates. At the first ballot, Waugh was eliminated. Put in its simplest terms, the player reportedly with the best cricket brain was out.

Can we presume that Boon, at an absolute minimum, got four votes — three from South Australia, one from Tasmania? If that were the case then Waugh got only the NSW votes, three.

The contest was now a head-to-head between Healy and Boon, no contest really, unless Healy's occasionally gritty behaviour was a niggle like a pebble in someone's shoe.

At that time there would have been any number of politically minded cricket people around Australia who would have thought it was a good thing that Waugh missed out.

Had he won the vice-captaincy it would have meant that of the 15-man team about to tour Pakistan not only were seven of them from NSW, but the captain and vice-captain, too. Plus the coach and physio. Those were numbers like John Howard had after the 1996 Federal election.

When you think about it, all that really happened with Waugh was that the Board backed the selectors' nomination for vice-captain, Healy.

But, why did the selectors nominate Healy if there was a feeling that Waugh's cricket brain was the smarter? It can only have been because of a lingering doubt about Waugh's form, or his intense approach to the game.

Politically, I'd say NSW shot themselves in the foot trying to change the captaincy agenda — not for the first time. Nor will it be the last time that any State tries it on. The penthouse beckons …

Steve Waugh's cricket was very similar to Rich's, a career that took off after a moderate beginning. Like Rich, Waugh benefited from a selection philosophy of perseverance, which only came under threat when he was dropped for the series against India in 1991–92.

The most derided decision on Waugh was his elevation to No.3 against the West Indies in 1992–93. Was his jump in the order by the hand of his captain Border, alone, or did Waugh stick up his hand for the job?

It doesn't really matter, the bottom line was the message it announced: Steve Waugh, you're a batsman! Up until then he had been assessed as an allrounder.

This graph outlines Waugh's batting performance in 10-Test splits and shows there is a good chance that the century he scored against the West Indies at the SCG that summer was something of a turning point in his career.

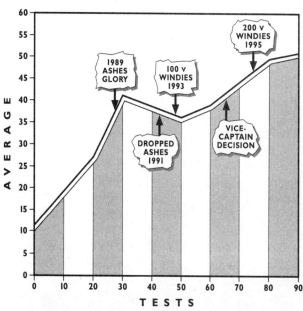

'Hindsighters' dwelling on the vice-captaincy vote would be mightily impressed by Waugh's form post-ballot, and up until the end of the 1997 Ashes series:

Inn	NO	100s	HS	Runs	Ave
50	10	7	200	2465	61.63

But who is to say how, if he had been offered leadership sooner, those pressures might have weighed upon his batting form in that period? We'll never know, but we do know that when testimonials are written to Allan Border and his toughness, Steve Waugh should rate a mention, too.

Steve Waugh plays serious cricket and his every moment on the field reflects that. Michael Slater is serious about his cricket, too, but he plays with something akin to gay abandon. Sadly for the game of cricket, it brought him down.

SLATER

The dropping of Michael Slater in 1996 and the dropping of Dean Jones, exactly four years earlier, generated strong criticism of the selectors. The Jones decision has been explained, but what of Slater — an irrational, callous, erratic judgment, or justified?

March 30, 1993

It is not too late in the afternoon in uptown Sydney, but already a coolish wind is swirling among the shadows of the skyscrapers. Laurie Sawle and I are strolling, yarning about cricket and those who play it.

That morning we have watched NSW tidy up the Sheffield Shield Final at the SCG. It was methodical stuff, like watching traffic lights change. NSW's last eight wickets had to knock up less than 50, a stroll. The sponsor's product would touch the sides real quick.

You always hope the climax of the Sheffield Shield Final will be a glittering, vibrant moment, but for the watchers this was pure anti-climax. It was achieved under a lukewarm early day sun, a suitable prop for the occasion.

The sweetest victories are the ones that happen late in the day. Hours of endeavour, litres of sweat, adrenalin pumping, eyes on high beam, brain bursting, an expectant crowd ...

Such are the ingredients for spontaneous celebrations — Tiger Woods winning the 1997 Masters at Augusta. But to have had to "come back the next day" to tidy up ... the NSW players must have felt like those platoons of cleaners who gather at sports stadiums the morning after a big event.

The vanquished were Queensland — again. As only they could in the days before their Shield glory, the Banana-benders had managed the impossible and buckled for 75 in their second innings on a straw-brown, dead pitch that had produced 652 runs by the time each side had concluded its first innings.

Another SCG spinner's paradise? Another heady haul for local hero Greg Matthews? Nope, seven for 41 to Wayne Holdsworth, all strut and searing speed, and the rest to a stick-man — young Glenn McGrath — who even then was showing favourable signs for the future. He bowled a lovely line all match, at pace, and got the ball to 'deck' away.

Laurie and I were on our way to help pick the 1993 Ashes tourists. We would meet up with Jim Higgs in a room at the Sheraton Wentworth Hotel. Jim was coming from Melbourne and was going to be late, which was why we were strolling. Jim's plane was destined for the Sydney airport holding pattern, which is an experience about as drawn out as an offspinner taking 'five-for' on a shirtfront.

Eventually we would be joined by Bob Simpson and Allan Border. Simmo and AB were flying in from New Zealand where the Australian team had been unimpressive, forced to a tie in the three-Test series, after winning the First Test by an innings and 60 runs.

Before that they'd seen the Frank Worrell Trophy snatched away — a 1–0 Test series lead against the West Indies had been reduced to 1–1 by the depressing, narrow loss in Adelaide, and that had become 1–2 in Perth when Curtly Ambrose went through the Australians, pretty much like a pig-rooting stallion set free in a paddock of willing mares.

Laurie was more forgiving about that collapse, and said the Perth pitch had reminded him of a lawn tennis court. "Where are you putting the net?" he had asked the groundsman prior to play. Laurie at his driest.

The tragedy of that series was that the Australian team had allowed themselves to get into the position of having to win the final Test — in of all places, Perth, the quickest pitch in the country — to win the series. 'Allowed'? The team would bridle at that mild criticism, but I'd said it at the time — we had slipped on the 'high wire' in the First Test in Brisbane. A few summers on the media still like to make the point that if Shane Warne had been in the team Australia would have won. Indeed. That's hindsight for you.

The reality was that we had Richie Richardson's team under the heel in that Test, four for nine in their second innings, then we'd lost the plot just because a few umpiring decisions went against us. Tempers overtook temperament, and a sure win became a costly and frustrating draw. Border and Hughes were reported for dissent, that's how badly we blew up.

In the Adelaide Test we had to make 186 in the fourth innings. Both match situations were character tests; we had the skill, the tactics and the team balance to win back the Trophy in 1993, but we still couldn't match the mental toughness that had kept the West Indies on top of world cricket for a couple of decades.

It's sometimes referred to as "knowing how to win". That didn't really surface until 1995 — we beat the best, the West Indies in the West Indies.

Our meeting at the Sheraton was to be a preliminary discussion, a sort of an agenda-setter for the main Ashes selection meeting which would take place the next day. Those meetings can cover all sorts of things, itinerary, new-look tour uniform, cricket form, naturally, technical strengths and weaknesses, temperament, team balance … and, Simmo and AB were adamant about one particular aspect of the team balance — David Boon would not be opening the batting again. He would bat at No.3, full-stop, exclamation mark.

Boon had opened with Taylor in four Tests against the West Indies and in the three in New Zealand. The No.3 job had been shared between Steve Waugh and young Justin Langer.

Why Steve Waugh had lost the No.3 job to the rookie, and Test debutant Langer in the Fourth Test against the West Indies at Adelaide after he'd scored an even hundred in the Third, baffled me. I could only assume someone started believing all that stuff about Waugh being hopeless against the short ball.

After all, Langer had only been chosen for the Fourth Test because Damien Martyn had withdrawn, injured. Even though Langer was a top order batsman with Western Australia the reasonable expectation was that he would bat in Martyn's spot in the middle order. A simple swap seemed more sensible than a batting order re-make. After all, if Martyn hadn't been injured would the centurion Waugh still have been moved away from No.3?

But, that was history. Now, Simmo and AB felt so strongly about Boon that they had even gone on the record in newspaper interviews, while the team was in New Zealand, to say as much. It wasn't so much the fact that they'd gone public that intrigued me, as the obvious question the comment raised: if they felt so strongly about Boon batting at No.3 why didn't they bat him there in the Tests in New Zealand? They could have.

They had three chances to open with Langer — which was exactly what they had done in the Perth Test (Taylor was 12th man) which had preceded the tour to New Zealand.

Most probably the New Zealand experience convinced them Langer wasn't the answer, that really there was no one else good enough to bat No.3, and even Steve Waugh was still a risk.

In our preliminary meeting, once Simmo and AB remained totally immovable about Boon, it created a new perspective to the Ashes selection, one that in the end was to have dramatic, but different effects on the careers of Langer, Dean Jones and Michael Slater.

When Damien Martyn had his training accident we could have gone back to Dean Jones, but it could only have been on the grounds of experience, because Deano was not faring well. In other words, a straight middle-order replacement.

We could have moved Boon to No.3, and everyone else down one in the order, and gone for Matthew Hayden, an opening batsman, who was scoring runs like bees gather pollen.

But some of us had doubts about his ability to make the extra step up in class. Not only that, it would have meant opening the batting with two like players, Taylor and Hayden — left-handers, neither of whom were expansive in approach. There was no complementary factor. The panel liked balance, mix-and-match.

We weren't inflexible, but we preferred to be consistent whenever possible. And, we were at a vital stage in the series. We decided to stay with the right-left combination of Boon and Taylor, and chose as Martyn's replacement Langer, a tough little bugger, gritty, no frills, and in form.

That was one aspect of the background to the Ashes selection. We were taking 17, and we'd decided the balance would be eight batsmen, two wicketkeepers, and seven bowlers. No worries with the 'keepers, Healy was the best and Zoehrer the next best.

There was a theory doing the rounds at the time that we should take only 16 players, therefore one 'keeper, the idea being that air travel is so swift these days that you can get the replacement over in next to no time. It's bunk, of course.

Firstly, what sort of fitness would the standby 'keeper be maintaining in the Australian winter; and secondly, what if the main 'keeper broke his finger during practice on the morning of the Test … hire an H. G. Wells time machine perhaps, to zip the replacement over?

If, in the future, the 16-man squad idea is pursued the obvious type of player to leave behind would be a batsman. After all, what harm could there be in allowing a wicketkeeper or bowler to get high-order batting experience in County matches?

The bowling selection was relatively straightforward, too. There were two spinners, Warne and May, and Hughes and McDermott were the strikers. Reiffel appealed as a seaming type who would do well in English conditions. Brendon Julian, it was hoped, was one for the future — tall, a whippy left-armer, a brilliant fieldsman and a handy, big-hitting batsman, probably a genuine allrounder.

The last bowling spot, reserve striker, went to NSW's Wayne Holdsworth. He'd had a hot summer and had been thereabouts for a couple of seasons. His haul in the Final a couple of days before probably tipped him in ahead of other candidates, one of whom was Michael Kasprowicz.

The batting … Border, the captain, Taylor, the vice-captain, Boon, Steve Waugh and Hayden were in for sure. Hayden?

Well, he had the right stats, no doubt about that: a ton of runs. He'd scored about 1200 and a long tour like The Ashes is the ideal one on which to send a young, in-form batsman. It's also a useful device to help a selection panel iron out any doubts that might be around about technique or temperament.

Mark Waugh had got the wobbles and been made 12th man in the Third Test in New Zealand; Damien Martyn had shown a couple of good signs in the series against the West Indies. We'd invested in them both over a period of time, the two batsmen you hoped could be your game-breakers, take the run rate up a cog.

Their occasional cavalier shotmaking was frustrating when it ended in failure, but we resolved to stick with them. After all, if you choose shotmakers you've got to expect that now and again they'll get out playing a shot.

So, that's seven batsmen. We wanted eight. Now, it got interesting, because we'd only chosen two opening batsmen, Taylor and Hayden, and we needed three. To send only Hayden and Taylor would be a huge risk … what if one, or both had a rough trot? Logic demanded that the final spot in our squad had to go to an opening batsman.

Langer? That was a reasonable consideration but it raised some tough questions. Could we really send away a team with three opening batsmen, all of them left-handers, all of whom played in the same fashion? The balance would be all wrong. (Just to support the adage 'different selectors, different opinions', in 1996–97 Trevor Hohns' selection panel chose Taylor, Hayden and Langer to bat Nos. 1–3 in two Tests against the West Indies.)

Could we send Langer instead of Hayden? Langer had played five Tests, Hayden none. And, surely it would have been consistent to send Langer who had played a couple of outstandingly gritty Test innings. Sheer weight of runs in the Sheffield Shield remained a compelling argument in Hayden's favour.

So, back-track … "Maybe we could take only two openers … Langer could be a utility player … but he's a rookie, like Hayden … what will we do in a crisis …?

Light bulb — "Boonie could open …!" But that was no longer an option. Simmo and AB, the team tacticians, had already announced they were having none of it. It is fair to say that if we had remained more flexible about Boon in the top order, rated him a utility opener, then we could have chosen Langer, or another middle-order player. Dean Jones?

Jones was still in the picture. Although he had played no Tests against the West Indies or New Zealand we had sent him across the Tasman to replace Langer in the One-day series that followed the three Tests.

But by confining Boon to No.3 in the Ashes selection we automatically eliminated Jones, or any other middle-order batsman. The last batting spot had to go to an opening batsman — we were back where we started.

Realistically that opener had to be a right-hander, preferably an aggressive one, to balance Taylor. Michael Slater was that right-handed opening batsman, the very last man chosen for the 1993 Ashes tour.

November, 1996

It seemed like only yesterday that Michael Slater, a free spirit, was kissing his helmet at Lord's, relaxed and happy, having treated us all to a maiden Test century that was a delightful display of crisp, attacking batsmanship.

In fact, nearly four years had passed, and the Australian selectors had just announced the team to play the West Indies in the First Test at the 'Gabba. Michael Slater's name was missing.

I was among a few million Australian cricket fans who thought, "That's a pretty tough call."

Think of it this way: David Boon had retired the previous season, leaving a major hole in the batting. Boon had been batting at No.3. It must have crossed the selectors' minds that there was a fair chance his absence would lead to some instability in the top order, possibly minor, but knowing Boon as we all did, more likely major.

But, even if they were unconcerned at that prospect, they should have been aware of another possible downside to Boon's retirement — the effect it could have on Mark Waugh. The pair had shared 11 Test century partnerships, the most of any pairing in the team, and just about all of them were recent history.

It's worth remembering that Waugh's Test career was in quicksand not very long after he hit his century on debut against England in 1990–91; he was dropped from the final Test against India the very next summer, but still managed to sneak onto the plane for a brief tour to Sri Lanka, where he made his four ducks in a row in two Tests. A period of mourning for the Mark Waugh fan club.

Any accolades that have come Mark Waugh's way in Test cricket have always pinpointed the fluency and grace of his strokemaking — an unbothered and exquisite style, like a gentleman gardner surveying, smelling and gathering in his rose patch. Tough was a word that was rarely used when Mark Waugh was batting.

Ten of Boon and Waugh's 11 century stands happened after Waugh's dark period. Question: just how much influence did David Boon's imposing, rock-like presence have on the fortunes of Waugh in his relentless rise from Test novice to Test tough guy?

Their partnership record inspired another question: how would the split affect the team performance?

Apparently none of this was of any great concern, because when the selectors said sayonara to Slater they split up the second most successful partnership in the team — Slater and Taylor. They had shared 10 century partnerships in Tests.

And, it was also one of the most successful opening partnerships in Test history. The top 10, based on most century stands, are:

Pair	Inn	Runs	50/100	Ave
Greenidge & Haynes	148	6482	26/16	47.31
Hobbs & Sutcliffe	38	3249	10/15	87.81
Taylor & Slater	57	3262	12/10	59.30
Gavaskar & Chauhan	59	3010	10/10	53.75
Lawry & Simpson	62	3596	18/9	60.95
Hutton & Washbrook	51	2880	13/8	60.00
Hobbs & Rhodes	36	2146	5/8	61.31
Gooch & Atherton	44	2500	12/7	56.82
Goddard & Barlow	34	1806	11/6	56.43
Boycott & Edrich	35	1672	8/6	52.25

Why was Slater pole-axed? Every media report on his sacking nominated 'form', a common theme which suggested a 'leak' from a high place. But there was scuttlebutt, too, a reference in a television magazine article about the advisability, or otherwise, of our Test cricketers doing 'live' television reports. There was a throwaway line about Slater "spending more time on the microphone than in the nets". The comment was allegedly made by a selector, who "preferred to remain anonymous". A nudge and a wink job.

The inference was that a microphone was somehow a contributing factor to Slater's dropping. As a former selector, I cannot believe that such a trifling issue would even be raised at team selection time and, if it was, then the chairman would certainly have given it very short shrift.

We should discount the theory that any of the selectors who dropped Slater, chairman Trevor Hohns, Jim Higgs, Steve Bernard, Peter Taylor or Andrew Hilditch, could be that petty. This was a Test team, not the Haberfield Under-12s.

So, we're left with 'form' as the main player in Slater's downfall, his 'bad form' and the 'good form' of other players. Just how bad was Slater's form?

The most mentioned aspect was the fact that he "hadn't scored a century in a Test for nearly a year". Sounds lousy, doesn't it? But the journalist concerned could easily have put it differently, and created a much less negative perspective — "He hasn't scored a double-century for three Tests." Sounds a bit better, doesn't it?

The fact was Slater hit 219 against Sri Lanka in Perth in December, 1995, and had played in only three Tests since, surely hardly enough time for any player with a Test batting average of 40-plus to convince any selector, no matter how hard a marker that selector might be, that he was a bad risk.

But such fine print just didn't suit the agenda — to justify the dropping of Slater in favour of Victoria's Matthew Elliott.

The most reasonable criticism that could have been made about Slater's career statistics was his performance against the West Indies — fewer than 150 runs in four Tests. But that invites comparisons with other batsmen's career records against the West Indies in recent years, and mostly they're average, as you might expect.

The most ludicrous criticism was that Slater had made the bulk of his runs against England, New Zealand and Sri Lanka — 1653 in a career aggregate of 2655. What if he had? I suppose you could pull out any modern batsman's career record and make exactly the same point. And, do we discount Lillee's wickets against Pakistan?

It was hardly Slater's fault if the Ashes series came around every couple of years, and there were a few weak nations around, as there always are. He could only do his job — score runs.

There was another mischievous line being peddled, too — that in his last 19 Test innings he'd only passed 50 three times. True, but ask yourself this: why pick on the magic number of 19?

The real perspective was that the Australian team had been in Test recess for eight months, playing Sri Lanka in Adelaide in January, 1996, before playing a lone Test against India in Delhi in October, 1996.

If form was to be such a decisive factor in the selection of a player with Slater's proven track record, it could only be the form in that Test in India, not some cobbled together record going back 19 innings — to the Perth Test against England in February, 1995, 21 months before!

He made 44 — not the magical 50 — in the first innings in India, the top score. He got a duck in the second, and played a loose shot. Should one loose shot, however loose, cost a brilliant young batsman his Test spot? Lou would have said 'no', but consider this: he played it when Australia were setting out in their second innings 179 runs in the red, and desperate to beat bankruptcy.

They needed to try to occupy the crease for a day and half to have any chance of saving the game and, saving the game meant a great deal.

It meant saving their reputation, because after beating the West Indies in the Caribbean, Australia had been letting the rest of the cricket world know that, "We are the champions!"

Ducks signify the ultimate failure, but only if you're looking in a score-book or at 'Daddles' weeping his way off the television screen. To a selector, though, it's just another number; 15 is as much of a failure as a duck. What worries the selector mightn't be the low score itself so much as the way it came about.

In Slater's case it raised a genuine concern about his shot selection, if not his temperament under extreme pressure. What if previously there had been similar concern on the panel about that? What if the coach, Geoff Marsh, had been in his ear about better shot selection?

On such a doubtful pitch, at such a crucial time for his team it was fair to say Slater had been reckless.

Once Matthew Elliott began 1996 with the same hard-nosed desire to score runs as he had finished 1995, and the selectors were unbending in their determination to choose him straight up, then it was Slater's position which came under notice.

After all, it's hard to imagine anyone on the panel offering, "Hey, why don't we drop Taylor the captain for Elliott?" Not at that stage, anyway.

Yet, Slater's dropping, the unofficial reason given for it, poor form, and the outcry it created, had an unfortunate knock-on effect — suddenly Taylor's batting form was targeted, and his steely temperament, his man management and his great captaincy form all forgotten.

Once the word was out that 'current form' was the reason for Slater's omission then form, and form alone became the media's yardstick for every other selection process.

There's nothing wrong with a background leak about a cricket team; se-lectors and administrators are just as capable of pushing a line about a crick-eter or the game as anyone else is.

It's just that 'the line' needs to be well thought through. It wasn't in Slat-er's case. "Have a look at his recent record ... long time between fifties, you know," was clearly the line from 'the leak' when it should only have been a reference to his suicide shot in India.

Any selector worth his salt will tell you stats are only a starting point in the selection process, and by themselves can be an untrue guide to any play-er's worth. Temperament, an intangible, can still be explained with a refer-ence to a material moment.

Of course, there was an alternative to choosing Elliott as an opener. If the selectors were also concerned about Ricky Ponting — and a subsequent Test selection showed they were, because he was dropped, and as unluckily as Slater was! — then they might have discussed Elliott coming into the team at No.3.

Was that a risk, asking an opening batsman to make his Test debut at No.3? Well, some selection panels — those from long gone days when there was no headlong rush to 'do it right now!' — have preferred to saunter to judgment; opening batsmen Bob Simpson and Les Favell are two who played out of position, as low as No.6 for Australia. So there were precedents.

Once the selectors started thinking they might drop Slater for Elliott they had to ask themselves some other tough questions:

- Can we open with two left-handers? Not really a problem, because Taylor and Elliott are hardly similar in style. There was little chance of them becoming becalmed.
- It's the first Test in a series against the West Indies, should we risk blooding Elliott now or wait until the Third Test at the MCG, his home ground? But, what if he loses form in between times?

And, as the summer went on, with the top order faltering, and Taylor in particular failing even though the team kept winning, they had to ask themselves the toughest questions of all:

- We haven't had a worthwhile opening partnership in eight Tests — did we make a mistake dropping Slater? Did we rob Taylor of his confidence, and therefore his form? Worse still, what if we've stuffed Michael Slater?

There would be few cricket people who would disagree with the theory that the most important session in a Test match is the first, even the first day. Of course, as the Test goes on that can change, but often fortunes on the opening day can influence the eventual result.

So, because form, or stats, became such a big issue in the Slater decision one Slater stat that should have been of vital interest to everyone was his performance in the first innings of any Test match:

Innings of Test	Runs	HS	50/100	Avge
First	1198	176	4/5	59.90
Second	655	219	3/1	46.79
Third	506	99	3/–	38.92
Fourth	296	103	–/1	32.89

<u>Question</u>: Why would you drop an opening batsman who could get his team off to the flying starts that Michael Slater did?

April 6, 1997

The same selectors who had dropped Slater met in the conference room at Sydney's Darling Harbour Park Royal. In four hours they'd completed the selection of the 1997 Ashes squad, which was quick by 1989 and 1993 standards.

Matthew Hayden was omitted, although he'd scored his maiden Test century not long before. Tasmania's Jamie Cox, an opening batsman, didn't make it, even though he'd scored 1,000 runs-plus in the Sheffield Shield with five centuries, and 200 against Pakistan.

Slater hadn't played a Test all summer and scored only 700 runs in the Sheffield Shield, yet he was reinstated. All of which makes you wonder — if form played such a major part in his dropping, why was he dropped in the first place, and why was he reinstated?

It makes you wonder about the minds of selectors, too. I think Laurie Sawle got us right when he said, "Selectors are a strange breed. It's all a matter of opinion, and everyone is entitled to their opinion. We take criticism as part of the job."

In 1996–97 the selectors certainly copped some criticism, but they were entitled to reply, "Our combinations beat the West Indies and South Africa and retained The Ashes didn't they, what more do you want?"

Players are influenced by many factors, a lot of them out of their own control, which makes them nervous if they're making a living from the game, as many are today. In modern times coaches have influence like never before.

YOLA

Cricket was once learned by batting for hours on a rough pitch hewn from a cow paddock graze, or bowling at a dustbin on a rocky road. Now most junior cricket coaching is done indoors, no breeze, on an artificial pitch in artificial light, and with a bowling machine. Is that desirable?

School was out, and the boys' voices, animated, were the first signal of their presence. They were coming from behind a tall hedge, all dressed in their cricket clothes, wandering towards the practice nets, chattering.

Then, the voice of a woman, a heavy European accent … I put two and two together and got five, it must be a mother talking to a son.

Then she appeared, carrying a cricket bag. Not his, hers. She was immaculate in sharp-creased cream cricket trousers, spic and span cricket shoes, shirt collar perfectly arranged outside the neck of a cream sweater with red piping. She looked every inch a cricketer.

Later, I learned she was a cricket coach, Yola Foister her name. A woman coaching cricket to young schoolboys is unusual, but Yola may have been unique. She was born in Romania in the '60s and this was Kent, England in the '90s! How did it happen?

Well … she arrives in England and, one late afternoon, she's walking through Regent's Park and sees a bunch of West Indians playing a strange game. She watches for a while then asks, "Hey, what are you guys doing?"

In no time at all she's accepted their offer to have a go … pads strapped on, looking not bad with a mini-skirt. It's love at first sight. Later, she is to play as a wicketkeeper, later again she studies for her coaching certificate.

Fact: anyone with the right piece of paper can coach cricketers these days — is that a bit of a worry, or is it a good thing that people from such a wide range of backgrounds are involved in spreading the word?

If I had a boy in need of coaching I'd like the coach to have experienced the game at a reasonably high level. That's not to say the best coaches have to have an outstanding record in first-class cricket — Lou certainly didn't have that credential.

But Lou did have outstanding credentials — he knew the fundamentals of the game and he was tolerant, and a good communicator.

The trend towards coaching indoors at the expense of outdoors is a concern. If not properly monitored it can be a sterile exercise, a military drill almost and cricket is not that sort of a game. It is a 'habit game' until the fundamentals have been mastered, but then cricket is about flair, and inventiveness, about facing up to a setback, like finding yourself in a deep hole yet still seeking success, working out how to climb out of the hole.

Cricket is practised and coached indoors more than any other outdoor sport. How often do you see rugby players practising indoors, or tennis players? Why do cricketers head indoors so readily, and not only when there's been some rain damage to their outdoor facility?

Laziness? There are no balls to be fetched. Softness? There is a dead true synthetic pitch, no changeable weather, no variables. Convenience? The nets don't have to be erected, there's no beating, hot sun and the drink machine is close by, beyond the net at mid-on, near the oven with the sausage rolls.

Cricket coaching has become a business and that means money. Indoor cricket centres have overheads that the outdoor nets in the local park don't. There is the electricity bill, the re-laying and maintenance of the artificial turf, the repairs to the netting, the wear and tear on balls, purchase/maintenance of the bowling machines, and the video.

If we accept that coaching rates per hour have limits then to maintain an effective balance sheet, or to increase turnover, the only realistic option is to preserve a strong client base.

That can mean keeping the client coming back, and coming back. Now that's not necessarily good for every kid. How sensible is it, for instance, that a lad of 10 years of age has been attending a one hour coaching class, one afternoon a week, after a day at school, for two years?

The kid has received nearly 100 cricket lessons. If he's not dog-tired mentally and physically then he's superhuman. Is that the parent's fault, or the coach's?

The game is about enjoyment. There's no point in playing without it, and that's not an old fashioned view in a so-called professional age, it's just commonsense.

Cricket coaches with indoor facilities need to carefully monitor not just a pupil's progress in the technical fundamentals, but his position on the enjoyment scale.

The video can be a crutch for a poor cricket coach. He sits down with the kid and watches it, slows it, freezes it, re-winds it, discusses it. It's probably made as much of an impression on the kid as an umpteenth re-run of Bugs Bunny.

But the coach without a video is right there with the kid, a trained eye on every ball, explaining then and there — instantly, while it's fresh in the kid's mind — what might be wrong, and, more importantly, encouraging the kid to do what's right by physical manipulation of the body position.

It might be self-satisfying for the kid to see himself on video replay, but when you think about it the kid is looking at himself from the wrong angle.

Hands-on coaching wins hands down in cricket. The video, even though it's the 'in' thing in modern coaching technology, should be used sparingly and with commonsense.

Here's hoping the modern coaching business, and its repetitive ethic, won't result in the Australian way, natural and fresh, being swamped by the English way, less expansive.

If coaching by the book is so important to success how can we explain Jeff Thomson, mechanically pure, and Max Walker, a Meccano set of arms and legs, bowling for Australia about the same time? Or, Doug Walters, who taught himself how to bat on that antbed pitch in his front yard?

If hand-eye coordination is a must to be selected for Australia, how do we explain Jim Higgs being a smart legspin bowler and a player with a very sharp tactical bent, but an ordinary fielder and a batting no-hoper?

They might be three good examples why the coaches of young cricketers need to be careful about making rash judgments too soon, and not just about whether the kid will make it or not. The kid who keeps wickets in the Under-10s often opens the bowling in the Under-16s. Neil Harvey was a wicket-keeper at school.

In fact, it is never too late to expect a career change of direction. At Cumberland, Lou played with Arthur Howell, the son of Bill Howell, who at the age of 25 was chosen as a batsman to play against England because he had scored well in NSW Country Week.

Teammates said Bill hit big because "he always used a bat about four pound in weight with a hole bored in the end and filled with lead". Bill went on to play 18 Tests for Australia — but, as a bowler because in that match against England he took five wickets after the 'chosen' NSW bowlers couldn't get anyone out!

Just because a young cricketer looks textbook-good, there is no guarantee that he will produce good results. Rick McCosker wasn't a pretty batsman to watch. It's that thing called temperament, and that's generally in a kid's nature.

It shows itself when the young cricketer finds himself in difficult situations that he has to work through, to come up with a solution that will give him a winning edge over his opponent.

John Gleeson, the mystery spinner, came on the first-class scene late, but he knew about 'the edge'. He once said, "The art of cunning is to make the opponent look for something that's not there …"

The very good cricket coach should appreciate natural ability and, if he needs to, he tweaks it, but he never introduces massive change seeking to create a clone of himself, or some high profile player, or some textbook example.

In his coaching notes, Lou made these points:

- *you can take a pupil so far and then it is up to him;*
- *a pupil should be taught to think as well as to play;*
- *he should be conversant with the administration side of the game, with the rules of the game, and with the ethics of the game;*
- *parents doting and otherwise should stay in the background.*

Translated for the '90s, the last point means, "Parents, butt out." Here's a classic case: I'm coaching an Under-12 team and they're in terrible trouble. Plenty out and plenty to get.

Our one hope is a lad named Phil, who for his age is a smart player. Got all the shots, a fair bit of ticker and, above all, a wealth of spirit.

Our No.11 is a lad named Arthur, one of those lads who is not quite uncoordinated at the game of cricket, but his style doesn't inspire confidence. I tell him that all he has to do is block the ball and let Phil do all the scoring.

This tactic is working exceptionally well when Arthur's father suddenly arrives on the scene and, after watching Arthur apply the team tactics faultlessly, calls out from the boundary, "Have a go Arthur!"

It gets worse. Arthur runs a single and, for the second time since he'd gone in, his protector falls out of his underpants, and onto the pitch.

As Arthur is walking back to fetch it, and reposition it — a sensible course of action for any young boy whose manhood one day awaits him — his father calls out, "For heaven's sake Arthur, leave it out!" What a dickhead.

THE THOUGHTS OF LOU

The cricket coach must endeavour to develop a deep love of cricket, for from that will spring all motivations.

Some cricket coaches neglect the mental approach to cricket and concentrate on the physical approach to the game. The successful cricket coach develops in the coached both mental and physical competence.

The perfectionist coaches are unreasonable, after all they certainly weren't perfection when they played cricket.

The boundary-riding coaches shout advice and produce a player lacking in self-reliance, as well as one unable to think for himself.

The mathematical coach demands the pupil place his feet parallel, 90 degrees this, 30 degrees that. It's confusing.

The coach should encourage all the coached to develop an analytical mind when playing a cricket match, or watching a cricket match.

Formal coaching should be started when the pupils have entered Year Seven at secondary school.

Unless the cricket coach is imbued with the spirit of cricket his message to the coached will fall far short of the required goal.

Purists say that an upright stance allows a batsman to move more quickly than when he crouches. If that is true why don't Olympic sprinters adopt an upright stance when starting their races?

Footwork enters one hundred per cent into all phases of the game — batting, bowling, fielding, wicketkeeping. The better the footwork the better the cricketer.

No cricket coach should lose control of his emotions in the presence of the coached. Displays of bad temper, sarcastic criticism, impatience, favourable treatment of some of the coached should never be shown by any coach.

If you are a spin bowler and have a big bodyswing the so-called experts will assert you are bowling too fast. It is essential if you want to be a great and a natural bowler, that your stock ball should be bowled at a pace governed by maximum bodyswing.

The worst runner between the wickets is one who is sure he can make his own ground — and hopes his partner can do the same.

Any player worth his salt will spend years of his cricketing life in accepting the continual challenge of trying to beat cricket's uncertainty.

Enquiry into why he succeeds as well as into why he fails should be deeply rooted in all cricketers, for without it no cricketer has any chance of developing into a first-class player.

Lou had some thoughts on the Australian coach, and whether it was necessary to have one at all. He said:

Coaches are needed to teach cricket to those who don't know how to play cricket. Surely first-class cricketers should be regarded as being able to play cricket or they wouldn't be selected to play at first-class level. It is suggested that a suitable person known as a trainer-consultant be given the job.

Lou was splitting hairs a bit there. He recognised the need for someone to play an advisory role, he just objected to the high profile title. He may have had a good point, because there is much more to the role at that level than just ironing out technical faults. In fact, if the emphasis was purely on the technical side the coach wouldn't last five minutes.

For instance, hard markers are entitled to wonder why the coach could not have done something to prevent, or at least shorten, Mark Taylor's slump. Taylor developed a problem on the 1997 Ashes tour, getting squared up to the short ball about middle and leg, and nicking to slip. Why couldn't the cricket coach eliminate that fault in the same way an athletics' coach irons out a runner's style?

Imagine the upheaval at the top level if the coach was blamed every time an individual suffered a form drop-off. As it is, he's only likely to cop blame if the team hits a losing streak, although Bob Simpson copped plenty when the team was winning!

The Australian cricket coach is more likely to be involved in organisation of practice and tactical measures, even selection than he is in constant technical instruction. He's an advisor. Or, a consultant.

Lou was a patient coach:

It was while we lived at North Parramatta that I coached Rich. I demonstrated each stroke — no ball was used. Rich played the stroke — no ball was used. I moved halfway up the pitch and threw a cricket ball on the right spot for each batting stroke. Rich played each stroke. Errors were corrected.

My aim was to make Rich a batsman-allrounder, with the bowling side being legspinning. My theory on the teaching of legspin bowling was that no pupil should become a legspinner until that pupil had learned his bowling fundamentals and variety as a medium pace bowler. He should not be introduced to legspinning until he was somewhere around 12 years old.

Lou believed that cricketers were entertainers, and that anyone connected with the game, whether it be administrators or selectors — or the media — they should be ever mindful that it was a game to be played with spirit. He said:

The strokemaker had delighted the spectators with an attractive fifty in 70 minutes. Then he attempted to drive the legspinner's delivery pitched outside the offstump, mishit the ball and was caught in the covers.

The negative pain-in-the-neck, push, prod, deflect batsman bored the spectator with 50 in three hours. Then he attempted to glance the offspinner's delivery to leg, mishit the ball and was caught at leg slip.

Some critics condemned the strokemaker for playing a false shot and accused him of throwing away his innings. No critic condemned the negative batsman for getting out.

Why is an attacking batsman always accused of throwing away his innings when he is beaten by the flight of the ball and he plays a false shot? Why is a negative batsman never accused of throwing away his innings when he is beaten by the flight of a ball and plays a false shot?

Lou had passed on when Michael Slater was dropped from the Australian team in 1996, but his philosophy was never more to the point.

A great batsman can hit a good ball and he upsets a good attack; he thinks of a scoring stroke when the ball leaves the bowler's hand, he is completely equipped technically, has good reflexes and maintains a controlled temperament.

Lou though, might have been inclined to re-confirm with Michael the absolute importance of the last attribute, but he wouldn't have dropped him to prove it.

LOU'S GOLDEN RULES

1. *Don't go around telling others that the captain lost the game. There are 11 in the team.*

2. *Do you play for your team or for yourself?*

3. *Do you condition yourself for cricket, or are you just a two hour fieldsman?*

4. *Don't forget, practice makes perfect.*

5. *Do you, without knowing the facts, condemn a player for a run of outs? Remember everyone has a 'trot' — and yours will come.*

6. *Do you criticise the selectors constructively, or just because you or your mates were the ones left out?*

7. *Don't be an 'average-chaser'. The game and the team always come first.*

8. *Do you blame the selectors or the chap who took your place if you are dropped? Or do you resolve to show, by your subsequent deeds, that you deserve reinstatement?*

9. *Do you keep an eye on the captain in the field, so that your position can be quietly altered without attracting the batsman's attention?*

10. *Do you allow any grievance, whether real or imaginary, to induce you to sulk or refuse to do your utmost?*

11. *Do you rise above yourself in adversity and help carry your side to victory, even when the position seems hopeless?*

12. *Do you agree that if your club is worth playing for, then it is also worth working for?*

13. *Do you nurse a grievance, or do you consult any member of the management committee, whose pleasure and duty at all times is to assist and advise members?*

Mackay, Queensland, 1975

There was nothing remarkable about the cricket oval at Finch Hatton, back of Mackay, in north Queensland; the pitch was malthoid, with deep birdbath furrows at each end where the bowlers' feet slid and dragged. The outfield was paspalum. There was no fence. I suppose that's how it happened, the accident to Michael.

He was almost like any other kid at the coaching class that summer's day. Fair hair, unkempt in the breeze, white pants and shirt, sandshoes and socks, green and gold cap in his back pocket. We see them in every park, every weekend.

On the fateful day Michael was fielding and, from a fair whack with the bat, he had to chase one to the boundary, a dozen or so red flags atop wooden stakes, spread in a vague circle. The ball was going fast and it looked like a certain four, but Michael still chased like a greyhound, head down watching the ball he knew he wanted to stop.

The other boys cried out to him to watch for the tractor but he didn't hear and the slashing blades of the gang mower caught his right leg.

I saw Michael a year after it happened. His freckles smiled at me when he said quite earnestly he wanted to bowl like Ray Lindwall. He said he could bat a bit, too. And, he was a good slip field. For a second I felt sorry for Michael because I knew that with his completely stiff right leg he could never really be a great in cricket.

His father recalled it all, how the mowers had slashed his son's leg, how one of the land's finest microsurgeons freakishly happened to be driving past the Finch Hatton pitch, how they got the ice from the drink machine in the changing sheds, and packed the leg, how they got along to the hospital.

And now here he was in front of me, steady on two legs, but wearing long white trousers to camouflage the scars that might have broken his heart; he took a six-stitcher and wheeled down a few. Not bad. Then it was his turn to bat and, stiff-legged, he survived. And he was right — in the catching drills he was a good slip field with good safe hands.

One of his mates worked his sandshoe toe in the dust and said he was sorry they couldn't bowl Michael ... but, by golly, he was handy with the bat in a tight situation, and at last they had a slip field because everyone else was scared.

In Michael is etched the fascination of cricket, the greatest game of all because it affords even the weakest the chance to be a strong player.

Consider tennis — the smash at the net which is played with such urgency that it floats off the racquet edge out over the baseline. But the uncertainty of cricket ensures that the ball which travels low and hard off the edge may be dropped. A second chance.

In golf to miss a putt is to miss the trophy. In cricket to miss the ball might serve only as a warning to a batsman to tighten his defence, if the ball passes wide of the stumps.

In soccer, to skew the ball off the wrong part of the foot may give the opposition a goal. In cricket the ball skewed off the bat may merely go for four past point instead of cover.

Michael can play none of those other games; but in cricket he can still express his sporting instinct. True, he may spend long days in the field eyeing enviously those lucky enough to take the new ball. But each of those new ball bowlers will run to him, grateful, when his safe hands hold a catch in the slips.

And, when he bats and the rest of the batsmen have failed and time is long and wickets are short, his teammates will flock to him if he is able to withstand the onslaught they could not.

That is the glory of cricket. Its uncertainty will strengthen Michael's character.

Character. Now that's what a selector looks for in a cricketer when he's looking for The One who can make the step up in class, The One who won't be intimidated by his opponents but who will instead intimidate his opponents.

CHARACTER

David Boon is a classic role model for any young cricketer. At times, coaching will have done something for his technique, but how can we explain the determined mindset that made him a champion of his era? That, he was surely born with.

They say a cricketer never forgets his first Test. David Boon's was at the 'Gabba against the West Indies in 1984, and he made 11 and 51. It was the Test when the Australian captain Kim Hughes decided to farewell himself. It created quite a mind picture: the young Boon in the dressing room after scoring a gutsy half century trying to save a lost cause, wondering innocently the whereabouts of his skipper, and someone saying, "Oh, he's in the lunch room resigning." A tough initiation, one likely to sharpen the focus.

Lou liked Boon: "Some batsmen can, and do produce their finest efforts when their team is in trouble," he said. "That is a sign of greatness."

November 18, 1988

It's the first Test of a new series and the new face of West Indian cricket is at the 'Gabba. His name is Curtly Elconn Lynwall Ambrose, a carpenter from the island of Antigua, 25 years old and six foot seven inches tall.

On strike is an old face of Australian cricket, David Boon. Boon remembers the moment: "Patrick Patterson broke down and had to go off. 'Swampy' [Geoff Marsh] and I were quite happy about that. We hadn't seen Ambrose before …"

Nor had anyone much. As a youth Ambrose had played tennis ball cricket in Swetes, his home village, and then a bit of English leagues, but minor stuff. A somewhat 'nothing career', then suddenly, with the first calendar page of 1988 barely turned, he took a record 35 wickets in the Red Stripe Cup and he was picked in the Test team.

Some cricket selectors are dreamers. They wander the parks hoping to find 'another Bradman' or 'another Lillee'. When David Boon retired the media immediately nominated Rick Ponting as 'the next Boon'. The search goes on.

But, imagine this — you're a West Indian selector and you've just had to cross the name Joel Garner off your team list because the great fast bowler's career has reached run-down.

Could you believe, even in your wildest cricketing fantasy that suddenly, out of a backyard in Antigua, would come a skinny 'Big Bird', a sort of a look-alike? Curtly Ambrose. The world got all excited when scientists managed to clone a sheep in 1997, but during the '70s and '80s the rest of the cricket world were convinced that the West Indies were cloning quicks!

It took Curtly the carpenter no time at all to decide hammering batsmen was better than hammering nails.

Boon continues: "I remember in the second over Curtly hit me in the ribs with a big offcutter ..." I remember it, too. I saw the moment, because it was my first Test, too ... as an Australian selector.

Watching it happen, then turning to watch it again in slow motion replay on the dressing room television, drew from me an involuntary wince. I watched Boon and wondered if he might deflate, the air rushing from his body like it would from a balloon that's had a hunter's knife thrust into it.

At the end of the over Boon and Marsh met in mid-pitch for a chat, as was their habit born of years of partnership. Boon summed up: "I said to Swampy, 'We're not going to get any rest here'."

That was Ambrose's ninth Test match and not too many more passed before he had earned a reputation — The Antiguan Assassin.

Opponents, or victims, had a particular mindset about the West Indian players of that era — Michael Holding was 'Whispering Death', Malcolm Marshall 'The Ninja', Viv Richards 'Smokin' Joe', Desmond Haynes 'Hammer'. Cricket's hit-men, a mind picture had them in dark glasses, dark hats and shirts, white ties, and all carrying violin cases, not cricket kits.

Curtly 'loaded' his bowling arm like a desperado would load cartridges into a shotgun. The ball in the left hand, held in front of the chest, then the first two fingers of the right hand wrapped about it, seam in the middle ... the grip, careful and calculated.

Clockwork Curtly had no hesitant, stuttering starting steps like Merv Hughes, no angled, crabbing run-in like Bob Willis. He was straight at you. Big step off the mark, balanced instantly, immediately into those long strides, high pump-action knees — like a Fosbury flopper approaching the high jump bar.

A split second before delivery he cocked his right wrist in a strangely horizontal way, directly above his head — a mannerism, like a rattlesnake's rhumba, possibly a distraction to his intended victim. And, there were the white wrist bands ... which distracted at least one batsman.

His follow-through flowed effortlessly and finished just a long arm's length from touching distance of the batsman.

Then The Look, often a moody stare, sometimes a wry smile after a frown, but always the eyes. Then, a turn on the heel, the quick walk back, the hitch of the shirt at the shoulder, the circle at the mark, the re-load, the full stride, the high steps … clockwork. Boon was right, no rest for the batsmen there.

Boon in his cricket socks could probably have head-butted Curtly in the chest. Boon is white, Curtly's black. Each hailed from a small island, but worlds apart. One's a batsman, the other a fast bowler.

Cricket 'enemies', yet they were similar cricketers in temperament, and professionally. And, cricket engendered in each a total respect for the other.

Each was acknowledged as a man of few words. Example: an interviewer to Curtly, in 1997 — Q: Which hamstring is worrying you? A: Both of them. Curtly on Boon, whom he rated the highest of his Australian opponents: "He was pure grit. Nothing seemed really to frustrate him. He was a hard man and a hard man to get out."

Boon was more expansive on Curtly:

His height gave the impression he was a lot quicker than he actually was, although when he was on song he was as quick as anything we had — Merv Hughes and Craig McDermott — but not as quick as Michael Holding or Malcolm Marshall.

As an opener against the new ball you always knew you were in a real good contest because you'd play at nine out of ten. His control and his ability to move the ball off the seam meant he was always at you, always giving himself the best opportunity to get you out.

I was always conscious that if I got a loose ball to try to get it away because I wasn't going to get too many. Ones were always very important against Curtly.

Once you got used to his little cock of the wrist picking him up [seeing the ball] wasn't difficult. Wasim Akram and Courtney Walsh were harder.

In all the times I batted against Curtly he never, ever said a word to me. He's not at all sour. He was at his best on a pitch with a little bit of juice — he ran through us in Perth in 1993, seven for one in 25 balls. I made a few runs, a forty and a fifty, but I don't think I've ever been as black with bruises.

He was relentless — perfect bowling on a pitch to suit. He didn't waste one ball. It might sound silly but I actually enjoyed facing him. I made it my business to go and sit next to him in their dressing room afterwards.

He's really a quiet, shy sort of a bloke especially around people he doesn't know. I've heard him giggling and carrying on with their blokes but socially with us, no.

We had a chat, not much ... how're things going, what he'd be doing when he went back home to Swetes, that's all.

I think he was great fast bowler. From 1988 until he hurt his shoulder 1994, he was magnificent.

In 1955 at Sabina Park, in Jamaica, Rich scored one of Test cricket's fastest centuries — it took him 78 minutes. That's remarkable, but so is this — he batted No.8, and his 121 was the fifth century in the Australian innings of eight for 758, in a match they won by an innings and 82 runs.

Colin McDonald, who had made his debut for Australia in the same Test as Rich — and one-Test wonder George Thoms — scored 127, Neil Harvey 204, Keith Miller 109 and Ron Archer 128. Unique.

In 1978 I was sweating it out in the press box at Sabina Park when the riot police effectively put down a crowd disturbance by (1) firing blanks, or rubber bullets; (2) letting loose the occasional whiff of tear gas; (3) vigorously wielding long batons made of wood, or hard rubber; (4) rattling the chain leashes of their german shepherd dogs.

Bob Simpson's team had looked like winning the final Test and the crowd hurled not abuse at the umpire they felt had made a mistake, but refuse ranging from rocks to iron piping to rubbish drums at the Australians who were standing in the middle of the ground, possibly feeling like Custer's cavalry.

And, I was in the dressing room with Greg Chappell at Sabina Park in 1973. Greg remembered the first day of the First Test like this:

It's a small ground Sabina Park, it can probably take about 18,000 people. But when we arrived at 9.30 there were already 25,000 inside.

Those inside were taking off their shirts and dangling them over the fence so their mates could abseil in without tickets. The light stanchions, reaching about eighty feet skywards, were jam-packed with people.

The atmosphere, the noise level, was unbelievable. I've never experienced anything like it. Uton Dowe was their great fast bowling hope.

No batsman, if he's honest, will tell you he likes facing fast bowling. Keith Stackpole was probably the one exception — he loved fast bowling. 'Stacky' was excited, the rest of us nervous.

As Dowe measured out his run the noise reached a crescendo and, as Dowe hit the delivery stride, for the split second it took the ball to travel from his end to Stacky's end an absolute and total silence broke out.

It was the most eerie feeling I've ever experienced around a Test match. It's one I'll never forget. It never happened anywhere else. Once the ball hit the bat that crowd noise went back to fever pitch and stayed there for the day.

In 1991 David Boon is batting before just such a crowd at Sabina Park, batting No.3 for Australia and facing fast bowling, Ambrose, Walsh, Patterson and Marshall.

Time, and all the repetitive references to the famous West Indian pace batteries can dull the mind, somehow fade what John Dyson called The Bruise Factor, make the ordeal seem so matter-of-fact now that it's just a memory.

But just take a minute to refresh your memory, to imagine what it must have been like facing those bowlers.

Human pile driving machines — thunk! thunk! Add some meanness in there, too. Batsmen, rubbing their bruises, physical and mental. Aussie batsmen could only dream … wouldn't it be great to play in a time machine team where the captain could throw the ball to Lillee, Thomson, Lindwall and Miller all in a morning's play.

According to Boon, Malcolm Marshall was the best fast bowler he ever faced — "He could move the ball both ways in the air and at great pace, and he was just as lethal from either over or around the wicket." Phew.

But that day in 1991 it is Patrick Patterson, fast and straight and angry, who nails Boon. Gets one under Boon's helmet guard, speed probably about what it takes to lose your licence and gain a fine on the freeway. Say 130km/h.

Slices Boon's chin open. Blood, and that Sabina Park crowd is baying for more. Boon needs stitches. But, Australia needs Boon. The longer he can stay with a faltering 'tail' the longer will be Australia's lead over the West Indies and the shorter the odds of an Australian victory.

Boon takes the 'stitches later' option.

Boon matched wits with the West Indies 40 times and Ambrose got him six times. Ambrose remains just outside the Top Ten best of all time (see top table overpage). He is in good company, as you can see. You may also notice they are all fast bowlers, except Lance Gibbs, the West Indian offspinner.

It says a lot for Boon's character, possibly even more than it says for his technical talent, that he was able to maintain an average of nearly 40 during a decade of confrontation with the most feared grouping of fast bowlers the cricket world might ever see. Of the elite list below Kapil, Hadlee, Botham, Marshall, Imran, Walsh, Akram and Ambrose all tried to sort out Boon.

The Top Test Wicket-takers					
Bowler	Matches	Wkts	5/10	Ave	S/rate
Kapil	131	434	23/2	29.65	63.92
Hadlee	86	431	36/9	22.30	50.85
Botham	102	383	27/4	28.40	56.96
Marshall	81	376	22/4	20.95	46.77
Imran	88	362	23/6	22.81	53.75
Lillee	70	355	23/7	23.92	52.01
Walsh	93	339	13/2	25.95	58.56
Willis	90	325	16/–	25.20	53.40
Akram	72	311	21/4	22.68	52.88
Gibbs	79	309	18/2	29.09	87.75
Trueman	67	307	17/3	21.58	49.43
Ambrose	72	306	18/3	21.46	53.89

David Boon in Tests				
Opponent	Runs	HS	50/100	Avge
Eng	2237	184*	8/7	45.65
Ind	1204	135	2/6	70.82
NZl	1187	200	8/3	47.48
Pak	431	114*	1/1	23.94
SrL	493	110	2/1	32.87
SAf	433	96	3/–	43.30
WIn	1437	149	8/3	39.92

A century against South Africa would have rounded out his career, as would one more catch to reach 100, but he conceded to the selectors' suggestion that at 36 years of age he was becoming a little pressed for time.

In all, Boon made 7,422 runs in Test cricket, No.13 on the list of all-time greats.

Another Boon ... we can only dream. It will never be and, nor will there be another Lillee, another Chappelli, another Dougie, nor another Merv, either H or S. Cricket people similar in style will come along, but never will they be identical.

For that has been the wonderful tradition of cricket — it has attracted an extraordinarily diverse range of individuals, not just in a physical sense but in the mental sense, all of whom, in their own unique way, perpetuate the uncertain qualities that make cricket the greatest game of all.

But, how certain is its future? Is Australian society today 'traditional cricket'-friendly? The lifestyle of the masses is a perpetual peak-hour rush, so little time to reflect, to weigh up the options.

And, what about the degeneration of The Bush, whose generations of thoughtful young men, well prepared to match the challenge of adversity, have been the steely backbone of our cricket? The bush cricketer might soon be like a bush bank, just a memory, a mirage on the horizon.

Our politicians constantly remind us that we are part of Asia now and, for once, we can believe them — the Hong Kong Sixes, the Singapore Sevens ... coming soon the Indonesian Eights?

If you happen to like cricket just the way it is/was, you might be inclined to ask yourself if the character of the game, as we know it, will survive the next few decades. There are some good reasons to be just a shade uncertain, even nervous about the possible outcome.

ACKNOWLEDGEMENTS

John Benaud thanks the following people and organisations for their generous assistance in providing information, assistance and photographs.

John Cranney, who is the 'great nephew' of the great 'Mudgee', and who lives in Parramatta, next door to the house where Mudgee spent most of life.

Harold Goodwin, who today coaches the Parramatta (formerly Cumberland) Under-16 A. W. Green Shield team, once one of Lou's pleasures.

Rene, Lou's wife, who remembers the early days as if they were yesterday, and maintained the family photo albums.

Rich, whose memory was often sharper than mine, and for his advice.

Penrith City Council Library, whose editions of the *Nepean Times* carried Lou's famous scoreboard.

Ross Dundas for all the statistics, truly a labour of love. In most instances they apply from May 1, 1997.

Merv Seres, for confirming to a former selector what he'd always suspected about Merv Hughes — he was unique.

Tom Morris and Tara, without whom a cricket tour to England would be a much less joyous affair.

Mike Pawley, who is still into sports goods selling but not greyhounds.

Col Blackman, who unearthed a photo of some tough team-mates from a club that's doing it tough in the '90s.

Bruce McDonald, for his World Series Cricket diary notes, and scorebooks.

Ian Field, Brian Hughes, and John Wood of Cricket NSW for the use of the Library and for access to the photographic collection, particularly those from the Bill O'Reilly collection and the Jack Chegwyn collection.

Norm Tasker of *Inside Edge*, and Daniel Lane for access to the PBL Marketing picture library.

Andrew Foulds of Fairfax, for unearthing photos of cricketing moments long gone, but well remembered.

Viv Jenkins, who probably watched as much cricket as any selector in the last two decades, and got most of it on film.

Patrick Eagar, who was in the Caribbean in 1973 and 1978 and retains photographic evidence of a hat-trick of memorable cricketing triumphs, the performers being Doug Walters, Ian Chappell and Jeff Thomson.

John Mikulcic of the Australian Picture Library who pulled strings on the other side of the world.

Bernard Whimpress, curator of the Adelaide Oval Museum.

Nicholson of *The Australian* for his cartoon comment in the Taylor chapter.

And finally, Lou. His philosophy on the game, conveyed in his teaching methods and perpetuated in his notes, inspired the book and ensured that its compilation was as enjoyable as playing the game was.

The following publications were used as reference points: Cumberland Cricket Club annual reports; Richie Benaud's *Wide World Of Sports Cricket Yearbooks*; *Australian Cricket* magazine, monthlies and annuals; *The Oxford Companion to Australian Cricket*; *The Wisden Book Of Test Cricket*; NSWCA *Cricket Yearbooks*; Fairfax Newspapers; News Ltd. newspapers; Australian Consolidated Press newspapers.